WALKING THE RAINBOW

AN ARC TO TRIUMPH

RICHARD RENÉ SILVIN

WHITMORE PUBLISHING CO.
PITTSBURGH, PENNSYLVANIA 15222

To the loving memory of my angel,

ROBERT D. MANN PH.D.

To all the other innocent victims whose full lives
and brilliant careers were prematurely and cruelly aborted.

"[*Walking the Rainbow*] is a terrific document! [Silvin's] full possession of the language allows [him] to draw from all angles and give voice to all demons. In this respect it is unique. [He] succeeds to confine to the reader three decades walking the rainbow through the multiple dimensions. It is sober and yet powerful. Never self-pity!"

—Leo Eckmann
M.D. Professor of Medicine

"*Walking the Rainbow* reveals a compelling visionary worldview that is directly relevant to how each one of us may more constructively engage, with hope yet without illusions, myriad pressure points we face in today's paradoxical world. René Silvin tells his fascinating story in context of his relational dynamics and complex role as a global health care executive, as a witness to loved ones who tragically succumb to AIDS, and his personal struggle with and unique insights into AIDS. I am struck by René's will to survive combined with his empathy and deep sensibility to what it is to be human."

—Ahmed Yehia
Chairman and CEO, Quantum Leadership Solutions, LLC

"[*Walking the Rainbow*] is stunning, both in quality and quantity. I simply could not put it down until completion. The loving caring way in which [Silvin] communicates about partners and friends is incredible. [He] writes of the compression of time--enjoying life to its fullest as one does not know what tomorrow may bring. [Silvin] inspires us to continue our quest. ... I am looking forward to [book] number three."

—Harold Bedenbaugh
First Vice President (Ret.), major investment house

"In Switzerland it is said that there is a treasure on both ends of a rainbow. It is true. There I found a man beyond class, completely multi-cultural and as personable as is possible.

"In both a professional and personal context, Richard is not ordinary, Whether in Switzerland, France, Spain, Germany, the UK, Australia, Canada or Singapore, everyone we met only said and thought positive things about Richard. The boy has one major drawback: He is incapable of making enemies."

—*Jean-Claude Salamin*

CONTENTS

Part One: The World Before AIDS 1976-1981

Chapter One: September 3, 1976............................3
Chapter Two: 1977...9
Chapter Three: 1978...16
Chapter Four: 1979...22
Chapter Five: 1980...29
Chapter Six: 1981...36

Part Two: Tim

Chapter Seven: 1982...43
Chapter Eight: 1983..49
Chapter Nine: 1984...56
Chapter Ten: 1985...63
Chapter Eleven: 1986..71
Chapter Twelve: 1987...78
Chapter Thirteen: 1988.......................................87
Chapter Fourteen: January 1-February 9, 1989.......111

Part Three: Bob

Chapter Fifteen: 1989...117
Chapter Sixteen: 1990..130
Chapter Seventeen: 1991....................................144
Chapter Eighteen: 1992......................................154
Chapter Nineteen: 1993......................................161
Chapter Twenty: 1994...170
Chapter Twenty-one: 1995..................................184
Chapter Twenty-two: 1996..................................189
Chapter Twenty-three: 1997...............................194
Chapter Twenty-four: 1998..................................200

Part Four: The Arc To Triumph

Chapter Twenty-five..219

Bibliography...233

"Ignorance more frequently begets confidence than does knowledge."
—Charles Darwin, 1871

PART ONE

THE WORLD BEFORE AIDS
1976–1981

CHAPTER ONE

SEPTEMBER 3, 1976

Beverly Hills, California

I stood outside one of the few tall office buildings in Beverly Hills with an energized sense of both anticipation and elation. At age twenty-eight, I had successfully negotiated the sale of my father-in-law's bankrupt hospital design company to American Medical International, Inc. (AMI). AMI was the first company in a relatively new industrial group called "investor- owned hospital corporations" and was one of three hospital companies listed on the New York Stock Exchange. The others were Humana—before it transformed itself into an insurance company—and Hospital Corporation of America (HCA), which was founded by Tommy Frist, the father of Senate Majority Leader Bill Frist.

Over the previous five weeks, AMI Chief Executive Officer Royce Diener and I had negotiated the sale to AMI of my father-in-law's small but well-respected firm. I had tried to peddle the firm to several other companies that seemed to represent a good fit, including consortium members with whom we had successfully collaborated on large projects. Our declining sales and deteriorating balance sheet turned out to be a consistent roadblock in our exploratory conversations with architectural and construction companies, with whom we had teamed, building hospitals in the United States, France, England, and Germany. In a last creative gasp, I went to the Library of Congress in Washington, DC, not far from our corporate office, and asked to see the annual reports of the three publicly traded hospital companies. Five years of reports were available for each company. I promptly spread all fifteen reports out on a large desk and read them carefully. It was clear that one company, AMI, had initiated a strategy to expand internationally, beginning with the United Kingdom, and was interested in telling its shareholders how many communities it served. That figure had progressed from twenty to thirty-five communities and finally, in 1976, to fifty.

Our little company served two hundred communities in three countries. While we did not own facilities, we consulted at many prestigious hospitals on both design and management challenges. The company's founder, my father-in-law, was in deep denial about our precarious financial condition. He was equally oblivious to the fact that, in the U.S., the funds allocated to hospital construction projects under an act of Congress called "Hill Burton" had dried up, seriously impeding our major source of revenue. Our sixty consultants and architects had dwindled to an overworked forty, and we were on C.O.D. terms with all our suppliers. On numerous occasions I would fly to clients literally begging for payments to be made because my payroll was due the following day.

Our lines of credit were extended because, three years before, I managed to obtain a design and management contract to run The American Hospital of Paris, one of the world's most respected and well-known hospitals, while it was rebuilt in several phases. Living in Paris and working at The American Hospital, I traveled to Cologne, Germany, every week to participate in team meetings relating to the construction of a one thousand bed, ultra-modern new university hospital. Unfortunately, these two lucrative projects were not able to cover the large losses incurred by the American side of the company, and we were faced with bankruptcy and foreclosure.

After reading the fifteen annual reports of the investor-owned hospital companies, I summoned up all my youthful courage and called AMI's C.E.O.

My heart pounded as the phone rang.

"AMI. How may I direct your call?"

"Ah, I'd like to speak to Mr. Diener, please," I said sheepishly.

"One moment please."

Another anxious moment went by while I heard a phone ring.

"Mr. Diener's office," said a soft yet professional voice.

"May I speak with Mr. Diener?" I inquired.

I looked across my desk at my partner, Ahmed Yehia, a childhood friend who had recently returned from a three-year stint at Proctor and Gamble, where he was a young product manger in the foods division. Amazingly, he personally committed to try to salvage me, the company, and my in-laws from bankruptcy and possible legal reprisals due to what our bankruptcy attorney had called "irresponsible misuse of creditor's funds."

The phone rang again.

I heard a deep, highly confident voice: "This is Royce Diener." I stared at Ahmed in astonishment, fully expecting to have been stopped well before actually speaking with a man of such relative importance.

"Mr. Diener, my name is Rick Silvin and I am the president of Friesen International in Washington, DC. Thank you in advance for taking my call," I said, hoping my trembling voice was not overly apparent.

"I know of your company. You fellows beat us on the American Hospital of Paris contract. What I can do for you?" he replied pleasantly. Again, I looked at Ahmed and shrugged my shoulders as if to say, "He actually wants to talk to us!"

"Mr. Diener, I see that you are leading AMI into becoming an international health care services company penetrating as many communities as possible," I said, still gazing at Ahmed in shock.

"Yes. How do you know that?" he asked.

"I took the time to dig into and interpret your last three annual reports," I said, gaining a tiny bit of confidence.

"Mmm, interesting. So, again, how can I help you?" he repeated.

The biggest moment since obtaining my MBA from Cornell University, and Ahmed's MBA from Harvard, both five years earlier, had arrived.

"We are working on several hospital projects in Europe, sir. Our corporate brochure highlights the fact that *we* serve two hundred communities." There was a prolonged silence.

I continued, my voice still shaky: "We are looking for a strategic alliance with a bigger, reputable company so that we may pursue larger, lucrative contracts in the Middle East. I'd like to come to Beverly Hills and explain myself in more detail. But, sir, I must put up-front the fact that we have gotten ahead of ourselves and are experiencing a severe cash flow problem."

That was code for "we're broke."

During the ensuing month, I shuttled back and forth to Los Angeles as a deal to acquire our floundering company was formulated. At one meeting, I handed my new hero a list of seven criteria to acquire the company. Six of these would handle the honoring of aging payables, irresponsible pledges to universities and charities and delinquent accounts, plus enough money for my father-in-law to retire comfortably. The seventh item on the page read:

"R. R. Silvin will stay for six months to train any manager AMI puts in charge of the company."

Diener had the paper in his hands and reviewed it in his careful manner. His handsome sun-tanned face showed no emotion. His pure white hair on a relatively youthful visage gave him a distinguished look of self-assurance.

"I'll not further negotiate the terms," he began. I could hardly believe my ears. Then he added, "Six items are accepted in their entirety— but item number seven is rejected."

I was dumbstruck. All I wanted was to extricate myself from a miserable and humiliating business and family experience. There was also a different hope—to achieve another kind of freedom. I knew I was gay and I wanted to "come out." I believed that establishing financial independence for my in-laws would also be the time to explain my sexuality. I assumed that I would have to vanish and start life over again in a different business sector and probably a different country.

"You'll work for AMI for five years, reporting to me, or there is no deal, Rick," he said. "It will take at least that long to see the emergence of a substantial international department."

"That's impossible, sir. I simply can't."

"Why?" he demanded.

"I cannot deal with one more creditor," I said firmly. "Do you realize that I get threatening calls at home in the middle of the night demanding payment for one financial obligation or another?"

Diener laughed aloud and picked up a phone.

"Get me accounts payable," he ordered. "Yes, this is Royce Diener. Cut a check to Friesen International for $225,000 and book it as an advance on the acquisition. Bring it to my office right away." He turned back to me adding, "That will carry you over until the deal is finalized. After which, there will be a new accounting department that handles all your payables, including the payroll. You will never, *ever* speak to a single creditor again. I promise," he affirmed.

"There is another–err–problem, Royce," I added. We had advanced to a first name basis during the negotiations. "I am gay and will be coming out of the closet," I continued.

After thinking a while Royce began, "I'm a Californian conservative." I imagined our deal flying out the window. "That means I am fiscally conservative and socially liberal. You are discrete and will be a fine representative for our new international division. You have not told me anything more significant than if you had said you were a vegetarian."

I so wanted to jump up and kiss him but restrained myself.

I was raised in homophobic Swiss boarding schools and had perpetrated the hoax of pretending I was straight. I had married while living a serious lie. It never occurred to me that any business executive I knew might comprehend all these parameters, be prepared to put them into perspective, *and* ask me to represent him professionally in a conservative industry. I wondered if I was dreaming. This new reality was simply beyond my wildest hopes and expectations. Ahmed and I, two young bucks, had successfully saved a family from bankruptcy and a company from disgrace while honoring all its debts.

I looked up at the modern ten-story black AMI building as the previous five weeks flashed through my mind. Today was *the big day*—signing my first Securities and Exchange-controlled transaction, which would end several years of horrendous financial and emotional hardship.

I rode the elevator to the top floor and entered the wood paneled lobby. I was friendly with the secretarial staff and knew all the senior executives, some of whom viewed me as a curious threat. I would be reporting directly to the Chief Executive even though initially I would "only" carry the title of Vice President. This represented an unusual break with traditional reporting lines, because I would by-pass the higher layers of Executive and Senior Vice Presidents.

I walked into the large boardroom. A huge custom-made wood table occupied the entire space. A door at the far end of the room led to a kitchen where a uniformed French chef tended to the needs of participants of meetings and served meals enjoyed by a select few elite guests. Some twenty piles of paper were neatly stacked along the periphery of the table, each requiring both my and Diener's signatures. Royce emerged from his office in a fashionable white suit. He smiled and put out his hand to congratulate me.

"Well, let's get this thing done. We should rejoice! After all, the lawyers nearly killed it several times in just a month," he said laughing.

I removed from my pocket a flashy pen I had bought along with a pack of Rothman cigarettes. I lit one with a DuPont lighter my aunt had given me ten years earlier. We each greeted the several attorneys who had prepared the numerous documents, a stock purchase agreement, a generous retirement package for my father-in-law, an employment contract, and settlement agreements to George Washington University (where Friesen had pledged $500,000 for a chair in Hospital Administration), another settlement agreement to The Kennedy Center in Washington, DC (for its building fund), plus several SEC required documents.

I followed Royce as we signed each pile of papers, feeling so relieved and excited about the future. I wondered what "gift" I might buy myself to celebrate. I did not need a car as Royce had already bought me a new green twelve-cylinder Jaguar XJS. I certainly could not envision a trip because I would be traveling constantly as of the following Monday.

Suddenly, unpremeditated, I settled on two gifts. One was healthy and the other definitely was not.

At the far end of the table, I crushed my cigarette into a Venetian glass ashtray and threw the nearly full pack of cigarettes into a trash bin.

"What's that about, Rick?" asked Royce.

"That's my gift to myself for completing the transaction," I replied proudly. We both laughed.

"Great idea," he added.

I did not tell him what I chose as my second gift. That night, after a celebration dinner, I would go to Los Angeles' largest bathhouse for the first time. The moment had finally come for me to begin my real life.

CHAPTER TWO

1977

Pines Harbor, Fire Island, New York

During my first year at AMI, I traveled constantly between Washington, DC; Beverly Hills; Europe; and—for fun—The Fire Island Pines. My boat was moored there in slip # 1, one of only four deep-water docks. I scheduled my business trips so I could spend a few nights every month on the slick new twin-engine Sea Ray, *Les Beaux*. The name was a takeoff on the delightful French village in Provence of Les *Baux*. It translates as "the good-looking ones." I *was* good looking, young, and had more disposable income than I had ever imagined. Importantly, I had not previously experienced any sexual act I enjoyed and, in the late 1970s, The Pines was a gay man's sexual Mecca–I dove in!

If I were transiting through New York, I'd fly into The Pines on the seaplane from Manhattan. If I could steal a night or two from Washington as a newly inaugurated non-stop flight from Washington National into McArthur Field in Islip was miraculously available. I worked hard and played just as hard. The contrast invigorated me and fed into the desire to do each distinct activity to the fullest and to the best of my abilities.

I had befriended a handsome young hustler in Washington who serviced several members of Congress. He was at the center of a secretive web of young men who earned their living similarly and that later became known as part of the "Capitol Hill Page Scandal." David was breathtakingly sexy and would meet me at one or the other jumping points to go over to Fire Island. If we arrived during daylight, he would lay on the bow of the boat as people gawked in awe of his muscular body and handsome face. Sitting at The Boatel's bar, every man there was willing—and delighted—to have several drinks with us. Late night substance-enhanced parties took place on the boat daily. Whenever we surfaced for air, we would enchant guests with stories of our previous week's adventures. David talked of his outrageous sexual experiences with Washington celebrities who were allegedly straight, and I revealed stories of my international travels. We were part of The A Group, and we enjoyed every second.

I knew most of the owners of the boats on the "gay side" of The Pines harbor. We all ate and partied together. On several occasions we were irresponsible and miraculously escaped severe injuries or fatalities. It was not unusual for a party boy to fall off a boat while skipping from one cocktail party to another. One night, after a drunken dinner on a neighbor's boat, I was dared to plane my vessel and cross the sandbar between Sayville and The Pines. When a boat accelerates, the bow raises. At higher speeds it may plane, thus flattening out and drawing (requiring) less depth. At the very most, only a few inches of water would be the difference between a foolish adventure and brutal injuries. Giggling in the wee hours of the morning, I maneuvered out of the harbor and pushed both throttles to their maximum. Many barely clad men stood on the bow in an attempt to make the boat plane which, inexplicably, it did while no innocent clam boat stood in our path.

But there was another phenomena gradually occurring: A few of the most energetic, all-night dancers were complaining of uncharacteristic fatigue and were returning to their boats or hotel rooms early. They all had one oddity in common—swollen lymph nodes in their necks, groins, or under their arms.

Washington, DC

Back in my Georgetown office in Washington, DC, Ahmed and I were hard at work trying to revive the company with the new capital at our disposal. We learned that, if well justified, Royce Diener approved all our business development plans as well as appropriate additions to the professional staff.

Several oil-rich Middle Eastern countries, notably Kuwait and Saudi Arabia, were in a race to develop their national infrastructure. That always included the construction of hospitals and, in some cases, complete hospital networks. We carefully monitored international requests for proposals (RFP) for every aspect of hospital development in the region and noticed that American firms were being left behind by the large European consortiums. We concluded there were two reasons for that: a lack of a proven track record and a new law enacted by President Jimmy Carter. The "Foreign Business Corruption Act" of 1977 was intended to "add morality" to business conducted by American companies overseas. Now that we were a division of a New York Stock Exchange company, it was of primary importance for us to strictly comply with this new, restrictive law. We knew, however, that the European consortiums had no such limitations and, worse, several Western European governments actually underwrote the substantial development costs that we all had to directly incur during the many months of studying for and, ultimately, bidding on these projects.

One of the most lucrative and, therefore, hotly pursued contracts was for the development of a health care plan for the country of Kuwait. Ahmed and I studied the RFP and prepared a proposal for Royce Diener's approval, which would allow us to compete with the usual front-runners. I brought the completed document to Beverly Hills and presented it to him.

"This is a significant amount of money, Rick," he said after careful review of the plan, which included several months of a development team's time and overseas expenses as well as the preparation of elaborate demographic studies, maps, and hospital models. "There are no guarantees you will be successful. In fact, American companies typically have not been awarded these contracts."

"That's true, Royce," I replied, "but a job like this will not only double our division's annual revenues and catapult us into profitability but, more importantly, position AMI to get the much larger hospital management contracts in the area that will be awarded over the next few years. And besides, Royce, we have a secret weapon."

"Oh, really, and what exactly is that?" he inquired.

"His name is Ahmed Yehia," I replied as Royce smiled. "As you know, prior to the Egyptian revolution, Ahmed's father was an enormously influential businessman in the region and is still known to many of the leaders and decision makers for his world view and integrity. We believe that, while this is insufficient to *get* the contract, it creates context and affinity that will be sufficient to get us in the door, to be heard and judged on our merit. With the funds described in this proposal, we will produce a crackerjack plan to present to the Kuwaiti Minister of Health."

"You are, of course, aware that three seats of my five-member Executive Committee are held by Jews?" he said, staring at me with a stoic and wise look.

"For now, they will be dealing with Ahmed and me. We'll have this discussion again if we are lucky enough to reach the stage of bidding for the management contracts once the hospitals are built."

"You know if you are not successful, these expenses will create a serious loss for the year. You will not reach your projections and your credibility may well be irreparably painted."

"Yes, I do, sir," I said, understanding what was implied.

"Good luck and keep me closely informed," he said as he stood to end our meeting.

During much of the rest of 1977, Ahmed stayed in Kuwait with his revolving team of expert demographers, consultants, architects, and model builders. I visited periodically until, in late November, to the surprise of the huge international construction consortiums, we were awarded the contract to set up the country's master health care plan, which would include the development and construction of six major modern hospitals.

In early December, I received a call from Royce.

"Rick, I want you and Ahmed to move to AMI headquarters in Beverly Hills. The consulting division can now stand on its own. Ahmed will oversee the Kuwait project from here. But I need you in Beverly Hills to begin the development of an international network of hospitals. Bring whoever is essential for Ahmed. We'll gather a team for international development here."

"When do you actually want me to move?" I asked, looking at a pile of drawings, papers, and contracts on my desk.

"As far as I know, there are many seats available on several flights tomorrow." The phone went dead.

I stared out at the Potomac River and the newly finished Kennedy Center. I recalled how we had struggled to survive on shoestring budgets while our now retired founder had vowed to contribute $250,000 for the Kennedy Center's construction. Given our precarious financial position, it was an embarrassing pledge that AMI had honored. By doing so, Royce had earned both my respect and appreciation for life, as during intermissions at

Kennedy Center performances, I had the added perk of using a private waiting room reserved for large contributors.

I knew that my days as a hospital design and management consultant were over, and I wondered what life in a rapidly growing large corporate structure would be like. Importantly, I would be involved in the acquisition and construction of hospitals our company *owned*—a huge difference from consulting for municipalities and governments with no long-term accountability. While I had managed one U.S. government-supported hospital in Paris, would I be able to run a new hospital network of "for profit" hospitals? Where would they be and how would our host governments view us? These challenges swirled around in my head.

There would also be an exciting and pleasurable additional change to savor—living in one of the centers of the gay world during its 'sexual revolution.'

Later that night, Royce called again.

"Rick, remember those available seats on the plane I spoke of earlier?"

"Of course," I replied. "I'll be in Beverly Hills Monday morning. My secretary will take care of packing up my apartment and sending my gear out later."

"You'll need to change those plans. I want you in London on Monday to meet Stanley, AMI's General Manager in London. The two of you will travel to Switzerland together. And we'll rent your condominium in Washington from you to serve as a corporate residence. I will naturally disclose this in the 10K, and it will have to be at market rates," concluded the ever ethically mindful chief executive who would never have knowingly violated his fiduciary responsibility to AMI's shareholders.

The author, boating at Fire Island.

The author working with a German government architect on
the new 1,400-bed Bonn Psychiatric Hospital in Germany.

CHAPTER THREE

1978

London, England, and Lausanne, Switzerland

AMI had recently made a significant investment in London, England, when it acquired the famous Harley Street Clinic from Doctor Stanley Balfour-Lynn, whose new role was managing director of International Operations, also reporting to Mr. Diener. Royce put Stanley and me in touch to investigate a possible expansion of private hospitals onto the European continent. I initially had some reservations about meeting the debonair, allegedly severe, and demanding physician-turned-hospital entrepreneur. After a wild weekend on *Les Beaux* at The Pines, I boarded a British Airlines Concorde and flew to London. Stanley sent his uniformed chauffeur with his Rolls Royce to the airport, which took me to what would become one of my homes away from home, Claridge's Hotel on Brooke Street. The following morning, the same dignified driver was waiting in front of the hotel to bring me to meet the mysterious Doctor Balfour-Lynn.

Upon arrival at AMI's luxurious offices on Wimpole Street, a block away from The Harley Street Clinic, I was escorted into his grand office. It was magnificently decorated with British antiques; a large, carved wood fireplace mantle dominated the room and tall floor to ceiling windows made the space bright and cheery. Stanley's huge desk in a far corner was bare of the typical stacks of paper and boasted a very visible sign that read "IT CAN BE DONE."

Stanley was reviewing his correspondence with his male secretary, Jeffery. The amusing procedure consisted of Jeffery opening each letter with a silver letter opener, showing it to his almighty boss, who would then, most often, order the document to be placed in a shredder located next to Jeffery. From time to time, Stanley would dictate a response and proceed with the show.

After a few seconds of witnessing this ritual, Stanley rose to greet me. He was immaculately groomed in a well-tailored blue suit, a monocle hanging from his neck. Although in his late fifties and balding, his skin was youthful, as were his movements.

"Lovely to meet you. Mind if I have a manicure while we chat," he said rather than ask. A manicurist was already seated and waiting, with her utensils, at a table in the opposite end of the office.

I instantly liked the extravagant gentleman and knew we would become great friends. His theatrics were both obviously superficial and very amusing. Equally apparent was his brilliance and gusto for excitement. While I intuitively knew we would do our best for AMI's European endeavors, I had no idea of how much fun we would have and how profitable our efforts would ultimately become.

While I sat across the table from Stanley and his beautician, we discussed the reason for my visit. We were going to Lausanne, Switzerland, to see a closed and historic previously grand hotel in the middle of the city.

Between the ages of seven and eighteen, I had attended Swiss Boarding Schools near Lausanne. In a way, I was going back to my roots and people I understood. We checked into what would become another of my new homes—the Lausanne Palace Hotel, a few blocks away from the boarded up Hotel Cecil. During my childhood, the grand old building was an operative but dilapidated hotel. It was now an embarrassment to the city. While it dominated a beautiful hill overlooking Lake Geneva and Evian, France, off in the distance, it had not been maintained in a fashion that attracted wealthy tourists, who preferred two other local hotels—the Lausanne Palace and The Beau Rivage at Lausanne's lakeside section of Ouchy.

AMI had previously entered into an agreement to acquire the property, subject to certain conditions we were examining. After two days of inspections with Lausanne's preeminent architect, Pierre Jacqerot, and meetings with an attorney who had worked on obtaining approval for the foreign investment, we decided to proceed with the acquisition. Believing that a change of venue would create some mental clarity, we left Lausanne to overnight at the new President Hotel in Geneva before boarding separate flights the following morning.

After dinner, we went to the hotel's bar for a nightcap, where we met two men. One would become my friend and partner to this day and the other would interject a practically unnoticed detail that would alter the future of health care over the following decades. While ordering drinks, an unusual-looking bearded, short, and well-dressed hotel executive entered the bar and introduced himself.

"Good evening, gentlemen, my name is Jean-Claude Salamin, and I am the hotel's night manager. How do you like your accommodations?"

"The new hotel is adequate," said Stanley in his fashion of distancing himself from "employees."

"Without being indiscrete," continued Jean-Claude undeterred, "may I ask what the nature of your business is here in Switzerland?"

"We represent a company that owns and operates hospitals," I answered, observing Stanley's discomfort at being questioned. "In fact, we are considering buying an old hotel with the intention of turning it into an acute care hospital."

"May I ask which hotel?"

"The Hotel Cecil in Lausanne," I responded.

"That's rather amusing. I live in Lausanne and am very familiar with the magnificent building and its unusual story. It is rather tragic that such a piece of Switzerland's history has fallen into disrepair and disgrace. I can imagine that monument restored to its former magnificence. But you said you own and operate hospitals. I do not understand."

"I owned an old hospital lodged in the center of London," interjected Stanley. "Our company restored and transformed it into an up-to-date hospital. We believe that the same efforts can make that old hotel into a first class hospital."

"We have a few obvious problems," I said.

"Again, might I query what those are?" asked Jean-Claude in his nearly perfect, yet heavily French-accented English. His charming blue eyes twinkled in the dimly lit bar.

"Well, the first is management," I said. "There are no graduate schools of hospital administration in Switzerland, and we plan to operate our hospitals based on sound yet locally adapted American hospital management techniques."

"The second?" inquired Jean-Claude.

"We are not sure the Swiss system of private healthcare is ready for a well-equipped, acute, highly technical hospital," I said.

"Well, I'll take the second concern first," answered a super-confident Jean-Claude, "If you create the finest private hospital in the Canton of Vaud, it cannot miss. But it has to be the *very best* run, equipped, and promoted facility. We are an overly insured population and supplementary private hospitalization policies are common here. No one has adequately filled that need. As for the second concern of finding an appropriate manager, I am your man! You can teach me these American hospital management techniques—no problem." Stanley and I looked at each other, wondering if we had met a complete nut or encountered one of the very best coincidences of our lives. The latter turned out to be the case.

"Excuse me, Messieurs," interjected a Frenchman sitting close by. "I am a physician from Paris. Perhaps we have something in common."

"What is your specialty?" asked Stanley.

"I am a pulmonologist," he replied, "informing certain authorities here, in Geneva, of a bizarre circumstance we have observed in Paris. Two women of the night have died of a rare and previously easily treated form of pneumonia. Speaking vulgarly, they were drowned by protozoa we all have in our lungs but which healthy immune systems can control. So bizarre!"

I wanted to inquire what exactly a "healthy immune system" was and how it was measured. But, understandably, the Frenchman's prophesy was of far less interest than our immediate business concerns that night in 1978.

Flying back to Washington, I read about the murders of Harvey Milk and George Mosconi in San Francisco. Harvey Milk was the first openly gay elected city official. He had run for a seat on San Francisco's city council on several occasions, each time gaining more votes and support. His rational no-nonsense approach to campaigning had gradually positioned him as a champion for not only gay rights but all human rights. He was serving his first term with another human rights advocate, Dianne Feinstein. The city's mayor, George Mosconi, was working closely with the pair to address what they saw as an alarming trend. The previous years had seen the rolling back of many gay rights in America.

A disturbed anti-gay conservative member of the city council, Dan White, had abruptly resigned his seat. When he asked to be reinstituted, Mayor Mosconi had refused to make an exception to the law and allow it. The enraged White had entered City Hall and shot and killed both the mayor and Harvey Milk. The homosexual community was in deep grief. Many feared that we had lost our hope to identify a "Martin Luther King-type" of leader who could galvanize the community and create a national awareness of the discrimination gay men and women had endured for decades.

The gay community had made some inroads in achieving acceptance after the Stonewall Inn Riot in Greenwich Village in 1969. That was an event that marked a change from silently enduring prejudice to demanding the rights offered all Americans under the Constitution. The violent late night demonstration occurred at one of those odd crossroads of history when many elements had come together to explode into a major episode. Unfortunately, in the ensuing decade much of the progress that was evident after Stonewall had deteriorated. Milk and his colleagues were working on reversing the conservative trend. His main crusade was to protect gay San Franciscans from being fired or denied lodging based on their sexual orientation.

The article enumerated several of Milk's requests, notably a demand that all gay Americans "come out." His position was that, as long as we hid our true selves and sexuality, we encouraged repression and discrimination. That idea became a requirement in my mind and I decided to follow the slain civil rights advocate's appeal. I would come out to my parents.

**From left, Tracy, Dicky, and the author aboard *The Norway*
shortly before Dicky's death.**

Chapter Four

1979

Los Angeles, California

My first year operating out of Los Angeles was a great learning experience both personally and professionally. At work, I had to quickly become skilled at surviving in an expanding, publicly traded company manned by many ambitious and some ruthless executives. I called the corporate office "the shark tank." Similarly, my personal life was completely different from my previous days. In Washington, DC, I was an obsessed workaholic, wedged in a tearing space between despair and hope and whose sole focus was to keep a small, fledgling company from tipping into a blank hole. I had not learned anything at graduate school that could guide me during such adversity. Ahmed and I ran the business by the seat of our pants, creating a new *modus operendi* week by week to find ways to meet our payroll.

As Royce had predicted, those days were completely over. While I worked and traveled more hours a week than anyone I knew, I was exhilarated. More importantly, perhaps, there were obvious fruits to our efforts. We were able to define strategies and set actions into motion to accomplish them. It took me a few years to profoundly believe the long-term projects we began would actually become realities. I had become too accustomed to setbacks due to lack of funds and fighting windmills that never stopped turning for long.

AMI's chief operating officer, Wally Weisman, was an understandable and ominous obstacle from the start. It was unprecedented for a vice president with profit and loss responsibility to report around a senior officer to the chief executive. Royce was the quintessential internationalist and Renaissance man. He knew the flexibility needed to create a network of hospitals in disparate countries presented challenges that the black- and-white thinking and unworldly Wally could not comprehend. While I tried to keep Weisman informed about my activities, a feeling of tension and visceral mistrust gradually emerged. It was clear to me from the beginning that my life at AMI was limited to Royce's tenure as its chief executive.

My large corner office at the AMI building in Beverly Hills was only a mile from West Hollywood and the trendy gay bars. Most evenings after work, I would drop by one of these gathering spots, usually Rage or The Revolver, for drinks while I watched the handsome, young men I nicknamed MDA's. This was a "*jeux de mots*" (play on words) of 'model, dancer, actors' and also the name of the new sex-enhancing drug that many of these beauties used.

On Saturday nights I would dance at Studio One, the largest gay bar I had ever seen or imagined. Located a few blocks from Rage, it occupied two floors in a large warehouse-type structure. The dance floor was approximately six thousand square feet, and by midnight it was jammed with men. The best disc jockeys played the latest disco music while we danced, usually shirtless. I felt a compelling desire for emotional connection with a view toward creating a special lifestyle of my own choosing. Several regulars looked more like world-class athletes and moved more like Olympic gymnasts than did dancers in other bars. The music was so loud that one could literally feel it pounding through one's entire body. As the night wore on, the sexual tension rose exponentially.

I rarely asked anyone to dance. Instead, I would either simply take the arm of a young man standing nearby and guide him onto the pulsating floor, squeezing through sweaty young men, or I would begin dancing alone. Before long one or more guys would join me, usually to dance for several hours. Both techniques worked more often than not.

One Saturday night, while standing on the narrow side pathways along the dance floor looking for a partner, I saw Tracy. His large green-blue eyes protruded from a handsome black face with shortly cropped hair. His smile was youthful and radiated a happy innocence that was hypnotic. His football player-like smooth shiny torso did, in fact, hypnotize me. We danced that Saturday night until closing, after which we went to my penthouse condominium on Ocean Avenue in Santa Monica, which had been professionally decorated and furnished while I was in Switzerland.

We developed a curious and happy sexual relationship. Tracy was a graduate student at USC (the University of Southern California) and had a part-time job. Busy and secure as we both were, neither one called, much less saw, the other during the week. We simply met at Studio One every Saturday and spent the night in Santa Monica. The following Sunday mornings we would part ways after brunch at a fashionable breakfast place somewhere on the West Side of town.

Most Sunday afternoons, after Tracy returned to his dormitory, I would walk the short distance from my apartment to Royce's impressive beachfront home. We sat by the pool or played paddle tennis. As day turned to evening, we ate cheese and fruit and sipped quality wines from Royce's well-stocked wine cellar. He never questioned me about my life away from work nor did he interrogate me about office politics. My admiration, appreciation, and love for him grew weekly.

Eastern Long Island, New York

Against Ahmed's advice, I decided to follow Harvey Milk's request and explain my sexuality to both my parents and a dear lady, Nonnie, who had been a huge influence in my very early years.

I began with her, in part, because I was most concerned about her ability to grasp the concept of homosexuality and, conveniently, she lived in Islip, Long Island, near the ferry docks to Fire Island.

I drove to her modest home near the village's Town Hall. During each visit I recalled with joy the happy times I spent in this small dwelling during most of my first six years, while my parents were in Europe. Nonnie and her husband, Mr. Lee, were poor but very loving. Nonnie tenderly bathed me in only a few inches of warm water to conserve energy. Any sense of security I have emerged during those years and from Nonnie and Mr. Lee's simple but flawless logic.

Upon my arrival, Nonnie would always serve me tea in one of the cups I routinely sent her from a foreign country to add to her cherished china collection. Each cup sat atop the piece of the packaging in which it arrived, with the stamps, so that she could easily recall its origin. I walked up the three red brick front steps where I had sat for many hours as an infant and knocked on the door. Obviously, Nonnie was ready and had our little party all set up. Nothing was different that day, but I feared the discussion certainly would be. Instead of enchanting her with tales of international travel and business, I would have to come out of the closet to her.

After taking my usual seat near her overstuffed rocking easy chair, I began, "Nonnie, you *do* know how much I love you, right?"

"Ayan," she affirmed in her unusual fashion of speaking.

"Well, I fear that I may have been hypocritical with you."

"There is not a lying cell in your body, René," she began, using my middle name, which everyone called me during my childhood. "You were as good as gold when you lived here, and I'll not be believing anything else." She chuckled and rocked back and forth in her chair.

"Nonnie, I am homosexual." I spat out the words before my courage disappeared. "Do you know what that means?"

"Oh, sure, René, I know all about gay men," she replied to my complete astonishment. "I watch Phil Donahue right there on that television every day." I laughed aloud as I noticed a frown appear on her face and watched her formulate her next sentences carefully.

"I am concerned about one thing, René. I never taught you a single thing about cooking and keeping house. I guess I should of. I wonder about who will be taking care of you and preparing your food."

My laughter turned into tears of joy as I jumped up and hugged her fragile body as tightly as I dared without hurting her.

The rest of the visit proceeded exactly as was the custom. When it was time to leave, she walked me the few feet to the front door, kissed me, and said, "Good as gold, René. You just always remember that. Good as gold," and she waved the Life-Line buzzer hanging from her neck. It allowed her to continue living alone with confidence since her recent stroke and was the best gift I ever gave anyone.

As I rode the ferry over to The Pines, I felt so relieved and thankful. I also had the unrealistic expectation that a similar discussion with my supposedly sophisticated parents would also be unproblematic. I planned to stop by their home in ten days when I returned from Europe.

Boca Raton, Florida

In their mid-seventies, my parents moved from a house to a condominium in a new high-rise on A1A across from the well-known pink Boca Raton Hotel and Club. They owned both places for two years while my father prepared the apartment and ascertained that *his* decision to downsize was correct.

My relationship with them was formal in the extreme. I barely knew them. I'd lived mostly with Nonnie during my happy first six years. After that, I spent ten years in strict and homophobic Swiss Boarding Schools. From there I went to Georgetown University and, later, graduate school, in addition to working most holidays in Washington, DC, as a bartender and chauffeur. I addressed my French father in the polite tense that was practically unheard of in the twentieth century. People who observed our infrequent interaction commented that we treated each other like formal strangers.

This estranged behavior had intensified during my days in Washington while Ahmed and I tried to save my father-in-law's consulting firm. After having received a *Washington Post* article about the impending liquidation, which had been sent by one of my board members, my father called and announced, "I did not bring a child into this world to drag our good name into bankruptcy courts. You will resign your duties immediately and identify another position."

"That is impossible, Father. Without my help, the company will definitely go down the drain. The family will be penniless, with no hopes of a comfortable retirement. With Ahmed's help, I feel there is a good chance of pulling this thing out of the nose dive."

My father, who had known Ahmed since early childhood, answered, "First of all, you both are too inexperienced to salvage such a mess. There is no one who will bail you out. If you end up without financial resources, do not think you can come to us for any assistance other than to find a place set at the dining room table to eat. Secondly, no business people in America can take seriously anyone with an Arab name like Ahmed Yehia."

As Christi Heffner, Playboy's successful C.E.O. recently said, "If I knew then everything I know now, I would have failed." Like Ms. Heffner, my innocent beliefs in managing the crisis won over a more experienced logic and led to success. But any furthering of a conversation based on differing views with my father was futile. In the next years, the fact that I "disobeyed" his order was not negated by the subsequent triumphant sale of the company to AMI, and he certainly never stated or implied any regret for his gloomy forecast.

On the flight from London to Miami, I tried to prepare myself and the presentation to my parents about my homosexuality. I silently rehearsed sentences that would, I hoped, absolve them of any misguided feelings of guilt—both genetic and environmental. I reached Boca Raton that evening and, after many flattering comments about their new home, I began my speech. "There are reasons for my recent divorce which you do not know. I apologize for not having been totally honest and up front with you. Please understand that what I have done is in no way because of any fault of yours but, rather, it is about who I am. I hope you will understand why and forgive me."

Blank faces stared at me across the living room coffee table. I looked out a picture window at the ocean, took a deep breath, and openly revealed my "fatal flaw," suspecting that I was merely confirming what my father already feared. "I am gay and would like to explain myself by answering any questions or concerns you may have."

After an uncomfortable and prolonged silence during which my sole focus was to disguise my inner terror of rejection, my father said, "I will be retiring to my room now. Your mother will join me. I am in no mood, at this hour, to discuss such a thing and will meet with you, in my office, after breakfast tomorrow."

With that, they both rose. Favoring an arthritic hip, my father limped away, my mother turned off lights, and I was left sitting alone in near darkness. After a sleepless night and a painfully uncomfortable breakfast, I met both parents in my father's den. They sat erect and created a mood similar to job interviews I'd had during my graduating semester at business school. I broke the icy silence. "I am sure this all comes as a shock, so please feel free to ask any question that may help explain things and I hope put your minds at rest."

"We have no questions, René, and of course we realize that this tragedy is no fault of ours. Simply a statement," began my father. "We cannot see why you did not stay married and take occasional vacations to do whatever you like. If you decide to live an openly homosexual existence, surrounded by hairdressers, that is your business. But understand you can *never* bring any—what am I supposed to call them, 'boyfriends'?—home to us unless you introduce them as your secretary."

Several decades earlier my father had lived on Cap Ferrat in the South of France near Nice. The villa was next door to the aging well-known gay author Somerset Maugham. Every evening Maugham and his "secretary," Allan, would walk by my father's house. Everyone knew that Allan was the author's lover but went along with the ruse.

"If that did not work for Somerset Maugham in the fifties, it certainly will not work for me in the eighties. I cannot introduce a partner as my secretary," I said as forcefully as I knew how.

"It's up to you. But those are our terms," he said. "I prefer to not discuss this subject any further."

And we never did.

I drove my rental car back to Miami airport, flew to Los Angeles and immediately went to the one place I felt at home, unthreatened, and in control: 8709, the gay baths.

CHAPTER FIVE

1980

Lausanne, Switzerland

In the early part of 1980, I spent a lot of time in London working with Stanley. We became close and frequently traveled to Switzerland together where the old hotel, now Clinique Cecil, was undergoing major renovations. (In French, the word "clinique" means private hospital as opposed to government national health facilities called "hospitals.") Immediately after we met him at The President Hotel in Geneva, Jean-Claude Salamin had been hired to run our inaugural Swiss facility. While in Lausanne working with Jean-Claude, we were actively involved in physician recruitment to ascertain that, upon completion of the construction, we would have an appropriate, qualified, and diverse medical staff.

Jean-Claude had spent several months in the U.S. visiting numerous AMI hospitals and working with executives at the corporate office in Beverly Hills to become familiar with the art of hospital management. From the beginning, it was obvious that he quickly understood everything we taught. More importantly, he instinctively knew which American management practices would work in Switzerland and which would not. Attempts to explain these subtleties to senior officers, especially Wally Weisman, were usually not successful. Wally and most of his senior department heads believed we could run European hospitals like American facilities.

Stanley had "adjusted" Jean-Claude's thinking in London, explaining important differences between community hospitals in the United States and acute private hospitals in Europe. The European strategy was to have high end, almost luxurious facilities and services to attract locals fortunate enough to afford relatively expensive supplementary hospital insurance to reimburse our costs. While the Harley Street Clinic was well appointed, Jean-Claude had higher aspirations for "his" Clinique Cecil, inspired in part from having run lavish hotels.

First and foremost was physician recruitment. That task in America is fairly regulated and, therefore, structured. U.S. hospitals cannot offer the types of incentives we could propose in Europe, such as free office space—or even financial inducements—if a renowned specialist would see and admit patients at our facilities. We needed to improvise new methods to attract our planned medical staff. As with all start-up businesses, we needed one famous physician to become primarily affiliated with us in order to start the ball rolling, which in turn would encourage others to follow. One summer day we had a lucky break.

During breakfast, at the Lausanne Palace Hotel, I read about a shakeup at The University Hospital in Bern, Switzerland's capitol. The paper mentioned a respected professor of medicine and surgery, Leo Eckmann, who was disenchanted with the city's major hospital's ability to fund new equipment. Jean-Claude walked—pranced, really—into the dining room to take us to a meeting in Geneva.

"Have you seen this article about trouble at the University Hospital in Bern?" I asked.

Jean-Claude took the paper and read the piece. "Let us try to reach Professor Eckmann from the car, we are late." We had one of the early car phones in Jean-Claude's prized BMW, which was parked in front of the hotel. "You drive. I'll try to find the professor's number," he said.

Within minutes we were connected with Leo Eckmann, who was willing to discuss the problems with us but preferred to do so in person. "Ask him when we can call on him," I told Jean-Claude in what became the typically disjointed three-way conversation.

"Now!" Salamin mouthed while still listening to the professor. I turned the car around and raced off in the opposite direction—to Bern.

Travel between Switzerland's cities by train or on their modern highway system (AutoRoute) is both fast and pleasant. In an hour we were in Bern and, shortly thereafter, sitting with a tall white-haired gentleman who spoke more like a charming philosopher than any physician I knew. To make things even more pleasant, he had a sharp, dry, English-like sense of humor. By the end of the day we had developed the basic terms for Professor Eckmann to leave Bern and occupy the ground floor of an attractive villa adjacent to the hospital we had purchased. We promised to reconfigure the space, creating both an office and a residential apartment. We also assured him that, with us, he would not have the bureaucratic problems obtaining budgets for modern equipment.

"I absolutely demand assurances that I will have the latest CT scanner at the clinique," he said.

"Guaranteed," I replied instantly.

"There are none yet in private hospitals in Switzerland," said Eckmann, still questioning our ability to purchase equipment that even the city had denied him.

"You'll have it *and* everything else we discussed," I assured him.

"By the way," he continued, "I am more interested now in a different specialty than surgery. Something I consider to be at the root of all medicine and an area that will be of increasing interest over the next decades. I'll be studying this subject carefully."

"And what might that be?" I inquired surprised.

"Immunology," responded Eckmann. "The topic fascinates me."

London, England

In April, AMI opened its third hospital in England. The Princess Margaret Hospital in Harrow was our foray into expanding the concept of acute care private hospitals from London to secondary English cities. If the expensive experiments were successful, I would use a similar business model in Switzerland. As such immediately before the hospital's opening I was both very interested and more involved with the final preparations.

Stanley had decided to name the hospital after Queen Elizabeth's younger sister, Princess Margaret. The unfortunate Royal had experienced a series of romantic disappointments, was always considered the "controversial Royal," and was struggling with alcohol abuse. As part of her Royal duties, Her Royal

Highness was Grand President of the St. John Ambulance Brigade and later Colonel-in-Chief of Queen Alexandra's Royal Army Nursing Corp.

Her drinking and her romantic experiences in the Bahamas were currently the subjects of considerable gossip. We correctly believed that the combination of her activities with medical charities as well as a need for a boost in her popularity might encourage her to lend her name and some of her time to our new hospital.

Stanley, Royce, and I were to greet the Princess at the front door of the modern and recently completed facility, to take her on a tour, which was to be followed by cocktails and lunch. As is customary, through the early days of a brand new hospital, and especially during a highly publicized grand opening, less acute illnesses are treated so as to not draw media attention to the usual growing pains of a new hospital. Consequently, the rooms along the patient floor we were to visit were occupied by attractive mothers carrying their newborns and other sub-acute patients who were all well enough to try to look their best.

As the long line of police vehicles approached, I noticed a baby blue Rolls Royce in the middle of the cortege. It was a small detail that surprised me, because at previous, somewhat similar events, I had always seen the guest of honor in specially designed large black cars. At fifty, Her Royal Highness was still an attractive, albeit slightly heavy woman, with magnificent blue eyes. As the back door of her car was opened, I held out my hand to assist her.

"Welcome, Princess Margaret," I said. "I cannot help but notice that your beautiful eyes match the lovely blue color of your car."

The forward complement momentarily took her aback, and she responded with, "This being a private occasion, I was able to bring the blue Rolls Royce. Had it been a Royal occasion, I'd have been obliged to ride in a black Rolls Royce."

"Happily for us!" I continued. "This car shows off your eyes," which filled with tears as she smiled and thanked me.

During the walk through the patient floors, the Princess commented, "My, everyone looks so well and happy."

"Well, you know, we are from Los Angeles. So I asked central casting to send us a selection of perfect looking patients to place in the beds just for you!"

She hesitated, but got the joke and burst out laughing.

Thus began an interesting relationship that included many meetings with her. At one Christmas party, which she always dutifully attended, I danced with her. When I brought her back to her seat, Stanley whispered in my ear, "That's the first time the Princess danced with the queen."

Los Angeles

Only a few of the very largest domestic AMI hospitals had been allowed to order CT scanners in 1980. None had ever made any kind of agreement with a physician, regardless of fame, like we were proposing. I knew that my promises to Professor Eckmann were of critical importance to Clinique Cecil's future but could also cause further jealousies. I discussed this with Royce upon my return to Beverly Hills. As usual he questioned me carefully. After reviewing the costs and expected benefits of all the expenses Professor Eckmann's arrival would involve, he allowed me to proceed and recommended we plan a major media event for the opening of Cecil's advanced surgery and radiology departments. He also advised me to overlook any jealousies, as they were always present in successful, active people.

As I was leaving the Chief Executive-turned-father figure's, office, he said, "You look drawn, Rick. Popping back and forth to Europe is taking a toll on you even at thirty-two years old. Watch it. Why not get a physical?" The comment hit home. I had felt drawn and decided to act on Royce's comment.

After work, I stopped by one of my usual watering spots, The Revolver, in West Hollywood. I picked up a gay newspaper that also had a classified section with advertisements from numerous professionals, including physicians, catering to a gay clientele. The following day, I called Doctor Robert Davis and booked an appointment. After two visits and results of the then-customary blood work, I met with Bob, who had quickly become a friend.

"I see nothing unusual in the blood work. However, you *do* have enlarged lymph nodes."

"What does that mean, Bob?" I asked.

"Frankly, I'm not sure," he answered. "I feel confident it is not lymph cancer." The remark struck that same nerve anyone sitting on a physician's table feels when hearing the "C word" for the first time. "But I am seeing this symptom in several of my patients, particularly those with other ailments. In contrast, you have no other problems, right? No digestion problems, no white-colored growths in your mouth, no unusual fatigue?"

"No," I said awkwardly. "I mean—you know—I travel a lot."

"I have a meeting with two other physicians here in L.A. who also have seen these phenomena in their patients," he continued. "I tell ya what; I'll call you afterwards and we'll get together and discuss what these physicians, Michael Gottlieb and Joel Weisman, have to say. They have larger practices."

A few weeks later, my secretary announced that Doctor Davis was on the line.

"Hi, Bob. What's up?" I asked joyfully. I had forgotten about the mysterious illnesses and was genuinely happy to speak with Bob.

"I have some information I'd like to talk to you about. How about a drink at The Revolver at seven o'clock?"

A few hours later, I met Bob. At first we talked about Ronald Reagan's victory over Jimmy Carter and how one of Reagan's greatest supporters, Jerry Fallwell, would like to see all gay men dead. We wondered if the civil liberties gay Americans had gained in the previous decade could be reversed. Then the topic switched from politics to medicine.

"René," he began, using my "away from work" name, "something very weird is going on. Serious, often fatal illnesses which used to be rarely observed are now being seen in both Joel's and Michael's practices."

"What kind of illnesses?" I asked.

"There are three really. A rare form of pneumonia...."

"Jesus," I interrupted. "I bumped into a French pulmonologist over a year ago who mentioned something like that."

"Well," continued Bob, "there are others. Have you ever heard of Toxoplasmosis?"

"No," I replied, confused.

"It's a rare problem, previously only observed in weakened cat and bird owners, that now seems to be attacking brain cells in gay men...."

I thought of the young friend I had on Fire Island who had rapidly become demented. "And the third?" I pushed on.

"A strange cancer called Kaposi's Sarcoma. It usually shows up as a smooth, painless skin lesion. Although it has been around forever, it used to only occur in middle aged Mediterraneans and was always slow progressing, usually not fatal. All that's different now."

Again I cut in: "Is it purple-like?"

"Exactly," he affirmed.

My heart skipped a few beats as I had noticed large purple blotches, what I thought were rashes, on a few friends both on Fire Island and in L.A.

"Joel suspects a correlation with low white blood cell counts. White cells help the body fend off illnesses, both viral and bacterial. Gottlieb, who has the huge resources of UCLA at his disposal, is counting something called T-Cells."

"What are T-Cells?" I asked, yet again learning new terminology.

"They are a lymphocyte, a type of white cell, and the main building block of the immune system."

I made a mental note to talk to my new Swiss pal, Leo Eckmann, about T-Cells when we met right after the New Year. Bob continued, "I was amazed to learn that these bizarre medical occurrences have now been observed on three continents. Here, mostly in L.A., New York, and San Francisco, almost always in gay men; and in Europe and Zaire, Africa. Some have started calling this 'a gay plague.'"

"That does not make sense," I said. "We are no different genetically than straight men. We all drink coffee! Is this a virus or bacteria?"

"I have no idea, René. All I know is that Hepatitis B is rising at an alarming rate, as are all venereal diseases. I think the sexual revolution has gotten out of hand. Sadly, I have no advice other than for you to come to me if you develop any of the symptoms I've mentioned."

"Sure thing. But what will you do if I develop one of these signs?"

"I have no idea," responded Bob, as a look of confusion and sadness came over his youthful face. "Just hope it does not happen. People are dying, René, and there seems little that anyone can do about it. That's all I know for sure."

CHAPTER SIX

1981

Lausanne, Switzerland

Clinique Cecil's new surgery and radiology departments were completed in the spring of 1981. During the planning of the grand opening party, I had come to understand that Jean-Claude had a real flair for the dramatic and looked forward to co-hosting what promised to be one of the city's major social events.

As usual, Jean-Claude picked me up at Geneva airport and we drove directly to the hospital. In the parking lot, by the entrance to the building, was a stretch Mercedes with a chauffeur and another gentleman in a dark blue suit standing near the door. Walking past them, Jean-Claude whispered to me, "A limousine with chauffeur and body guard always means a foreign dignitary or royalty has come to see Professor Eckmann."

After two days of meetings, mostly with Jean-Claude and his new finance director, and on the day of the celebration, I met Professor Eckmann in the hospital's "living-room," which Jean-Claude had made sure to restore to its earlier hotel grandeur.

The lounge felt like the main drawing room of a historic luxury hotel. In one corner was a full bar, staffed by a uniformed waiter who served cappuccinos, alcoholic drinks, and other beverages to guests and visitors. A great oval section in the middle of the far end of the room had large, beautiful etched windows with art glass details. Elegant yet comfortable, furniture had been arranged so that the occupants of the room could look out over Lake Geneva and see the French city of Evian in the distance, lying just beneath snow covered mountains.

Before the big event, Leo, Jean-Claude, and I sat in a quiet section of the room and discussed the professor's activities at the hospital. His arrival as a primarily affiliated member of the medical staff had created the desired effect in the medical community, and several other prominent physicians were now also admitting their patients. Leo raised some administrative and many medical staff issues, which Jean-Claude and I addressed point by point. When all the business matters had been covered, I directed the conversation to a more personal level.

"How do you like living in the Villa?" I asked.

"It's very pleasant," he responded in his deliberate pronunciation. "It could be more so if I had a bit more cooperation from the architect. He insists that everything be painted white!" The gentle hint was noted.

"Please explain all the details." I said.

"Let's go over to my flat and I'll show you what I would like to have accomplished."

Leaving Jean-Claude to attend to the caterers, we crossed the busy street to the villa, also being refurbished, and entered Leo's apartment, which was full of antiquities and exotic art collected during his many visits to Asia and Africa. After he described the design concerns, Leo poured two glasses of wine and invited me to sit in a large, brown leather chair. When he was seated in another I said, "Leo, please tell me more about your interest in immunology."

"Well, my grandfather was an immunologist in Czarist Russia before the term was even used. My father followed in his footsteps. They taught me that the strength of the immune system is at the basis of all health. I have made interesting observations ever since. For example, did you know the immune system weakens as one ages, which is principally responsible for the onset of many illnesses?"

Ignoring his rhetorical question, I proceeded. "Have you been following the odd illnesses being observed in the States, largely in the homosexual community?"

"Of course I have. But we have cases in Europe and even right here in Switzerland. I make a point of speaking with the physicians treating several of these patients."

"What are your conclusions?" I asked, hoping to finally hear some promising news.

"Many more questions than conclusions…. But there definitely is a link between the cancer, pneumonia, and digestive and nervous system problems. I'm sure there is an assault on the immune system. What we need are funds for research and *quickly*. This is not going away—more cases are being seen every week!"

"Sadly, our new president has cut the proposed Center for Disease Control's research budget from $320 million dollars to some $160 million," I said, quoting frightening statistics I had read on the recent overnight flight.

"I assume you have a personal interest in the subject," he asked, leading me to revealing more details.

"Yes, Leo, I do. I have friends who have exhibited many of the symptoms of what I have heard called 'the gay plague,' and my doctor pointed out that I have enlarged lymph nodes." The brilliant and intuitive professor got the messages loud and clear.

"Believing that this is directly linked to homosexuality is idiocy. Note that I said 'directly.' There may be some behavior, drug, or product consumed that is creating a battering of the immune system, in addition to the lack of necessary rest, which also weakens the body. I assume that these unknown causes are somehow linked to sex but it's not what I'd call a typical 'sexually transmitted disease' because there is no manifestation whatsoever on the genitals and, remember, sexually transmitted diseases are bacterial and easily treated."

"Is this not a bacteria?" I asked, misusing the plural of bacterium. It was the same question being bounced around at the time in many hospitals and research laboratories.

"That is not yet known for sure, but I'll place my bet on a virus. We have to identify it!" he said, raising his voice almost to a shout.

"Will you be my physician?" I asked bluntly.

"I'd be delighted, but remember, my theories are often controversial and I make both medical and—let's call them—paramedical recommendations," he concluded and began a twenty-year relationship that often turned inexplicable facts into some sense. "Now let's go to the party. I heard you will speak!"

"Do you not want to examine me?" I asked.

"Why? You said you have enlarged lymph nodes. That's enough for now." Over the following years, Leo never examined my body but he certainly challenged my mind. "Let's go and see this spectacle!" he said as we both left his warm inviting apartment.

The evening celebration certainly was a "spectacle." Waiters wearing spotless, white jackets served delicious hot and cold hors d'oeuvres and a selection of wines and Champagne. Small groups of dignitaries and physicians were individually escorted into the radiology and surgery departments. Reporters from Switzerland's three "sections" (French, German, and Italian) were in attendance, as was a local television news crew. The *piece de resistance* was waiting inside a new Mercedes ambulance, which had the hospital's name painted most prominently on the side and was waiting in the parking lot.

Jean-Claude had arranged for the director of Lausanne's well-known museum to allow us to collect an Egyptian mummy, transport it to the hospital, and place it in our new Siemens CT scanner—the first one in a private Swiss hospital. After the examination, our proud new radiologist spoke to the group in the main lounge. "We have learned several things about the mummy many of us have seen at the museum. Now that we have looked *inside* this treasure, I will begin by referring to 'it' as 'she.' In addition, and to the curator's amazement, there is a four-centimeter needle in the mummy's chest cavity that may, when the data is analyzed by an international team of experts, explain the cause of death.

The guests were all duly amazed, as exhibited by many exclamations and muffled conversations. The newspaper and television reporters all gave the honest stunt great coverage which, in turn, brought our new hospital very much into the minds of most Swiss citizens.

Los Angeles, California

By the summer of 1981, the still unnamed phenomena was being spoken about in many medical circles. A Center for Disease Control (CDC) task force had determined a link between the major illnesses of Pneumocystis Carinii, Kaposi's Sarcoma, and Candida, and created a new term grouping them as "Opportunistic Infections." "OI's" now defined the heretofore-rare infirmities that attack the immune system. But, sadly, since the problem was so largely focused on the homosexual community, it did not ignite much concern in the general public. A conservative wave was taking over in Washington, DC, and it was clear that as long as "normal Americans" were not at risk, there was no reason to prioritize research programs.

A new, temporary name for the scourge did not help. "GRID," or "Gay Related Immune Deficiency," reinforced the belief that this was a problem which solely effected homosexuals and, therefore, was not to be taken very seriously. Worse, some ultraconservative members of the Religious Right felt vindicated in their belief that God would eventually "get even" with the heathen homosexuals. In their minds, it was perfectly all right if the problem eradicated all gay men as long as it stayed clear of the general population. Stories of deviant behavior abounded as a link to sexual activity emerged and a theory about "Patient Zero" took root. The title was attributed to a handsome gay Air Canada flight attendant, Gaetan Ducas, who frequently visited the bathhouses in Los Angeles, San Francisco, and New York. It was wildly rumored that Gaetan, who had shown symptoms of KS for two years, engaged in unprotected sex with several thousand partners a year.

The Pines Harbor, Fire Island, New York

As the ferry from Sayville pulled into the harbor, I was eager to see all the sights I had missed. *Les Beaux* was moored on our port side, and the Ice Palace, with its bar, restaurant, and dance floor, was on the starboard side. There was something that caught my eye as we disembarked. A booth was set up near the dock with a large sign that read, "GIVE TO THE GAY CANCER."

As I walked along the boardwalk to my boat, the excitement was again dampened as we passed a beautifully restored antique Chris Craft belonging to a friend I had not seen all summer. At the boat's stern, I met the harbormaster who I knew well and inquired about the lovely old-fashioned boat's owner.

"He died in July, René, of the gay cancer, which spread to his lungs. We are having a fund raising drive this weekend."

That night, while eating a late dinner at an open-air roof top restaurant, I talked with former acquaintances about the gay plague, about whether my friend had died of KS or of pneumonia and about patient zero. Everyone there knew someone who was ill and were all on the lookout for any signs of the gay cancer. Sleeping around was no longer a joking matter; the period when one measured success by numbers of conquests was over.

PART TWO

TIM
1982–1989

CHAPTER SEVEN

1982

Lausanne, Switzerland

By January 1982, The World Health Organization announced that there had been thirty- six reported cases of the gay cancer in Europe, five of these in the very small country of Switzerland. The CDC had weighed in with their American tally of one hundred eight and had requested funds for their Opportunistic Infection and Kaposi's Sarcoma task force. The unanswered appeal for $830,000 represented an infinitesimal part of the multi-billion dollar National Institute of Health (NIH) budget. There simply was no interest in studying, much less preparing any prevention, for an illness that affected only gays.

Back in Switzerland, I continued to enjoy building the physician and client base of Clinique Cecil, working closely with Jean-Claude and Leo Eckmann. Jean-Claude's flair for publicity never took a vacation, as demonstrated on the first day of my January visit.

"Did you know that we have on the property the oldest Great Sequoia in Switzerland?" he asked out of the blue.

"I assume you mean that huge tree near the physician office building," I replied. "I love it but was unaware of its distinction."

"Well, it's sick. I see this as a great opportunity for good publicity. The expert we consulted said that it would slowly die and that the only hope was to use an expensive treatment developed in California."

"Okay," I said, wondering where this was leading.

"Think about it! We are a California-based company often criticized as being insensitive to local concerns."

Still not quite getting it, I continued. "You know perfectly well that you do not need my authority to incur that kind of expense. Just take care of it."

"Here *is* what I do need your authority for. I want to invite the best tree doctor in California to come *here* to treat Switzerland's oldest tree. I'll have a huge coverage of the event in the press. Now do you understand?"

"Brilliant," I exclaimed, realizing that we would get some excellent publicity. "But while we are on the subject of approvals from Corporate, you must re-read AMI's new Policy and Procedure Manual for hospital administrators and begin to comply. Wally Weisman, the chief operating officer, has pointed out many areas of non-compliance."

"You know that the American and Swiss systems are fundamentally different, as are our strategies. You tell Wally I wake up every morning and figure out how I can break one of those silly rules," Jean-Claude concluded.

Thus began a multi-year struggle I undertook to mediate Jean-Claude's contempt for the American side of the company, mostly as personified by Wally Weisman, and our instincts for what was needed to continue the now-evident success in Switzerland. Wally was not the only executive Jean-Claude teased. He had responded badly to Stanley's indignation that Queen Elizabeth had not been received with sufficient pomp during a recent visit to Geneva.

Jean-Claude, who was not *allowed* to call Stanley by his first name, responded. "You must understand, Doctor," he began, seizing the opportunity to provoke a violent reaction in anyone he felt had been illogical. "We respect real work and accomplishments here in Switzerland. So we feel that your Queen is really of no greater significance than my housekeeper!" That verbal recklessness had cost me a special trip to London to convince Stanley that Jean-Claude was doing his job and should not be "sacked"—the British term for fired.

In what was becoming my custom before I left Switzerland, I asked to have a personal conversation with my health advisor, Professor Eckmann.

"Leo, have you come closer to understanding the cause of the immune problems we have discussed?" I asked.

"No, but I am more and more convinced it is a virus. May I give you a quick course in virology?" he asked in his typical way of beginning conversations, one that would remain memorable for life.

"Please do," I urged.

"Well, virology has been studied for nearly a hundred years, mostly in Europe, notably France. The Pasteur Institute, in collaboration with the ancestor of your friend, Doctor Mérieux, and another brilliant researcher named Roux, were sure of the destruction viruses cause and differentiated this from bacterial illnesses. But it was not until the middle of the century, with the discovery of the electron microscope, that we could *see* viruses. Once we had the ability to watch them, we could much better understand their activity in the body. This led to the discovery of a sub-category called 'slow viruses.' If, indeed, we are dealing with a virus, I feel it is both slow and relatively difficult to contract."

"That's all good news," I said naively.

"Yes and no," he continued. "A slow virus can be in the system for years before manifesting itself. So it can be innocently spread. Worse, it can 'mutate' or transform itself, becoming a new virus with different characteristics. If a virus is easily transmitted from human to human, the world health authorities take action to avoid what is called 'a pandemic,' like we had here in Europe during the early part of the century. Immunology requires the identification of a virus in order to create a vaccine *from* it. In the history of virology, no serious viral condition has ever been solved by medications. It is useless to try to kill or to stop the virus, especially a mutating one. Rather we need to *change the host* so that the virus becomes ineffective. That is what a vaccine does. Think of the polio vaccine: The virus still exists, but it cannot hurt anyone who has been *immunized*. Back to the problem at hand," continued Leo, "there is a physician in Miami who believes that a transfusion caused his patient to develop Pneumocystis pneumonia. Sad as this may be, if it is true and *if* it is the same virus, the world may finally wake up to the fact that calling this a 'gay plague' is archaic and very dangerous. Once there is a spread to the general population, we may finally get much needed research funds! For now we are at the mercy of some political radicals on both sides of the ocean. Extremists, like your Reagan and France's Le Pen, would like to turn their heads away from medicine and see you all disappear. It's outrageous to link a human behavior to a virus, but that is what is happening."

Like many future lectures, delivered with consistent charm and knowledge, I never forgot his exact words and thought later about how accurate this visionary man was.

Los Angeles

One Sunday afternoon, at a tea dance in West Hollywood, I saw a young man who took my breath away. He was the typical tall, dark, and handsome wholesome boy. He had silky black hair, the same rich texture of a healthy young Indian Brave, as well as sparkling blue eyes and olive skin that looked like satin. I could not take my eyes off of him while he was speaking to a small gathering of other real lookers. When he broke away from his friends and walked passed me, I took hold of his arm in a bold attempt to start a conversation. This startled him and the first look that Tim shot at me was one of annoyance. But a conversation began and before long, I learned that Tim had only been in Los Angeles for six months and was very much enjoying being one of the hottest looking boys in town.

To my surprise, Tim agreed to accompany me to the beach in Santa Monica and watch the sun set. While there, he took off his shirt, revealing a very well-built lean athletic body including the only perfect six pack I ever saw. As the sun fell into the Pacific, Tim did cartwheels on the beach while the golden light made his blue eyes sparkle and his hair glisten. I watched his acrobatics believing that I had seen the most perfect example of a healthy all-American young man. I was completely dazzled and invited him to join me on a weekend adventure to Catalina Island. There I discovered that Tim did, in fact, have the perfect body with one exception. He, too, had swollen lymph nodes on his neck and under his arms. It occurred to me that I was no longer waiting for something better to walk into my life and, also, beauties were certainly not immune from whatever was happening to us.

From then on Tim and I saw as much of each other as possible. Tracy had graduated and left town and I was enamored with Tim. I learned that he was from a typical Indiana family and had been the captain of his high school's basketball team, which made him something of a local celebrity. He was the first in his family to get a college education and, to his mother's dismay, the first to leave Indiana. He was living in a distant suburb of Los Angeles working at a job he hated at Kimberly Clarke, mostly controlling inventory in a large warehouse. He was not "out" to his family and had no plans to have that conversation with them.

Tim was the first dedicated body builder I knew, and he quickly encouraged me to begin going to a gym with regularity. I joined West Hollywood's new large Sport's Connection, also referred to as the "Sport's Erection," due to the many magnificent men who worked with weights, went to new aerobics classes, and used the spa facilities. When I did not have a business lunch scheduled, I'd use my mid-day break to work out with a trainer at the nearby club. As I left, I always bought a protein shake and a salad and wolfed them down in my new Mercedes 500 SEC while racing back to the office. I had never previously enjoyed clubs, had not even known about health clubs, and I certainly loved this new experience.

By late winter, there were increasing hints that the new illness was not limited to the homosexual population. Every morning I read the *Wall Street Journal,* which my secretary would place on my desk. On February 25 I was struck by an article titled "New, Often Fatal, Illness in Homosexuals Turns up in Women, Heterosexual Males." I faxed it to Leo. It was followed a month later by an article in the *Los Angeles Times* that basically said the same thing. I knew the new information would be the subject of a conversation with my sage advisor when we next met. In the meantime, the CDC reported the cases in the U.S. jumped to two hundred eighty-five in March. The illness' name was being altered routinely as the search for its origin and targets were being investigated. It went from "GRID" through several mutations of its own and in July the CDC finally named it "AIDS," for "Acquired Immune Deficiency Syndrome."

Unfortunately, two contradictory forces were at play. The CDC's efforts to inform the general population were countered by politicians who still believed it was an illness that only sought out certain "undesirable" minorities. The new member to join that group were Haitians, which created a pathetic nickname for the disease of "The Four H's"—for homosexuals, heroin addicts, Haitians, and hemophiliacs, presumably in descending order of undesirability.

The case was made perfectly clear after the advent of a second mysterious illness called Legionnaires Disease, so-named because of an outbreak of a sometime fatal, respiratory problem during a Legionnaires convention in Pennsylvania. Perhaps because the latest illness only attacked "good Americans," NIH spent $34,000 on each fatal case versus $3,200 per AIDS deaths.

In France, the right-wing Le Pen, mentioned previously by Leo, was relentless in his efforts to make his constituents believe that good Frenchmen were safe because the illness was limited to the Four H's. It seemed that an international race for homophobia had begun when a slogan emerged during the gubernatorial campaign in New York between Mario Cuomo and Ed Koch: "Vote for Cuomo, not the homo."

By the end of the year, Tim and I were seeing each other every weekend I was in Los Angeles. I was developing a deep affection for this youthful, energetic, and naive young man. The number of Americans diagnosed with AIDS had risen to six hundred ninety-one, of which two hundred seventy-eight had died. There still was no ability to determine how many were infected. Leo's theory about slow viruses made sense when the term "pre-AIDS" emerged— this referred to the period from when an individual was exposed to the virus, showed some of the well-known symptoms, but had not had any opportunistic infections.

At a Christmas dinner I cooked in Santa Monica, guests of whom included Bob Davis and several of his patients who were also friends, Tim asked if our swollen lymph nodes could be considered "pre-AIDS."

"Since there is no way to know if you guys have been exposed, I'd have to say no. None of my patients have had 'pre-AIDS' for long before progressing to an OI. The good news is that research is being well coordinated between the French, at Pasteur, and NIH. Also, there is more evidence of a spread to the general population—hemophiliacs. It's also been reported in babies in New York. The government just can't stay quiet now. I'll bet there will be real progress soon even if the majority of Americans hate and fear gay people."

Tim and I ended the year on that optimistic note and began talking about his moving into the Santa Monica condominium and his long-term goals.

CHAPTER EIGHT

1983

Europe

By 1983, we were further expanding our International activities into Spain and considering a move into Australia. My monthly trips to Europe now always included visits to Spain and often on to Australia. Before leaving Switzerland, I never neglected a personal chat with Leo. "There are small advances in understanding the mystery," he told me one winter day. "Pasteur and one of their main scientists, Jean-Claude Chermann, believe it is a 'retrovirus' and not the virus that causes leukemia. Pasteur is also convinced that there is evidence it has been around for a number of years."

"What is a retrovirus?" I asked, readying myself for another brilliant lesson.

"I'll try to make this simple," began Leo. "A retrovirus not only attacks and kills its target but it *invades* those cells. After destroying them, it explodes into the body, releasing *many more* 'killers.' Chermann has been studying retroviruses for years. I will make a special effort to meet with him soon. The illness has now been observed in sixteen countries. I cannot understand why more efforts for research and education are not being made. But I now believe that we are dealing with a blood disease and not a venereal disease."

On the flight to Barcelona, Spain, I read that the reported cases of AIDS in America had crossed the 1,000 mark. I looked around me in the first class section of the plane. The usual variety of people was traveling—male, female, old, young, handsome, unattractive, etc. Was I the only person on the plane with "contaminated blood," I wondered. And, if so, would I not happily change places with anyone else on the flight regardless of age, education, or social condition?

Our first entry into the Spanish market was to acquire a 50 percent interest in the famous Clinica Quiron in Barcelona. For three generations, the well-respected private hospital had belonged to the Mestre family, the ancestors of whom wrote the first book for medical students. Joaquin Mestre and his administrative team realized that the hospital needed an infusion of capital that was unrealistic for a family to meet. As a result, discussions with us lead to AMI becoming equal equity partners. I was particularly fond of the hospital administrator, Antonio Vancells, and his young assistant, Gabriel Massfurrol. Antonio was not only a competent manager and diplomat, but also a renowned sculptor who had been commissioned by the Spanish Royal family to create busts of several of their loved ones.

My times at Quiron were always rewarding. The people I worked with were more cultured and well-rounded than any other executives in my experience, with the exception of Royce. While challenging, our board meetings were productive and resulted in an unusual collaboration of differing experiences resulting in successful efforts to renovate the hospital and return it to its earlier greatness. It always gave me a laugh when other members of the hospital's board referred to me as "Don Ricardo." Beginning with my first visits to Barcelona, I frequently met two of the hospital's regular famous local patients, Xavier Cugat and Salvador Dali. Later, I secretly made exceptions to our rule of only treating acute cases and allowed both artists to enjoy a personalized more long-term care in the facility. The hospital's dining room had a walled-off executive area where the hospital administrators would meet after work, at earlier hours than the Spaniards were accustomed to, merely to accommodate my schedule. There, we had many wonderful meals, often including famous patients and Catalonian friends.

In the spring of 1983, Pasteur was closely watching ten AIDS cases in an effort to identify the virus and, in America, Congressman Henry Waxman of California was trying to create greater awareness of the dangers AIDS posed. As a member of the House Subcommittee on Health, he was the first to request federal funding specifically identified for AIDS research.

Los Angeles, California

Around this time, I received the first communication from my father since our discussion of my sexuality. In the interim, he had relied on my mother to relay all information to me. His communiqué actually was a copy of a letter he had sent to my brother. It explained that 1983 was a great year for our family because we all turned milestone ages. He would be eighty, my mother seventy-five, my brother forty, and I would turn thirty-five. As a result, he was "informing" us that we were all to meet in Rotterdam, Holland, in late summer, for a twelve-day family cruise through the Norwegian Fjords and on to Leningrad. The letter was signed, "Your loving father, John Silvin."

I had *never* taken a two week-long vacation. The prospect of spending my first real holiday—longer than a three-day weekend—with my parents certainly was not what I had imagined. But, after considering the effort he was making, I responded, also in writing. I explained that this would be my first prolonged absence from work and I joked saying that, in a rapidly growing firm, anyone who left for two weeks ran the risk of returning to the office to find someone else sitting at his desk. Finally, I informed both parents that I was entering into a relationship and could only make such a "wonderful'" long trip if my "friend" could join me.

After a period of silence, the second round of letters began. "Your mother and I have carefully considered your difficult request. We can accept you bringing this friend along but only if, as previously mentioned, he is introduced as your secretary." My brother was copied on the correspondence.

By return mail, I told him that this was unacceptable. I reminded him of how silly that game had sounded decades earlier with Somerset Maugham and that I had no intention of humiliating Tim in a like fashion or, for that matter, the entire family. Again, after a period of silence, I received a copy of a letter to my brother that included a check for $5,000 made out to me. The letter explained that, "because René is being difficult" they had canceled the reservations for the cruise. The total cost of the vacation per couple, including the double cabins for my brother and his wife, was $10,000. The value of my brother's gift was enclosed. "As for

René, since it was never intended that he be accompanied by any-one, I am sending him $5,000." It was signed "John Silvin." This must have hit a nerve in my brother who subsequently sent me $2,500 trying to "even things out."

I was crushed and asked my friend and physician, Bob Davis, to recommend a psychologist I could consult. He suggested a gay colleague, Doctor Bernard, who I began seeing regularly regarding my relationship with my father; my being gay in a hostile corporate environment, with the exception of my boss, Royce; and about my serious insomnia and use of sleeping pills. I was using pills in the belief that they could lessen my frequent, horrible nightmares, but that proved not to be the case. In fact, it took longer to wake up from an episode which had made me take them, resulting in more sleepless nights.

When I brought Doctor Bernard the letters regarding the pro-posed family meeting, I saw that he had a difficult time containing his laughter. But, over the ensuing two years, he was extremely professional in assisting me with my list of problematic subjects, including the unfolding of how to deal with what was not yet called HIV. One of his first recommendations was that I start attending meetings hosted by an enlightened psychologist who met with groups of gay men, mostly with health issues, at West Hollywood's community centre. Her name was Louise Hay, and she had just moved her rapidly growing gatherings from her back porch to a larger forum. Her classes and those of another forward thinking psychologist, Marianne Williamson, were being called "A Course in Miracles"!

Melbourne, Australia

Stanley and I had already made several reconnaissance trips to Australia. AMI had acquired its first hospital on the continent, in Melbourne. While we were the industry leaders in developing hos-pitals outside the United States, we had entered the Australian market late. Hospital Corporation of America (HCA) had set up a subsidiary in Sydney and had acquired three small hospitals. We chose Melbourne, Australia's second city and the capital of Victoria Province, as our entry into this ripe new market as we were con-vinced we could here become the dominant private health care providers more easily than taking on HCA in Sydney.

We were studying building a new hospital in a rapidly growing affluent suburb of Melbourne. On this trip we met with a disconcerting piece of news. Our attorney advised us that our arch competitor, HCA, had acquired a piece of land in the area and had begun speaking with a local architect about building a community hospital. At first, it appeared that we would not be the only player in the Province and our strategy may have failed. By the next day, Stanley had developed a bold Machiavellian plan. We immediately made an unconditional offer on the property we had identified as optimal and hired a young architect in town. Before we left we instructed the design firm to *immediately* erect a huge billboard on the site which read, "COMING SOON, NEW AMI HOSPITAL."

"You must understand, gentlemen," began our architect, "it may take a year to finish the construction documents and to obtain the necessary permits."

"That may be," replied Stanley, "but how long will it take to arrange for two large bulldozers to start moving earth around in the center of the property?"

Our architect understood the plan and was willing to comply. As we left the office, Stanley turned at the door and said, "By the way, it won't take a year. It will take nine months. *It can be done.*"

Later we learned that HCA had abandoned its plans to build a hospital in Victoria. On the long Quantas flight back to London, I read an article in Sydney's newspaper that talked about AIDS and which described several local occurrences. The reporter went on to say that the number of cases in the U.S. had gone from 1,000 at the beginning of the year to an estimated 3,000 by the end of 1983 and that approximately 650 Americans had already succumbed to the illness. He went on to extrapolate what a similar progression would yield in total number of Australian cases and fatalities within two years.

Lausanne, Switzerland

Before returning to California, I made my usual visit to Switzerland. Jean-Claude and I were evaluating the possibility of expanding the Swiss operations into other cities. Consequently, much of my time spent with him was driving around the country. On one road trip to Bern, we asked Leo to join us and the conversation quickly turned to AIDS and what Leo was learning.

"Gallo, at NIH, still believes that the virus which causes AIDS is the same as the Leukemia virus. The scientists at Pasteur do not agree. This debate is dragging on. But, fortunately, both research teams are now freely exchanging data. I'll attend a conference in Geneva in a few weeks at the World Health Organization on the subject, and I hope to obtain much more information. Apparently, representatives from more than thirty nations will attend! Of special interest to me is the fact that Pasteur will soon have an antibody test."

"What's that?" I asked.

"Once one has been exposed to a virus, the body develops what are called 'antibodies' in an attempt to fight the invader. The body may or may not be successful but the antibodies are always present. We can detect their presence with something called 'ELISA' tests that will be instrumental in determining if someone has the virus. I want to know when the test will be commercially available and how accurate it is. Maybe we can finally begin testing large groups and, with national education programs, inform people of their status and reduce cross infection."

"Who is Elisa?" asked Jean-Claude.

"It is not a person," laughed Leo. "It stands for Enzyme Linked Immuno Sorbent Assay. It is usually reliable, although there are more complicated tests that are even more reliable, such as RIPA tests or Radio Immuno Precipitation Assay. Let's hope Pasteur makes one available in early 1984. I am sure there are many asymptomatic people who are carriers while the virus has not yet manifested itself. Given the history of the crisis, many people are infectious without being sure or even having any idea of the dangers they pose. Testing, along with education, will reduce—let us call them 'innocent' transmissions by healthy carriers who have been exposed to the virus. Have you ever heard of Typhoid Mary?"

"All I know is that she lived in New York and was accused of spreading Typhoid Fever before the First World War," I answered.

"Yes, that's correct," continued Leo, "but she was a 'passive' carrier. She demonstrated no symptoms of the illness whatsoever but the bacteria was continuously detected in her stool. It took health officials a long time to determine that her immune system was strong enough to prevent her from becoming sick. That did not mean she was not infectious. The concept of a healthy carrier emerged from her tragic life and also gave birth to the debate of balancing the rights of the sick versus the risk of contagion to the healthy. We are lucky that the virus that causes AIDS is relatively hard to transfer from human to human. If it were airborne or even transmitted though ingestion you would all be quarantined!"

"There has been some talk about that from the religious right extremists," I said.

"Yes, as usual, they speak from ignorance in order to spread their fears," replied Leo as he shrugged his shoulders.

The November 1983 meeting in Geneva would be the first of an ever growing, hugely attended international gathering of AIDS researchers and practitioners that Leo would always closely monitor. Unfortunately, national education programs were nowhere even *close* to the horizon. Equally as distressing was the fact that no antibody test was released to the public in 1984. Leo's delight at the collaboration between NIH and the Pasteur Institute would also be somewhat unfortunate. Soon the organizations would become enemies rather than scientific collaborators, which would further delay the progress of scientific and clinical knowledge.

Chapter Nine

1984

Los Angeles

At the beginning of the year, Tim moved in with me to the condominium on Ocean Avenue in Santa Monica. I felt a deepening paternalistic affection for him and regretted that he was unhappy at his job with Kimberly Clarke. One evening I asked him what he would like to do if he could choose any career or profession.

"That's easy!" he replied. "I'd like to be an interior designer."

"Okay," I said. "Why not look into L.A.'s best design school and consider applying for admittance for their next semester?"

"I can't give up a job that pays me well and go to school," he said.

"I'll make you an offer you can't refuse," I continued. "If you get accepted to a program you want, I'll pay the tuition and take care of housing and entertainment expenses. All you have to do is find a part-time job for pocket money. I want to be your partner, not your parent, and giving you an allowance would make me feel very uncomfortable."

Tim was thrilled and by spring he was admitted to the UCLA Extension Interior and Architectural Design program. We installed a drafting table in our guest room, which became Tim's work space and was quickly full with reference books, furniture catalogues, fabric samples, and supplies. Tim's enthusiasm and obvious talent thrilled me, as did watching him at work behind the architect's table (almost always in a bathing suit). Tim was hired as a part-time assistant to a designer on the trendy Melrose Avenue. She rearranged her street front office to seat Tim at a desk in the showroom's window. I think she knew that more people would stop to look at Tim than at the furniture displays.

Our international operations were expanding rapidly and I traveled constantly. In addition to Europe and Australia, I now made regular stops in Singapore, where we were building a new facility, and in Argentina and Ecuador, where we were studying the markets. Switzerland, however, was the focal point of my interest because of the relatively high capital investments and the corresponding returns. Jean-Claude was on the lookout for us to expand into other cities. Within eighteen months we would own hospitals in five Swiss cities.

Gstaad, Switzerland

Ahmed and I traveled together only on a few occasions. Mostly he was at work trying to secure a huge hospital management contract in Saudi Arabia while I was developing facilities we would own and operate elsewhere. His long-term strategy to earn AMI a reputation of reliability and good performance in Kuwait had paid off, and he was negotiating a three-year $213 million contract to run The King Khalid Eye Specialty Hospital, which later became well-known as KKESH. When AMI was awarded the contract, Ahmed embarked on a vast international recruiting effort to identify, hire, and relocate every employee from janitors to surgeons for the specialty medical center.

In March, we planned a long weekend together in Switzerland on our separate ways, me to Singapore and Ahmed to Saudi Arabia. We had both attended Le Rosey boarding school in Switzerland, which was having a large alumni meeting in Gstaad to celebrate its one hundred-year anniversary. We loved to ski and had many common friends and family members scheduled to be at the three-day event, including our respective brothers.

The Palace Hotel in Gstaad is a grand imposing castle-like structure that dominates the quaint small alpine village. The hotel's owner, Ernst Scherz, was also a former "Rosey boy" and had made sure that we were all well received and pampered. There were gala dinners every night at the hotel, followed by speeches and awards, as well as a choice of lunch locations. Ahmed and I ate lunch at mountain top restaurants and skied as much a possible. While my brother, John, was among the participants, Ahmed's brother, Aziz, did not show up. Every evening, before dinner, we would try to reach him at his apartment in Geneva—to no avail.

After the fantasy fun-filled weekend, I left for Singapore. Ahmed decided to stop by Aziz's apartment on his way to the airport. There he discovered a horrible scene. Aziz, who had been plagued by serious depression, had committed suicide. I received the news upon my arrival in Singapore and promptly turned around and flew back to Switzerland, with the same flight crew that brought me over two days before, to attend my childhood friend's funeral and lend some small comfort to Ahmed and his mother.

Progress on understanding the virus—even giving it an accepted, international name— was slow. The Pasteur Institute called it LAV and made a patent application for its improved ELISA antibody test, while Gallo at the National Cancer Institute (NCI) still believed it was linked to leukemia and named it HTLV III.

On March 30, the infamous Patient Zero died in Quebec, Canada. Those of us who had frequented some of his regular venues wondered uselessly if we had met him years before. On April 23, the *New York Times* reported that the CDC felt Pasteur had isolated the virus. With all players now aspiring to win a Nobel Prize in medicine, any hopes of a tight Trans-Atlantic cooperation were rapidly disappearing. In April, the number of reported cases in America rose to 4,100 with 1,807 deaths. Two months later, those figures were amended to 5,000 cases and 2,300 fatalities while Secretary of Health and Human Services (HHS) Margaret Heckler debated whether the Americans or the French were more advanced on their respective quests to understand the virus. Gallo, the CDC, NIH, and the Pasteur Institute were consumed with winning, by being the first to clearly identify the virus and have an antibody test. Scientific advancement suffered as a result of that unfortunate competition.

That spring a piece of news again gave us all some hope that AIDS would enter the mainstream of conversation and thinking.

One of America's most popular and well-known male celebrities, Rock Hudson, was diagnosed with Kaposi's Sarcoma. For months he tried in vain to conceal the news, which was rapidly spreading among anyone interested in the progression of the tragedy. But he did fool one important friend: Nancy Reagan. At

The White House in August, in response to the First Lady's question regarding his gaunt appearance, Hudson claimed he had contracted food poisoning while shooting a film on location in Israel. Once again, the gay world lost an opportunity to accelerate acceptance and research. This sad event coincided with the Democratic National Convention in San Francisco where Jerry Falwell said we all "needed to return to moral sanity" and not to "favor homosexuals" in any medical research. Finally, these two events ignited some public protest in California and New York.

People afflicted with the illness, as well as their friends and family, pooled resources and raced off to Mexico, France, and other countries following reports of miracle drugs and bizarre treatments. One such weird action was an injection of ozone into the anus! Others talked of eliminating the virus by heating the patient's blood. Contradicting rumors of how the virus was transmitted flourished. Some believed it was transmitted through casual contact such as kissing or touching, while others took an opposite point of view. Gallo even said that only one out of one hundred people who were exposed to the virus would progress and actually contract the disease. This news was discounted when the CDC further revised its statistics and the number of cases crossed the 6,000 mark.

Ronald Reagan's first term was drawing to a close and it became painfully obvious that he had not once publicly uttered the word "AIDS" or made a single policy speech on the issue.

One exiting bright spot was the advent of the Los Angeles Olympics. AMI was the official provider of medical and emergency services. Royce was presented with an Olympic torch as the flame carrying Olympiad ran past his house and various executives were given well-located seats to numerous events. I had requested, and been granted, two seats to both the opening and closing ceremonies, which Tim and I regaled in using. This was made even more luxurious due to an AMI allocated parking space that permitted us to avoid traffic jams and shuttle busses. Between the two bookend events, I went to Europe.

Switzerland

We had entered into an agreement to acquire an old, previously well renowned hospital in the Capital city of Bern. The "Klinik" (the German word for private hospital) Beau Site had to be completely renovated up-dated and re-equipped. Wally Weisman and I had an unpleasant discussion on the subject of whether we should run a radically scaled down hospital operation during construction or shut the facility completely. I argued strongly for the former in order to create better acceptance of an American company "taking over Bearnaise health care." A local reporter had included a humorous cartoon in an article that implied we would not run a hospital in keeping with the traditional, conservative norms of the citizens of Bern. The article was titled "McMedical?" and the drawing was of a patient in bed with an IV running into his arm from a Coca-Cola bottle. Seizing the opportunity, I invited the reporter to dinner. I praised her humor and we became friends. Subsequent articles were much more positive and she often called me to get our opinion or explanation of an incident or decision.

In my argument with Weisman, I explained these events and considerations. I argued that terminating employees in Europe is much more difficult, costly, and damaging to corporate reputations than in the States. At a dinner meeting, I pointed out that we would recoup the operating losses incurred during construction from the good reputation we would gain by announcing we were not callously laying off employees in an "American fashion."

"I don't give a Goddamn! Blow 'em all out of the water!" he ordered.

Later in the meal, while being served by a somewhat flamboyant waiter, Wally exclaimed, "I had better be nice to that fag or he'll spit in my food and I'll get AIDS."

I could not contain myself. "Wally, you are the chief operating officer of a hospital corporation, not a trucking company. As a Jew, you too are part of a minority that has been the victim of ignorant prejudice throughout history. How does it feel when Jews are referred to with slurs? Please be more understanding."

His face turned red and I knew that the deepening rift between us had accelerated. It also did not help that I had to bring Royce into the discussion of closing Klinik Beau Site and rule in my favor. When *that* meeting was over, I glimpsed in Wally's eyes what he would do to me as soon as Royce retired and he became the chief executive.

While in Switzerland, I had my personal medical discussion with Leo Eckmann. I produced my list of questions for him to clarify.

"Are contaminated people infectious between couples?" I asked, wondering if Tim and I had to practice safe sex since we were both already infected.

"First of all, we call you 'sero-positives,' not contaminated," he corrected me. "I presume the answer is yes. You see, if the virus mutates there could be different strains. If so, you and Tim could cross infect yourselves which would further weaken the immune system."

Happy to use his new word, I continued. "There are differing opinions about whether all sero-positives will get AIDS. What is your opinion?"

"Again, allow me to correct the terminology. We call it 'progress' and refer to a 'latent period.' I assume that the vast majority of sero-positives will progress. The time spent in the latency period is, as of now, completely undetermined. Of equal importance are the various phases the illness takes after it has progressed by gradually damaging the immune system. How old are you?"

"Thirty-six," I replied.

"I assume we will have a therapeutic vaccine shortly. So, if you live to be forty, you'll live to be eighty."

"What's a therapeutic vaccine?" I asked, regaining my composure.

"All vaccines may not be beneficial to someone who already has the virus. A therapeutic vaccine would specifically benefit sero-positive cases."

Once again, Leo proved to be way ahead of typically accepted medical thinking. Unfortunately, being an optimist, he was significantly off on the timing required to discover a vaccine, therapeutic or otherwise.

Barcelona, Spain

Before returning to California, I made my usual stop in Spain. Clinica Quiron was well on its way to profitability, and we acquired a controlling interest in a second facility in Barcelona. By now I had an increasing fear that my years, perhaps months, were numbered. Bob Davis had recently said, "Face it, René, in two years, we'll all be pushing up daisies." After work, I asked Antonio, our hospital administrator-turned-respected sculptor, if he would carve my bust so I could leave it to my parents upon my death.

"I'd be thrilled," he replied, "but it will take at least six sittings." While Antonio reviewed his technique and which medium he wanted to use, I calculated that it would take eighteen months for me to visit Spain six times. I hoped that I could live a year and a half in order to complete the bust.

A year and a half later, a larger than life sculpture in extinct black Belgium marble, mounted on a Plexiglas base, was completed. Although I thought the piece looked more like Joaquin Mestre, Quiron's former owner, than it did me, I felt that another step in "getting one's affairs in order" had been accomplished.

On December 31, there were 7,699 reported cases of AIDS in America.

CHAPTER TEN

1985

Los Angeles

The year began with conflicting mental attitudes. Some friends had died, more were sick, and there was a general consensus that anyone who had been sexually active in the gay community would soon follow. Offsetting this was the great satisfaction I was getting from my career and the progress in AMI's International Division. We now owned and operated hospitals in England, France, Spain, Switzerland, Greece, Singapore, Ecuador, and Australia. Most were successful and all presented many challenges, which I found invigorating.

Naturally there were difficulties, mostly caused by corporate politics. Stanley resigned and founded a company to own and operate extended care facilities in England. I hoped that the growing U.K. business would be turned over to me, but Wally Weisman had a different position. Wally felt comfortable in London, an opposite reaction to his experience in all other countries in which AMI was active. He wanted to be in control in England.

While discussing which airlines we preferred, I touted the comforts offered on Swissair. Wally responded with, "I hate Swissair—just give me a good hamburger on TWA." This attitude did not go unnoticed on the few trips he made with me, resulting in my managers being quite happy that our division was separate from London.

The poor fellow, albeit intelligent and diligent, was not in any way an "internationalist" and had no ability to develop the much needed cultural flexibility all successful multinational corporations must acquire. In a board room compromise, AMI's British operations were assigned to him, and all other owned facilities reported to me who, in turn, continued to report to Royce, the chief executive. Ahmed handled the large Saudi Arabian management contracts in addition to his responsibilities as AMI's chief marketing officer. While this was no ideal organizational chart, I had no choice but to accept it and to run my hospitals as best I could.

Over the years, a large corporate office had developed in London. It became headed by a young Tennessean protégé of Wally's, Gene Burleson. Within a short period of time, Gene developed spurious, sophisticated airs and attitudes. He went from an innocuous assistant hospital administrator, not having ever enjoyed a cup of tea, to talking about "the legs" on the Port he nightly consumed and the style of his chauffeur's uniform. He even developed a phony English accent, which many observers ridiculed. Wally visited London regularly, where he and Gene enjoyed extravagant luxuries. The sad overall organizational result was the odd fact that the company had two philosophically very different International Divisions.

I was building my international oversight office in Beverly Hills. It was lean and efficient, in large part because of my chief operating officer, Marliese Mooney. I had recruited her from Humana, a fierce competitor in the hospital business and she, in turn, recruited a number of excellent executives from Humana. Our International Division in Beverly Hills looked like a mini-Humana staffed by a financial director, nursing director, hospital administrators, and systems experts, many of whom were former Humana employees.

Both health care giants, AMI and Humana, had begun health insurance companies in the misguided belief that the two divisions (owned hospitals and health insurance) could be mutually supportive and reinforcing. In fact, it rapidly became apparent that they were anything but that. If efficient, the insurance group begrudged any profits the hospitals booked and vice versa. This resulted in a competitive and destructive environment.

During a mounting international concern, approaching hysteria about the progression of AIDS, I buried myself in my work, perhaps in a form of denial. Every month I went around the world for board of director and management meetings, as well as for discussions with influential political leaders. For many months I was away from Los Angeles for two to three weeks at a time. This did not create ideal conditions to develop a strong partnership with Tim, who was hard at work in school.

Shortly after Ronald Reagan was sworn in for his second term, and as the number of AIDS cases in America reached 8,000, the Office of Management and Budget (OMB) actually *cut* AIDS spending from $96 million to $85 million. Equally disappointing was the fact that the usually forward-looking CDC did not fund a proposed unit, which was suggested to be called "Operations AIDS Control." These negligent decisions coincided with increasing documentation of heterosexual transmission of the virus, incidence of the disease in the U.S. Army, and a new awareness of the risk of sharing IV drug user's syringes.

One evening Tim returned home from a late class to find me trying to cook dinner blindfolded.

"What on earth are you doing, René?" he asked.

"Bob Davis told me that our friend, Don, is now blind because of CMV. I am practicing being able to cope if that happens to me."

CMV, or cytomegalovirus, was a much-feared untreatable opportunistic infection that induced a rapid progression to blindness in AIDS patients.

With that we hugged each other, fell to the floor, and had the first of many therapeutic cries.

The antibody test became available to the general population in March. Tim and I went to Bob Davis' office the very first day physicians were allowed to send blood samples to the approved central laboratory. The ensuing days were anxious as we both tried to carry on, as best as possible, with our respective routines. After all, we were regularly attending Louise Hay's positive lectures. Perhaps there were two miracles assigned to us. Eventually, my secretary said that Doctor Davis was holding on the phone. In a rare act, I shut the door to my office and picked up an extension in the room's sitting area, near the picture windows that overlooked the mountains behind Beverly Hills. I drew a deep breath.

"Hi, Bob," I began. "How are we all doing?"

"Two years, René. I'm sorry."

"What about Tim?"

"Same thing. I'm sorry, but we all knew the probable outcome."

"If Tim calls, please say you do not yet have the results. Promise? I want to tell him myself."

I looked out at the beautiful hills filled with stunning homes. Turning 90 degrees I could see the Pacific Ocean in the distance. I wondered how many people would be receiving this news today and over the next few days. At least, in one way, we were the lucky ones. There were many who had not lived long enough to experience this day. I left the office and went home to prepare a nice dinner for Tim and me. Why not?

When Tim arrived, I had a bottle of Champagne in a large ice bucket placed on the living room coffee table. His eyes sparkled as he saw it.

"Are we celebrating?" he asked.

"Actually, in one way, yes." I replied. "We are both positive...."

"That's good, right?" he interrupted.

"No, Tim, it's not good." The words tore out my heart, as did the changed look on his face. "It means we have been exposed to the virus." I took his hands in mine as he began to cry.

"So what's the Champagne all about?" he said, choking back tears.

"We both *knew* this was the expected outcome. The Champagne is to celebrate the fact that we are here today—*right now*—alive, feeling well, looking out at the ocean, with lots of time together and things to accomplish in life. Let's open this sucker, take our glasses across the street, sit on a park bench, and look at the horizon, knowing we are not alone and we are alive."

We sat in the park a long time. We cried and even laughed. We decided we would have a professional photographer take a picture of us in that very spot as soon as possible. We talked about Tim's graduation the following year and the possibilities of his creating a dual design office in L.A. and Gstaad, Switzerland. We contemplated following many wealthy Americans by going to Paris for an experimental treatment Jean-Claude Chermann was investigating called HPA 23, made well known because Rock Hudson was trying it.

Although it represented little direct importance, we discussed the mounting feud between French and American researchers. The "two" viruses (LAV and HTLV) were too similar, and rumors mounted that Gallo had stolen the French virus. Congressman Waxman remained our lone voice in the desert trying to get Congress and the Administration to become actively involved in research and education. In contrast, Health and Human Services

Secretary Margaret Heckler made a *faux-pas* and revealed her inner thoughts by saying that AIDS had to be addressed "before it reached the heterosexual population." Apparently she did not know what everyone else did: It already had. All together, the situation looked bleak and depressing. I felt we had no choice but to try as best we could to continue with our personal and professional lives.

The news did not improve all summer. In June, Mother Theresa was awarded the Medal of Freedom at a White House ceremony. While AIDS was not mentioned, she immediately proceeded to George Washington University Hospital, ten blocks away, to visit their AIDS ward and offer support and prayers to the patients. Finally, in July, increased gossip in Paris regarding Rock Hudson's diagnosis caused the American Hospital to ask him to leave. I was ashamed by the fact that I had run that facility nine years before.

One rainy July evening, I returned to our condominium to find Tim watching the news. "Rock Hudson just arrived back in Los Angeles, apparently near death," he said. "He chartered a 747 for the trip home."

"You must be mistaken," I said. "A 747 is a huge plane. It must have been a different aircraft."

Tim shrugged his shoulders as if to say *whatever.* But it was I who was mistaken. Consistent with a stream of bad advice, someone had recommended the stricken actor spend $250,000 to return to Los Angeles by private charter aboard a plane designed for several hundred people.

Zurich, Switzerland

By mid-1985, AMI's success in Switzerland was known throughout the investor-owned hospital industry. The first competitor to get a share of the market was Humana, which acquired a hospital outside of Geneva on the boarder town of La Tour de Meyrin. The facility had been offered to us, but our feasibility study indicated that the price asked would not allow AMI to generate the returns we were used to in Switzerland.

Even so, considering the relative wealth of the Swiss population and the high percentage of people insured to cover the costs of private hospitals, Switzerland was Europe's most lucrative market. Zurich, the country's largest city, had one old out-of-date private hospital that belonged to the Union Bank of Switzerland (UBS). Along with Humana and our other American competitors,

HCA and NME (National Medical Enterprises), which were not yet in the international market, we were all trying to figure out how to be the first to establish a hospital in Zurich, a facility we all knew would be destined to become Europe's finest.

Consequently, Jean-Claude and I spent a great deal of time in Zurich. The only requirement to build a hospital in Switzerland was to own a suitable site and obtain a building permit specifically identifying an advanced set of architectural drawings. These permits were awarded by the city's mayor. Unlike Humana, which was operating in a suburb of Geneva, our strategy was to be located in the center of our target cities. Property values in Zurich were among the highest in the world, along with Tokyo, Japan. Therefore, a huge investment on good faith was required to reach the point at which a building permit might, or might not, be granted.

On each of my trips to Europe, Jean-Claude and I would look at possible though expensive sites in Zurich. More importantly, we would call on the city's powerful well-respected mayor, Thomas Wagner. We always told him of our activities and plans and the properties we were currently studying. The mayor became both a friend and an advisor, explaining which neighborhoods were the most problematic and which were the most desirable.

On one trip, we were going to see a shut-down hotel in an upscale residential area within the city, Hotel Im Park in Zolikon. During breakfast with Jean-Claude, at the Dolder Grand Hotel, we noticed both Humana's Geneva hospital administrator *and* an HCA executive, seated at separate tables. We feared they were also aware of the Im Park site's desirability. As I walked past their tables I said, "Nice day here in Zurich, isn't it gentlemen? Is there a hospital convention I was unaware of?"

After a few hours at the site with an architect and city planner, we were sure that it was *the* location for our goals. The land was both large enough and easily accessed from all parts of greater Zurich. The hotel was not on the national registry of historic structures and could, therefore, be demolished. On one corner of the property stood a magnificent but run-down villa, which had belonged to the Mussolini family prior to the end of the Second World War and was Mussolini's destination when he was apprehended and killed. It was a historic landmark, but, given its location, we were certain we could build an appropriately sized and designed hospital around it. As usual, we ended our day with a visit to the mayor's office. After the usual pleasantries about art and wine, we asked his opinion of the Im Park land and, more importantly, the likelihood of his granting us a building permit there. He was positive about the site's desirability and cautiously optimistic about our ability to obtain the necessary permits, *if* we owned the land and had a set of drawings.

Jean-Claude and I returned to the hotel and called Royce in Los Angeles. After describing our find and reviewing the various costs, notably the purchase price, Royce asked his usual appropriate questions, "We have never spent that much on any site. Are you sure this is our best bet?"

"Not only the best, Royce, but possibly the only suitable site," I responded.

"What is the likelihood of you getting a building permit?" he continued.

"Mayor Wagner was as positive as he could safely be, while still remaining impartial."

"Do you *feel* you can get the permits?" he insisted.

"Yes, I do," I said confidentially.

"You realize what will happen if you do not?" he stated more than asked.

"Yes, sir, I do."

We made an offer to acquire the property, which, in turn, was accepted. While both Jean-Claude and I knew that our jobs were at risk, we experienced a feeling of elation, even as we contemplated the huge amount of work and roadblocks ahead. We were correct about the former; we seriously underestimated the latter.

By fall the number of AIDS cases had passed 10,000.

Tim and the author after receiving HIV diagnosis.

CHAPTER ELEVEN

1986

Switzerland

Because of the developing Zurich project, I was in Switzerland at least once a month. We hired a well-respected and politically accepted architect, Karl Steiner, whose first challenge was to prepare a schematic plan of the proposed project. Before we even reached that point, the neighbors organized in an emotional, concerted effort to stop the project. Their primary compliant was that, while the old hotel could legally be demolished, any new structure should basically look similar. Hotel Im Park was scattered into three structures, connected at the base. No efficient hospital could be planned in an even vaguely analogous group of buildings.

Our architect suggested that the first schematic of the new hospital look similar to the hotel. The logic was to placate the neighbors and then to alter the plan once we had established a working dialogue with their representative. I explained the strategy to both Mayor Wagner and to Royce, who was very concerned about getting locked into an inefficient design that he constantly referred to as "three lumps." It was a gamble we were prepared to take and one that I had to frequently justify.

Even though I was spending more time in Zurich than in Lausanne, I never missed an opportunity to review the medical and political developments regarding AIDS with Professor Eckmann. The press in Europe contained almost daily articles about the origin, cause, and future of the disease. I wanted to know Leo's opinion on how AIDS developed.

"How can a new virus begin?" I asked him when we met for dinner.

"I rather doubt this is a new virus," he said. "It certainly is a new illness and a different manifestation of the virus. But I believe the virus has been around for a long time."

"As you know," I continued, "I have seen clues for eight years."

"I believe it has been around a lot longer than that," continued Leo. "There have been sporadic, documented cases of the same series of opportunistic infections we now call AIDS. I'm sure there were pockets of immune suppressed illnesses and I'd bet that the LAV virus was one virus that caused them. This theory could be easily proved *if* we had proper storage of blood samples prior to the 1960s. Sadly, that is not the case."

"Okay," I said, fascinated with this theory. "Then why did it suddenly blow up?"

"I don't think it was sudden," Leo explained. "I believe that something gradually upset a balance that coexisted between human beings and a silent virus. Fatigue created by all-night parties, promiscuous sex, and already unhealthy male prostitutes, notably in Haiti, were key elements which helped create a weakened host for a virus that was waiting to attack. The *real* plague existed in rats for generations before conditions were ripe enough for it to jump into humans. The same set of conditions happened here. Unfortunately for you, the disease initially exploded in the international homosexual community. But, as we already know for sure, AIDS will continue to spread to other groups; I'll guess malnourished, impoverished populations because, again, these are weakened potential hosts with inadequate hygiene, waiting to become ill."

"What is the future of treatment?" I asked.

"In the absence of a vaccine, there will be several levels of activity. The first is prevention, of course. Second is what I would call immune building, In other words, taking advantage of products which are proven to strengthen the immune system. Products like the ones that are now used after serious surgeries or marrow transplants. Finally there are, and will be more, anti-viral medications. But remember what I have already told you: No serious viral condition has even been solved with anti-virals. You need to change the host through a vaccine. The dilemma is that there is not much profit in vaccine research and production, but there are huge potential profits in the development and continual, long-term use of anti-viral therapy. Also, there is huge profit potential in developing medications to treat the *symptoms* of AIDS. There are already new treatments for the digestive and respiratory manifestations of LAV. You can expect to see many advances in treatment for sure. Think about it. It has been the same with cancer. We have improved chemotherapy regimes as well as many new medications to make oncology more tolerable. But we have made little, if any, progress in understanding and treating the causes of cancer."

After my visit with Leo, I felt so grateful for the education, but also felt quite depressed about what I, Tim, and many friends would experience in the coming years. Most of them would not have the benefit of a wise physician who was also an historian and a philosopher.

By mid-year, the "two" viruses (HTLV 111 and LAV) were recognized as one and internationally renamed HIV (Human Immunodeficiency Virus). At the same time, it was becoming widely accepted that there were several strains of HIV and that the easiest way to determine the virus' effect and damage on the immune system was to measure the CD-4 lymphocyte, also called the "T Helper Cell" and commonly referred to as the "T-Cell."

Los Angeles

Tim graduated in the spring and the ceremony was held and celebrated at UCLA. I bought him a silver gray Corvette, which he had always wanted. I had it parked on a lawn, near the building where the graduation took place. I had a huge red ribbon crisscrossed over the car and a big red bow on the roof. If we were only going to live a few years, I wanted Tim to have any material possessions I could afford. When we walked out of the building I said, "Look, Tim! Some lucky fellow got a Corvette as a present! Let's go over and check it out!"

He walked all around the car until I held out a key and said, "Hey, why not see if this works?"

Tim was so overcome that he had to sit down on the grass because he was afraid he would faint. That occurred twice during the spring. The second time, I had obtained tickets to the Academy Awards. When I picked up Tim he looked so handsome in his tuxedo and was so excited about going to the event he had always dreamed of. As we got out of a rented limousine and began down the red carpet, we were sandwiched between Shirley McLaine and

Faye Dunaway. Tim grabbed my arm and said he was about to faint. I responded with, "Just take a deep breath, put one foot in front of the other, and be grateful that everyone is wondering who *you* are. After all, you are the prettiest one here."

The following week, President Reagan bombed Libyan President Khadafi, killing several members of his family. As I heard the news on my car radio, the phone rang. It was my secretary telling me that Stanley Balfour-Lynn had died. It was a rainy night in Los Angeles. I pulled over to the side of the road and thought about this amazing man and how very lucky I was to have known him.

AMI had completed a modern hospital in the city of Quito, Ecuador. Every time we opened a new facility, I would send a team from the corporate office to work with our newly recruited local hospital administration. The water and uncooked food in Quito was dangerous, resulting in several of my staff returning to California with amoebic dysentery. Eventually, we sent all the needed water as well as many other supplies to the apartments we rented to house the team. After my first trip to Quito, I also developed severe intestinal problems. I followed several courses of treatment of an unpleasant arsenic-based pill called Flagil. Time after time I would complete the required number of days on the medication only to have the symptoms return. After losing twenty-five pounds, I underwent several tests and met with Bob Davis.

"René, there is no current evidence of amoebas in your system. There is something called recurring amoebic dysentery, but I think this now is a yeast infection in your intestines, a sign of a weakened immune system."

He prescribed an antifungal medication and put me on a severe diet. Eventually, looking like skin and bones, the horrible symptoms subsided. I was sure I had experienced my first opportunistic infection, especially because many people commented on my appearance. Royce's concern was both comforting and alarming. I feared what Wally might be thinking.

Zurich, Switzerland

The story of the proposed new AMI hospital was of great interest throughout the city of Zurich. It was the topic of discussion everywhere we went, even when people did not know who we were. Our regular meetings with the neighbors of the Im Park site were difficult, but did gradually result in a spirit of cooperation. Eventually the "three lump" plan was scrapped. Although the strategy of easing into the neighborhood was successful, the new plan was more expensive to construct. The site would have to be excavated to contain four underground levels at the highest part of the property, but by doing so we could prepare an efficient design. Finally, with the consent of the district commissioner, we were able to present the drawings to the city and apply for a building permit.

Jean-Claude and I waited outside the city council meeting the day of their vote on the project. I paced around the huge hallways while Jean-Claude tried to joke about what our next career would be once the project was rejected and Wally made sure we were fired. After what seemed like an eternity, we were called into the meeting.

"We are willing to grant your company a building permit for the hospital project," began the mayor, "but with certain understandings."

"Thank you, sir. What are they?" I asked.

"First, you will have to construct a bomb shelter large enough to house all employees of the new hospital." I had been informed that this concession was being required of many large new projects. We had already calculated the extravagant cost. The hospital could still become profitable after several years but the feasibility study was less and less convincing. I feared the cost of further concessions.

"Yes, we accept the condition to include a bomb shelter of adequate size to protect four hundred fifty people in the event of a thermonuclear attack. What else, sir?" I asked.

"You have to add a new highly sophisticated energy conservation system." We had feared this also, due to the cost. It would require between nine and ten years of greatly reduced energy bills to recoup the investment.

"Very well," I said, hoping beyond all hope that was the last compromise.

"And finally," Mayor Wagner stated, "the Mussolini villa cannot move."

"I'm not quite sure I understand, sir," I began. "The plan calls for us to move the villa off the site, construct the underground areas of the hospital, replace the building back to its *exact* current location, and, finally, totally renovate it."

"That is what we do not accept," he said. Before I could further question him, he continued. "The villa must not move *at all* during construction. You will have to support it in place while you excavate underneath. Specific surveyor's sightings will be located to ascertain the villa does not move one centimeter during the construction phase. The city's architect assures us this can be done, but at great expense to you."

I was astounded and tried to imagine the price. I did understand that I had nothing to lose by accepting the condition. Any response other than an immediate acceptance would further delay our breaking ground. The financial studies would be recalculated, after the price had been computed and presented to Royce. I would also have to be fully prepared to be ridiculed and see the project, and my job, terminated.

"Granted," I said, hoping my knees would hold me up.

"Congratulations and good luck. We will have the lawyers draw up the agreement. I expect monthly progress reports to the city building department," he concluded.

Los Angeles, California

At an executive meeting in Los Angeles ten days later, I explained what occurred during the Zurich city council meeting. I had a new set of financial projections, which incorporated all the additional features. I had also increased the yet-to-be-built hospital's occupancy rates to slightly offset the added expenses. Obviously, I had reviewed the presentation with Royce the day before.

When it came to vote on whether to move forward or abort the effort, Wally spoke. "This will be the most expensive hospital AMI has ever built, both in the absolute and on a per-bed basis. The site preparation alone is over two million dollars. I also note that the projected initial occupancy rates are higher than any start-up facility has experienced." Looking at me he asked, "How sure are you that there will be no further escalation of the construction costs and of these *very optimistic* occupancy rates?"

I responded, "There certainly will be many problems to address during construction over the next two years. I feel we have the best team to address them and I place my reputation on the fact that we will achieve the financial results in the first three years as described in the report."

After the vote went in favor of proceeding, Wally closed the discussion with, "I want my concerns to go on record."

He looked me squarely in the eyes as if to say, "Another possible nail in your coffin, Silvin."

Jean-Claude Salamin and the author, above at the construction
site of Im Park Hospital with Mussolini villa in background,
and below, at the opening of Clinique Cecil.

CHAPTER TWELVE

1987

Los Angeles

The year began with conflicting emotions and information regarding any progress the world was making on AIDS research, education, and acceptance. Religious leaders clearly had furthered their agenda in repressing any helpful conversation of the disaster. They had been successful in establishing the feeling among many of their followers that the "homos deserved what they got," even though there were adequate statistics to prove that the virus had no sexual preference. Albeit in a clumsy manner, President Reagan finally uttered "the word" (AIDS) and, after an awkward joke about funding, he explained his position on the pandemic. He made no mention of education and chose to focus on testing. Sadly, no funding initiatives were proposed. These missed opportunities were partially offset by the huge attendance at the Third International Conference on AIDS and Surgeon General Koop's remarks where education and acceptance were emphasized. Because AIDS was decimating the art world, including Hollywood, several celebrities, notably Liz Taylor, were speaking out. She was clear about her support for Rock Hudson and other friends, showing genuine emotion as she presented Surgeon General Koop with an award for his efforts. Civil rights leaders were beginning to make significant headway in organizing the collective voice of frustration including a controlled but well-observed protest when Vice

President George Bush gave the opening remarks at the AIDS Conference.

I had subconsciously concluded that Tim and I needed to live our lives to the fullest—to expect the worst and hope for the best.

Wally Weisman had been named CEO Designate to assume the position of Chief Executive the following year upon Royce's retirement. I was not the only member of the senior management group to be saddened, but not surprised, by the news. Many had hoped Royce would appoint an outsider to assume the reins and lead the company out of new financial difficulties.

The Reagan administration implemented a new Medicare reimbursement program called diagnostic related grouping (or DRG). Hospitals could no longer bill the government for services on a cost-plus basis, but would be compensated by a fixed amount of money determined by which DRG was assigned to the patient. All health insurance carriers followed the example, which put enormous pressure on the investor-owned hospital industry and rewarded the low cost. AMI had a couple of significant investments that were drawing negative reactions from our shareholders, notably the institutional investors. One was turning out to be a failed foray into the insurance business and the other, another of Wally's pet projects, was a corporate college.

Wally decided to discontinue the insurance company's development and shut it down, taking a $100 million charge against 1987 earnings. Coinciding with the collapse of our stock price, a few substantial investors made significant investments in the company in the hope of taking over an imperiled company that, under different leadership, could emerge as a new industry leader. The well-known Bass brothers, from Texas, and a wealthy Miami-based physician-turned-hospital and bank owner, Lee Pierce, had managed to put the company in play, which meant that a takeover was possible. Tension in the executive offices at the Beverly Hills headquarters was palpable and a most uncomfortable working environment emerged. The company's great growth era, in which entrepreneurial spirit was rewarded, had been replaced with a bureaucratic "cover your ass" approach to business. I found myself savoring the constant trips to Zurich, even though it was detrimental to any personal life I had hoped for.

At Sea, Mid Atlantic

On numerous occasions I would begin my day in Beverly Hills, having made evening and weekend plans with Tim, only to be informed of one crisis or another at one of our Swiss hospital construction sites. By evening, I would be on a flight to Zurich, after having apologized to Tim and the few social friends we had who were willing to cooperate with my schedule. My one huge thrill was to synchronize any emergency trips with an Eastbound crossing of the *QE2,* if it occurred over a weekend. I kept a sailing schedule in a drawer on my desk, which I consulted periodically.

One Wednesday I was informed of an unscheduled meeting at the Mayor's office in Zurich to be held the following Tuesday. The *QE2* was to set sail from New York the following day and, after five magnificent days at sea, land in Europe in just enough time for me to prepare for, and attend, the meeting. I took a red eye flight to New York and went to the Cunard office to purchase a last-minute best available cabin for that day's departure. The popular trips were always heavily booked, especially in the best cabins and suites. However, some of these desirable accommodations routinely became available on the eve of the trip, due to passengers' unforeseen personal or business events. I was delighted to find such a case upon my arrival in New York, which gave me just the right amount of time to buy the ticket, walk by the ship to admire the curve of its bow towering over the pier, catch a quick nap, and board for the customary 4:00 P.M. sailing.

My "Queen's Grill" cabin, so-named because of the special dining room to which passengers in these accommodations were assigned, was immediately adjacent to a suite occupied by a handsome young couple, whom I initially assumed were on their honeymoon. After dinner, on the first night at sea, the slender buxom blonde from the neighboring suite sat next to me at the ship casino's bar. She began a rather forward and inquisitive conversation, which caused me to be evasive in my responses and to abort the obvious flirting as soon as possible. Two similar chance encounters occurred the following day. Again, I prematurely terminated them.

During the subsequent two days, I had comparable meetings with her James Bond-like companion. One get-together was in the ship's gymnasium, followed by a steam room run in and a meeting in several of the ship's bars over the next day and a half. Again, the conversation was intrusive and very forward, and again my reaction was to abbreviate each session. Over the weekend, I had several phone conversations with Jean-Claude, as well as a number of exchanges of telegrams relating to the construction in Zurich.

I became aware of just how odd this trend had become when, on the third day at sea, the handsome but intrusive couple's suite was vacated and the striking pair vanished from sight. My cabin steward gave me an odd reason for the unusual mid-Atlantic behavior. The day we disembarked in Southampton, England, I saw the duo enter an unmarked yet official-looking black Rover. Several months later, I ran into the mystery man at one of my favorite bars in Los Angeles and we began to chat.

Los Angeles, California

"Fancy meeting you in a joint like this," I began. "Where is your beautiful friend?"

"She was a colleague, not a friend," he answered. "How is that hospital in Zurich coming along?" he asked to my amazement, as I had carefully avoided any mention of my business with either person.

After a hesitation, he continued. "I used to work for the British Secret Service. We had a credible report of a terrorist threat on the *QE2* to occur on that particular crossing. There were several teams aboard, lodged in cabins throughout the ship and posing as Cunard staff. At first, you met the profile and we were primarily assigned to surveilling you."

"Why me?" I asked.

"You were alone in a high-end cabin and you purchased the ticket the day of the trip. Then we reviewed a tape that showed you sitting on the pier several hours before embarkation. You didn't help matters by trying to slip away from us. When we concluded that the soft touch was not going to work, I made the move on you in the gym. I hate to tell you, we searched your cabin and monitored your calls and telegrams. When we discovered the nature of your business, we moved to a cabin adjacent to a second suspect."

It was an amazing tale, but one which fit the very odd events. Meeting this gentleman gave me an interesting diversion from my scheduled meeting with Wally the following day.

———————————

It was clear on entering his office that a confrontation was going to happen. "I'm not happy with the progress in Zurich and the occupancy rates in Bern and Lausanne," he began in an abrupt manner.

"Wally, we are ahead of the construction schedule in Zurich and on budget. The summer occupancy rates are cyclically below average in Switzerland, and I am perfectly confident we will meet our targets for the quarter and the year. I have kept Royce very closely aware of both facts and...."

"I am the Chief Executive-designate and Royce is on his way out!" he pointed out emphatically. "From now on, you will only report to me. If I tell you something different than Royce, you will follow my instructions! And I am telling you to improve the operations in Switzerland. So that you know, I will be firing Jean-Claude today!"

I felt under personal attack. Jean-Claude had been promoted to country manager with the various hospital administrators reporting to him. I had also appointed him to the position of Corporate Vice President. When I was able to catch my breath and try to organize some thoughts, I answered, "Wally, Switzerland's performance will be on or above target at each hospital. And, I'm sorry, but firing Jean-Claude will be a catastrophic error economically, politically, and for the morale of all the staffs. Whose side are you on?"

"Do you understand I have the power to blow anyone I like out of the water? Jean-Claude has mocked me and everything we have tried to accomplish in bringing this company into a multi-billion dollar league. I don't give a rat's ass about staff morale or the political implications, and I won't allow one more Swiss Franc to be spent than what has previously been approved. You can forget making any new capital expenditure requests."

"I'm sure you don't mean that," I continued. "There will be many essential investments required to achieve operating targets as we open the new hospitals. And, again, it's not in your interest to fire Jean-Claude before all five hospitals are opened. Then you can fire us both, if you wish. In the meantime, you may want to ask the Swiss holding company's board members what they think of losing Jean-Claude at this stage of the development."

"I don't need anyone's approval or consent. It's a done deal. Goodbye, Rick."

I knew very well that both Jean-Claude's and my days were numbered. I was completely committed to the staffs and the politicians we had befriended in Switzerland, and I was determined to do my best to live up to our commitments even if it meant my early departure from AMI. I met with Royce fully aware of what rage that would elicit in Wally. As always, Royce heard me and solicited my opinions in significant detail. Royce then prevailed upon Wally not to alter our existing plans or to fire Jean-Claude, at least for now. But what recourse would I have after Wally really was CEO and my boss, I wondered?

Royce and I also agreed that an AMI with Wally as CEO would inevitably divest itself of the International Division with the possible exception of the U.K. The best strategy from a shareholder's perspective was to move the International Oversight Office to Switzerland in order to establish it as a true Swiss company capable of operating independently from the corporate office in Beverly Hills; to open the three new hospitals that were coming on line over the next months; and, finally, to identify the best possible buyer for the entire International subsidiary. That would likely be a Swiss group, given the relatively high asset values of the Swiss properties.

"What do you think of *my* trying to buy the company?" I asked.

"All offers will be reviewed carefully. If you really feel you can embark on such an adventure, go right ahead. But, remember Wally will become CEO and we will also have to pursue all options."

Athens, Greece

One market we had tested to determine if a hospital company with our strategy could be successful was Athens, Greece. We took a 35 percent interest in the capital city's largest private hospital, the 350-bed Hygia Hospital. We quickly learned that we had been duped into the acquisition and that we had little hope of controlling the rampant corruption that existed at all levels, starting with the Board of Directors. Erroneously, and at great expense, Wally had insisted that we hire one of "his" domestic hospital administrators and move him and his family to Athens. While we were able to achieve a break-even, we never met any profit projections. My trips to Athens were extremely difficult and contentious as I sat through all day board meetings punctuated with arguments and accusations. On a few occasions, I received death threats, since I represented the largest American employer of Greeks in Athens. When a threat seemed somewhat plausible, because of a difficult resolution we were proposing at the Board level, a bodyguard at the airport would meet me. He would remain with me throughout the usual two-day visit and even sleep in front of my door at the Intercontinental Hotel.

On our fall visit, Marliese Mooney, my chief operating officer, and I were met by the hospital's assistant administrator, who was one of the very few people we trusted. His dour demeanor was quickly explained by his request to come up to my suite and tell us some disconcerting news.

"One of the hospital's ambulance drivers has been taking bribes," he explained. "The butcher is his brother-in-law, and we are buying his inferior meat. We have hired other relatives of his, including mechanics and electricians, all of whom are sub-par."

"Have you told your boss, Ross, the administrator?" I asked.

"Well, that's the problem," he began. "The driver is sleeping with Ross' daughter and has ingratiated himself with the family."

"I'll take it up with Ross," I said.

"Well, you need to know another problem as it relates to them. The driver also sleeps with Ross!" Marliese burst out laughing and I shook my head. Another one of Wally's decisions had ended in disaster. I would have to fire the administrator at the same time while we were trying to make changes to the physicians' remuneration package, which would reduce certain Board members annual income. That difficult decision had been made and we were not about to alter our plan. Marliese and I agreed that I should lay low until the following day's shareholder meeting, when I would bring the new pay package for the doctors to the shareholders for a vote.

One of Athens's most powerful professors of medicine was also on the hospital's Board of Directors. In his usual arrogant fashion, he tried in vain to reach me to fend off our plan. However, he did reach Marliese.

"You must stop Rick from making an irresponsible and reckless proposal to the shareholders tomorrow," he said. "You know, I am an old man and Rick is very young and reckless. If he does this, he is a fool."

"Well, Professor," Marliese answered, "no one can talk Rick out of what *we* plan to do. And, in America, we have an adage that says, 'There is no fool like an old fool.'"

The following day I conducted the shareholder meeting on the seventeenth floor of the tall hospital tower. Just as the contentiously debated issue was ready for the crucial vote, Athens experienced one of the worst earthquakes in its recent history. People jumped under desks, ran down stairwells, and hid under door thresholds. Marliese and I were practically alone on the dais. We looked at each other and burst out laughing. When the group reassembled, the motion did pass by a slight majority, an important step for us to enable us to sell our holdings without taking a loss. As we left the meeting, Marliese told the Professor, "Now you know that Rick has special powers."

Los Angeles, California

As the year drew to a close, I continued to plan moving the key elements of the office, Tim, and me to Switzerland. AIDS had now attacked 36,000 Americans and caused 20,000 deaths. There was no reason for me to take "measured risks," since Tim and I were well into Bob Davis' prediction of "two years."

When I told Bob of my plans, he said, "Obviously, you can obtain excellent care at your facilities in Switzerland. The average is two hospitalizations before death. There are new treatments which you need to look into." His prediction of "excellent care" proved to not be quite accurate.

"Really, please tell me about them," I asked.

"A physician in Bethesda is studying a treatment using a product called Peptide T and an old Burroughs Welcome medication, AZT, seems to have some effects in retarding the progression of the virus. It's being renamed Retrovir, which is a clever name, but I doubt it is in any way a magic bullet."

Fortunately, I did not feel inclined to investigate either possibility until I could review the news with Leo. I'd be in Switzerland for much of the next months and would probably soon be living there. I'd also be living with AIDS, which was the new expression used at the support groups conducted by Louise Hay and Marianne Williamson, as well as by many HIV-positive people. My usual evenings, previously spent at bars, were now used attending the meetings held by these two inspiring and brilliant ladies.

The author (right) in Greece with AMI International's Chief Operating Officer Marliese Mooney and Susan Harrison, director of nursing at Hygia Hospital in Athens.

CHAPTER THIRTEEN

1988

Lausanne, Switzerland

During the early winter months of 1988, I spent more time in Switzerland than in California. At least once a week, I would meet Leo for a coffee in Clinique Cecil's opulent lounge. Jean-Claude had installed a trout tank there for guests to select a trout, like at the Palace Hotel. The action had earned us an article on the front page of the *Wall Street Journal* in the left-hand column, which read, "AMI's Swiss Hospitals Install Trout Tanks." On one occasion, in that very spot, Wally had criticized us for not having a public address system throughout the hospitals. Jean-Claude proudly and defiantly said, "You see the cash register on the bar? That is the only noise I will allow in our hospitals. This is not LAX, Wally." The stress between them had obviously reached the boiling point.

"Leo," I began our conversation seated by the now famous cash register, "please tell me about Peptide T and AZT."

"Well, Doctor Pert in Bethesda has an interesting theory with Peptide T. Although she is brilliant, they focus their work on the activity of oxidizing agents. I prefer the viral hypothesis. AZT is now being commonly prescribed, but it is very toxic, particularly in the high doses currently being administered. I strongly advise you not starting any such treatment in your current condition. I do recommend that you and Tim begin regular intravenous infusions of human immunoglobulin."

"What's that, Leo?" I inquired.

"It is a blood by-product which I use to boost the strength of elderly patients after surgery. The French use it on hemophiliacs, at least those who can afford it. I, myself, take it from time to time when I am run down. If it helps weakened surgical patients, I am confident it will strengthen you. Think about it. The more little soldiers we can put on the front line to fend off the virus the better. But, since the dose I would like you to take every month will require 14,000 blood donors to produce, you can imagine the cost. It has been observed in Paris that 50 percent of all hemophiliacs are HIV positive and yet only a few progress to AIDS. I think immunoglobulin infusions are partially responsible."

Tim and I began to use this prophylactic action regularly. It was finally accepted as treatment for advanced AIDS cases in America five years later.

One morning, while looking over occupancy rates in Jean-Claude's office, he erupted while reading his mail, "Look at the kind of ridiculous complaints I receive!" he declared.

I read a very angry letter from a dissatisfied client and asked, "Who is Pierre Nussbaumer?"

"The family represents a major Swiss fortune. Pierre is our age and the son of the family's business empire's founder," he responded.

"Let's call him and ask him to please meet us for a drink at the hotel whenever it's convenient for him."

That evening, I met a most charming and intelligent man who, after airing some very valid criticisms about his lovely wife's treatment at the hospital, went on to set the basis to become a friend and supporter. I had been very secretive about my sexuality in business circles but somehow Pierre's questioning allowed me to be honest. "How does your wife handle your constant traveling?" he asked.

"Well, Monsieur," I said, still being formal, "I have a partner, not a wife, and *he* finds my schedule challenging, to say the least."

Pierre's reaction was so liberal, "un-Swiss," and so refreshing. "We'll be delighted to meet him and take you both to dinner the very first night he joins you in Switzerland," he said, with obvious honesty and enthusiasm. "I'll count on you to let me know."

"We plan on moving the company to Switzerland within a few months," I said. "There will be plenty of opportunity for us to get to know each other soon." Pierre then gave me useful advice on where to live in the area. Over the next months the four of us spent many wonderful evenings and a few weekends together in Gstaad and France.

Beverly Hills, California

The months before moving to Switzerland were spent preparing operating forecasts, detailed pro-forma financials, and book values for all International hospitals. With my financial officer's assistance, I prepared a two hundred-page book that would become the prospectus we could use to interest buyers in the entire business. The book value of the overseas facilities was approximately equal to the charge against earnings that AMI would declare at the close of our fiscal year in August. I felt the forecasts to reach profitability at the three new hospitals in Switzerland and to improve other facilities' performance were optimistic but achievable. Determining the estimated variables of occupancy rates, uncollectible accounts, and certain unpredictable start-up costs became a frequent discussion among Wally, Royce, and me. Although we did eventually reach an understanding on all estimates, the conflict had become apparent. Overly optimistic forecasts would help both AMI and me identify financial backers, while reasonable projections would be easier for me to achieve as the executive ultimately in charge of operating results.

By late springtime the forecasts were all agreed upon, as was the desired sale price, net of debt, of $98 million. Several key members of my international team, as well as Tim and I, scheduled our phased move to Switzerland over the summer and I listed my Santa Monica condominium for sale. At my parting meeting with Wally, he said, "I'll give you a few months to come up with a buyer and I hope you have some idea of the magnitude of the venture and adventure you are embarking upon." That may have been the one profound statement he made to me during my brief tenure reporting to him. My emotional farewells to the loyal International staff remaining in Beverly Hills paled in comparison with leaving Royce, who was boss, mentor, and beloved father figure.

I thought of something Tennessee Williams said: "I lived out in Santa Monica and had a ball until the money ran out." I too lived "out" in Santa Monica and had a ball until Royce retired. It was time to leave, and I knew it.

As Tim and I prepared to move, we discussed the many obvious uncertainties about our careers as well as a growing list of health issues. Several medications to restore immune system functioning were being thrashed around. Among these were Interleukin 2; Leo's Immunoglobulin infusions; and Imuthiol, also called DTC, which was manufactured by the French pharmaceutical giant, The Mérieux Institute. My father's family and the Mérieux had been close friends for three generations and I planned on asking their advice.

During our initial months in Europe, Tim planned to master a working knowledge of French while I focused on the leveraged buyout of the hospital group. We both followed whatever immune support therapies Leo recommended. We flew to Europe on the Concord. However, it was difficult to have any conversation because Tim was mesmerized by Diana Ross, who was sitting across the narrow aisle from him.

Switzerland

Tim and I rented a charming villa in the middle of the vineyards above Lausanne which my new friend, Pierre, had found. Like the hospital, it had a spectacular view across Lake Geneva at the French Alps in the distance. With the owner's consent, I allowed Tim to redecorate the house, even though we did not own it, in the hope of his establishing himself with a completed design project in Switzerland. We also rented an apartment in Gstaad, where Tim hoped to identify clients searching for interior design talent with a modern Californian flair. I spent most days away from Lausanne, in one Swiss city or another, as well as making quick trips to our other European hospitals.

It was imperative that I obtain permanent resident and working status in Switzerland. Leo warned me that an HIV test was now part of the mandatory physical exam to apply for the all-important documents. Upon questioning, we learned that there was still one Canton (State) in the very decentralized Swiss Confederation that had not adopted the added blood test.

"We're going to Lugano in the morning," he said one afternoon. "The Canton of Ticino is the only one that does not have HIV on the list of blood tests. You don't have syphilis, do you?" he joked. "I have spoken with the medical director of the Canton and told him that we hoped you would not have to wait in line in Lugano, as we could not pull strings at The Canton of Vaud. He was quite willing to have you go for the physical there without having to queue up.

It will cost you a dinner at the best restaurant in Lugano for us, the doctor, and his wife."

The plan worked perfectly. The Canton of Ticino added the HIV test to its list of blood work the following month.

My friendship with Pierre took root and grew quickly. His attractive, liberal, and sophisticated wife, Michele, tried very hard to make us feel at home and to introduce us to their unusual trendy friends. Pierre took an interest in our efforts to find backers to acquire the company and gave us numerous excellent suggestions, "If I was you," he said one night at dinner, "I'd resign my position at AMI and pursue the purchase as an outside independent party. I don't think you can serve two masters simultaneously. Up until now, you have represented AMI, but it will become increasingly difficult to do so and you will open yourself to criticism." The difficulties I had encountered with Wally in coming to agreements on occupancy forecasts were a case in point. Unfortunately, I did not heed his sound advice.

While the rental house was torn apart, Tim and I lived at the Lausanne Palace Hotel. Late, on one of our first nights in Lausanne, I was awakened by a call from Wally who advised me that, consistent to what I had read in the *Wall Street Journal,* Lee Pierce was still trying to take over the entire company. He told me that Doctor Pierce was particularly interested in seeing all the European hospitals. I was to cancel any activities for the ensuing week and accompany Lee Pierce, and an attorney with whom he was traveling, throughout Europe. Wally proceeded to enumerate a list of important individuals associated with our activities, arriving from Miami the following day, who I was to introduce to the team.

I knew that when Doctor Pierce practiced medicine, his partner, Doctor Brooks, had been imprisoned for hiring a hit man to kill his wife. Nevertheless, with an open mind, I met Doctor Pierce at Geneva airport and reviewed the travel plans I had made. I had hurriedly set up appointments with the hospital's administrations, select board members, and local authorities in several cities. Within the first hour of our planned week together, it was clear that Doctor Pierce would present an image that was not at all in keeping with the culturally adapted and politically correct stance we had worked so hard to achieve in each country. At restaurants he insisted on paying with one hundred-dollar bills, which created unnecessary attention to us as vulgar Americans. On the second day of the trip, and after having already heard many grotesque racial slurs and bad homophobic jokes, we entered the charming little Swiss city of Aarau, where we were building a new hospital.

Doctor Pierce turned to his lawyer, both sitting in the back of the company's Mercedes, and said, "Can you imagine what just five niggers from Miami let loose in this town could do to it in one year? It would look like Harlem!"

I instantly decided I would cancel dinner planned that night in Zurich, with my friend, Mayor Thomas Wagner, as well as several other appointments. There was no way I could introduce this hideous man, who was announcing his plan to take over the entire company, to individuals I had cultivated over the previous years. If such an acquisition were to occur I would leave the company, but, until that time, I was willing to run the risk of creating any ruse necessary to save face. I called the Mayor's office from the car and, in front of my American guests, but in French, simply told his assistant we had to change our plans and that I would explain at a later date.

"Mayor Wagner will not be joining us for dinner tonight," I told Pierce, hanging up the phone. "He had an emergency and left Zurich. But we will have a lovely evening, and I'll take you through the new hospital tomorrow."

"But we *will* meet the producer of the TV station which is covering it in Switzerland's version of '60 Minutes,' right?" he asked.

"I'll confirm that in the morning. There was some doubt about their availability," I said, in what was to become a recurring phrase that week. Jean-Claude had managed to arrange for us to be featured on the well-respected weekly national program the following week.

At dinner that night, the four of us, including Jean-Claude, were seated in a corner table adjacent to an empty table for two. After ordering our meal, I gasped at the sight of Mayor Wagner and his wife being escorted to the neighboring table. I jumped up to meet him and quickly said in Swiss German, "Please trust me on this strange encounter. There is a good explanation, and I will call you tomorrow. For now, please understand that I am not going to introduce you to our guests."

Jean-Claude was hiding his face behind a dinner napkin stifling laughter. There was no need for any lengthy explanation the next day. The mayor understood enough English to be totally shocked by what he overheard during the meal. Lee Pierce was talking about a trip to the African kingdom of Ghana, where the U.S.

Ambassador said he would meet the country's Queen that night. "Is she a real queen or just another fat nigger?" Pierce boasted he had asked. I looked over at the mayor, whose expression and hand motions thanked me for sparing him the experience.

Barcelona, Spain

When our little group reached Barcelona, I explained that the two hospitals under our management had turned to profitability and were the only acute-care private hospitals in Spain to command that honor. Antonio, the senior administrator and my sculptor, proudly spread out the two hospitals' financial statements on his desk for Pierce to examine.

"Let me understand this," Pierce said after looking over the documents. "Do you mean to tell me you have a total of four hundred beds and only cleared a million dollars last year?"

"Doctor," began Antonio, "we have reversed a million dollar *loss* into this profit and will be improving these results next year."

"Frankly, Antonio, I see no reason for you to get out of bed in the morning if it's to only make a million bucks," answered Pierce, as he got up and walked away.

My friend's face turned white with shock. He took me aside and said, "Thank you for canceling lunch with Mestre, the hospital's previous owner. You know, I have nearly killed myself for AMI. But I beg of you, do not let me nor my staff fall into the hands of a man like this."

"All I can promise you, Antonio, is that I will do my best," I said, putting my hands on this dear gentle man's shoulder, feeling his pain.

Switzerland

After the Miami delegation left Switzerland, I proceeded with the effort to identify a substantial backer for the leveraged buyout of the International Division. Since Union Bank of Switzerland (UBS) owned the only other private hospital in Zurich, it seemed likely they would be interested in fending off the huge competition our new well-staffed and equipped Klinik Im Park would present. I managed to set up an appointment with the three-member top management committee at the bank's headquarters in Zurich.

As Jean-Claude and I walked into the impressive building we chuckled at the well-known sign on the floor which simply read "BANK." We both knew that, in Swiss tradition, the executives we were about to meet would have detailed informational dossiers about us.

"What do you think these chaps will think about me being gay and living openly with another man in Switzerland?"

"Obviously their research has already revealed that," answered Jean-Claude. "If we pull this deal off, they will sweep the sidewalks in front of your faggy shoes as you walk down Zurich's main street, the Bahnhoffstrasse."

We had stopped laughing by the time we were formally ushered into a large boardroom where the three top Swiss bankers waited. Each had a file in front of them. After a few polite introductions, we took our seats across the table from our hosts and the chief executive officer asked, "Mr. Silvin, please tell me about your pre-college schooling. We Swiss like to know our future partners backgrounds."

"Well, sir," I replied, "I attended Le Rosey boarding school in Gstaad from 1959 to 1966 when I graduated and...."

"But what about three earlier years at school in Villars," he interrupted as he thumbed through his file.

I answered this question as well as several others while his point was well made: *"We know all about you so let's not try to fool each other about anything."*

A copy of the thick prospectus we had prepared stood in front of each inquisitor. I easily responded to many questions because I knew every detail of our operations and how each Swiss Franc, Spanish Peseta, Greek Drachma, Singapore and Australian dollar were allocated. We also tactfully proposed a joint venture between UBS' aging hospital, Hirschlanden, and our new Im Park. Jean-Claude added many confident details about the famous medical professors we had housed in the beautifully remodeled Mussolini villa, confidently adding that the transformed Villa itself was to be written up in Zurich's paper, the *NZZ*. He also mentioned that he and I would be interviewed live on the Swiss "60 Minutes" program that week. He was now making *our* point: *"Watch out fellas, we are about to blow you out of the water in your own backyard, if you don't team up with us."*

At the end of the meeting, it was clear there was serious interest in our proposal. "As you may know, Switzerland's largest insurance company has two executives on our Board of Directors and we are also represented on their board," said the bank's chief financial officer. "Will you make a similar appearance as soon as possible with some executives at Zurich Assurances?"

The following day, we had an almost instant replay with the senior members of the large insurance group as well as officers of Switzerland's largest electric company, EOS. Day after day we were introduced to a growing list of board members and corporate executives of each company. The original feeling of being grilled for information changed into an atmosphere of teamwork and culminated with a specific offer to loan us the Swiss Franc equivalent of $98 million, at differing interest rates based on several variables, to acquire the company. Five of the executives we dealt with were in Klink Im Park's lobby while I discussed the hospital and its service on Swiss television that week.

Beverly Hills, California

I flew to Los Angeles after confirming a meeting with Wally. I went alone, of course, because there was no point in aggravating my new "boss" by bringing Jean-Claude to Beverly Hills. When I reached his office and reviewed the offer, I was stunned at his reaction. "Actually, Rick, that's your problem," he said. "The price has been raised to $114 million."

The elation I had experienced over the previous days evaporated as I answered. "Wally, we had an agreement. You and I will both lose all credibility if we change the terms now. Even *if* UBS agrees to increase its loan package, I am not sure the group is viable with the added interest expense caused by a $16 million increase in price."

"That's your problem, Silvin. I'm not concerned about credibility with UBS. Swiss Bank Corporation is *our* bank. Anyway, the company is worth more than we originally thought."

Switzerland

As feared, I had an embarrassing meeting with UBS that ended with a formal and permanent goodbye. I had the distinct and upsetting feeling that my likely partners believed that I had prior knowledge of the news I brought them and was involved in a corporate

---

plot. It was clear, however, that something was being withheld from the discussion.

It took Jean-Claude and me less than a week to update the prospectus in order to justify the interest expense on $114 million and to obtain a meeting with an infamous, Swiss Howard Hughes-type entrepreneur, Werner Rey.

Jean-Claude and I met him at his heavily guarded lakefront villa near Geneva. It was a luxurious property in front of which I had practiced competitive rowing two decades earlier when I was in boarding school nearby. Mr. Rey was a dry, right-down-to-business type man who conducted discussions with no polite introductions or pleasantries. A much quicker and less detailed series of meetings followed which, again, resulted in a specific proposal to bring to California. This deal would acquire the company in his name. Jean-Claude and I were also presented with employment contracts, if the deal was successful, as well as equal finders fees of 12 ½ percent of the Swiss company's equity.

Beverly Hills, California

Again, I immediately requested to meet with Wally. We decided that Mr. Rey's financial officer and a representative of their bank, SBC, would join us in Beverly Hills a day after my arrival. In a bizarre meeting laced with *deja vu,* Wally advised me that he decided to raise the purchase price to $126 million.

I took a deep breath and said as calmly as I could, "Wally, two people are currently airborne on their way to meet with you regarding a deal you, yourself, suggested. How can we change the terms now?" I asked.

"You figure it out. It is evident that the price we are asking is inadequate, which is why you are able to raise commitments for this much money so quickly."

I was devastated when I met Mr. Rey's representatives at AMI's headquarters the following day and tried my best to explain the upsetting news. We spent the subsequent two days analyzing the new figures, resulting in a cold parting of ways and an agreement to meet again in Geneva the following Monday. Wally's parting words to me were, "This is a still a very good deal for this fellow Rey. It will elevate his reputation in Switzerland since he has a criminal record."

"No, Wally, he does not have a 'criminal record." He was indict-ed and cleared of all charges in a bank deal a few years back," I tried in vain to clarify. "To condemn him for that is like finding Lee Pierce guilty because his partner tried to kill his wife."

"Still, it is in his best interest to accept the new price. But if he does not," be advised, "we are raising the price to $135 million."

"That's outrageous," I said. "There is no way I can find a rep-utable buyer to undertake the risks associated with new start-up hospitals carrying that much additional debt."

"Integrity is in the eye of the beholder, isn't it?" he continued. "In fact, feel free to talk to the devil himself as far as I am concerned."

The following day, completely exhausted, on my way back to Geneva, I read the *Wall Street Journal,* which carried a front page article explaining that another suitor had registered with the Securities and Exchange Commission announcing his intention to acquire AMI. He was another physician-become-hospital investor named Roy Pesch, the son-in-law of Chicago's aging billionaire insurance king, W. Clement Stone. We were well aware of Doctor Pesch because he had acquired two Swiss hospitals twenty-four months earlier. Jean-Claude had brilliantly undercut all their devel-opment plans as well as recruited several cardiologists and cardiac surgeons who they were trying to hire in order to inaugurate a major cardiac program. After this, Pesch had become somewhat of a joke in the hospital business in Switzerland. Nevertheless, I knew my days at AMI were fast drawing to a close and thought I had just discovered the very "devil" Wally had referred to.

Switzerland

During this period of failing shuttle negotiation, I used to return to Switzerland by flying from L.A. to New York and connecting to Swissair's flight 111 to Geneva. I played a silly game with myself to see how long it would take from touchdown in Geneva to transit through the extremely efficient airport, exit the parking lot, and be on the nearby highway to Lausanne. This morning it took only eleven minutes for what could take an hour in Los Angles or more in New York. Once on the AutoRoute speeding West, I phoned Tim.

A weary voice answered. "What's wrong?" I asked.

"I was up all night, René," he said. "I have cramps in my stom-ach and can hardly stand up."

I called Leo, who luckily was in Lausanne, picked up a doubled over Tim, and went straight to Clinique Cecil. A CT scan revealed nothing unusual and an intravenous antibiotic and pain medication temporarily soothed Tim and relieved the symptoms. We went back to the villa in the vineyard in early evening, where Tim and I went to bed, both worn out. In the middle of the night, Tim awoke in agony and, during a heavy, late-fall snowstorm, I slowly drove our Mercedes Puch Jeep down the mountain to the hospital. Leo met us and admitted Tim. Again, by morning, the symptoms subsided. Leo consulted an abdominal surgeon who saw no reason to operate, choosing instead to keep Tim on high doses of antibiotics and immunoglobulins.

"Is this a first AIDS-related hospitalization?" I asked Leo, thinking of Bob Davis' "two hospitalizations followed by death" prediction.

"Probably," he answered. "I think we need to keep a close eye on Tim and to begin Retrovir and AL 721."

"I have never heard of that," I said.

"It's an Israeli drug made from egg yolks which may have some benefit. You have to understand, René. These are not cures—only possible temporary solutions."

My head was spinning. The divergence between the crazy-making process of selling the company, Wally's unpredictability, and now Tim's first hospitalization put me into a sort of trance I would come to know well over the next decade. I could only survive by operating with a personalized version of an auto pilot, trying to carry on as best I could. That day, I had to attend a board of directors meeting at the hospital in Bern. I went to Tim's room to tell him I was going to Bern but would be back that night. In front of his door stood a small table, atop of which was a breakfast tray. Carrying the untouched meal into his room I said, "The nurse must have forgotten to bring this in to you."

"They are afraid of getting AIDS, René," he answered. "Only one nurse comes in. The rest drop supplies outside the door and run away," he said, his eyes filled with tears.

"You must be mistaken," I said, totally surprised. But I went to the nursing director's office and, with the administrator who replaced Jean-Claude when he became Swiss Country Manager, we discovered that, indeed, Tim was correct. The hospital had never had an HIV admission and the nursing staff's ignorance had paralyzed them. As I left for Bern, our director of nursing called the Canton's University Hospital and arranged for a team to come to

Clinique Cecil and educate our nurses, aides, and housekeepers as quickly as possible, explaining the risks and myths of HIV contagion. Bob Davis' thought that we would receive excellent care at our own hospital was only partially correct. The physicians were prepared to deal with Tim, but the nursing and housekeeping staffs had never been trained or experienced in HIV care. Tim's admission changed that, but the experience further convinced Tim that he was uncomfortable in Switzerland and, faced with failing health, he wanted to return to the United States.

During the Board meeting in Bern, my auto pilot took over, and we discussed the hospital's problems and achievements. The completed, totally renovated hospital had reached a high occupancy rate and achieved a break-even way ahead of our projections. In the middle of a discussion, a secretary entered the room and whispered in my ear,

"Monsieur Weisman is on the phone, Monsieur."

"Please tell him I am in a meeting with the board and will call him back within an hour."

"I already told him that, Monsieur," she said. "He insists on speaking with you *now*."

I excused myself and went to an office where I picked up the phone.

"We need to sever and sever forthwith, Silvin," began Wally. "Meet me at the AMI office in London tomorrow." The phone went dead. I sat in stunned silence much of the rest of the board meeting and even attended a get-together with the medical staff afterwards. When I got into the car to drive back to Lausanne and to see Tim, I called my secretary.

"Please book me on an early flight to London tomorrow," I told her.

"I already have," she said.

"How did you know I need to be there?" I asked.

"I have received calls from many of your people in Spain, Greece, Singapore, and even Australia telling me that Wally had ordered them to meet you both in London tomorrow. All your top people are on their way already so I took the liberty of making your arrangements, since I did not want to interrupt the board meeting."

Sitting in Tim's room at the hospital, I held his hand and told him I had to be away over the next twenty-four hours.

"René, I'm frightened. Please take me back to America," he begged. "I feel like a leper here and I hate it."

"I think we'll be going home very shortly," I answered. "We'll make plans when I get back from England in a day or so. I promise. Hold on until then. You're still my big hunk, just remember that."

Jean-Claude drove me to Geneva airport for my flight to London. Once again, he proved his amazing ability to turn adversity into humor. He had stopped at our favorite sports equipment store to buy a thick piece of mountain climber's rope that he tied in the shape of a perfect hangman's noose. I appreciated the joke and, after the hectic and crazy events of the preceding six weeks, faced with Tim's mysterious sickness, I relished wearing it into the meeting with Wally.

"Your charming little tête-à-tête with Wally is the bad news," he said. "I have good news too."

"Oh, really? I'd love to hear some good news."

"Roy Pesch has agreed to meet with us the day after tomorrow in Geneva. He is on his way here from Chicago."

After a few moments of silence, I said, "It's worth a shot. Perhaps Pesch will save his Swiss hospitals, we will keep our jobs, and Wally will be rid of the nightmare of a hostile takeover by Pesch. It may just be a classical win-win-win. But it is far more likely that I will soon be unemployed *and uninsurable*. How much do you think it will cost me to pay for Tim's and my health care from now until the end?"

Jean-Claude could switch from buffoon to brilliant mathematician in a second. "A million dollars," he answered.

"Get our attorney to prepare an indemnification letter stating that Pesch will pay us each a million dollars if we get fired for speaking with him. If he signs it and, *if* I still have any authority when I return from London, we'll meet with him and help him draft an offer."

"Wally may end up kissing your feet. Make sure you give him my warm regards," he said laughing as we pulled up to the departure zone at Geneva's airport.

London, England

When I got to the AMI office in London, the secretaries were visibly agitated. A few shot nervous looks at me and one whispered that the International executives were grouped in a meeting room, but that Mr. Weisman was waiting for me in Mr. Burleson's office.

Sporting my hangman's noose and trying to be calm, I entered the same office where I had had so many wonderful, amusing, and productive meetings with the late Stanley Balfour-Lynn. The sad state of affairs our company had reached still had a way to go under the leadership of a man best categorized as the ordinary.

Wally looked more disheveled than usual. His few reaming strands of colored hair, usually combed from one ear across his bald head to the other side, were is disarray. "Even you can't think this is amusing, Silvin," he said.

"Actually, Wally, I do," I began. "No one will comprehend the perverse self-sabotage inherent in our actions of the last weeks nor will anyone understand why you yanked all these highly paid executives to London on an expensive whim. Is this your idea of how a low-cost provider should behave?"

"None of that is any longer your concern. I want your people to be in the room when I officially terminate you. You have too tight a relationship with them. I do not believe any other situation can convey my intent and signal a clear transfer of power to Gene. Being there will be your last official duty at AMI. Your usefulness is over now that the Swiss hospitals are operational and, anyway, you would never be able to raise our new asking price of $140 million."

"That's where you are wrong, Wally," I said, playing my last card. "But I thought you were now asking $135 million."

"That's changed," he said flatly.

"I actually think there is only one chance for you to get that amount. I won't put my name on the line to justify the price because no rational person will pay it. However, there may be an emotional reason for a given party to do so."

"Who's that?" he barked.

"That's for me to know and you to find out. Give me a month." I correctly bet that Wally could never imagine turning a predator, as he perceived Roy Pesch, into an ally, finding mutual ground based on self-interest. Offering Pesch the International Division, even at Wally's outrageous asking price, was beyond his periphery.

Wally's face took on a blank stare and he answered, "Okay, two weeks."

Statements like that made Wally feel potent.

"Now let's go see *my* staff," I said. "I'm looking forward to your explanation to these individuals in the habit of justifying the cost of every trip they ask to make, even to important professional seminars."

We entered the nearby meeting room where more than a dozen worried faces, all close associates whom I had hired over the years, stared at me inquisitively. Wally made a clumsy explanation of the company's need to divest itself of the International Division, how sorry he was that the group was experiencing insecurities regarding their futures, and that he would have further news for them all "in the near term." Then, retreating into his comfort zone, he asked each administrator and country manager to give the assembly an update on their activities. Everyone complied amidst blank stares. Few listened and no one understood why they had traveled overseas for such a useless meeting.

My aborted public "execution" had been postponed at an estimated cost of $150,000, not including opportunity cost.

Switzerland

Jean-Claude had André Kaploon, our personal attorney, draw up the document we had discussed for Doctor Pesch's possible signature. We went by the attorney's office to read it. André had been baffled by the recent events and said that Pesch would be in his office after lunch. We agreed that, if Pesch indemnified us for talking with him, we would meet to discuss the Swiss operations. We all knew that we were walking a fine line between high treason and pulling off a miracle. André said, "You will either be heroes or zeros." Once again, I had no reason to take measured risks.

Before even reaching Lausanne, André called to say the documents were signed. We turned around at the next exit and went back to Geneva to meet the man we had heard so much about and who had been seriously outmaneuvered by Jean-Claude and me. We gathered in the exact same suite Royce Diener occupied on several occasions at the Richmond Hotel.

Roy Pesch was a jovial-looking overweight blond man with charm and social skills. He was the exact opposite of Lee Pierce–his archenemy. While both physicians had become hospital owners and both had risen to great fame, one was a delight to meet, the other a social burgh. The two competitors now wanted to own all, or at least the International Division, of AMI. I had learned a lot about him from an article that appeared on September 25 in the *New York Times* titled, "The MD Who Would Be a Tycoon." Among other things we learned was that his late wife, Donna, had left him $250 million.

As we hoped, Doctor Pesch explained that he was primarily interested in the International hospitals, opening the door for our presentation. "Frankly, Doctor Pesch," I said, "why bother pursuing an acquisition of the whole company. For a fraction of the price and many less headaches, why not buy my division. I'm sure Gary Winnick, your consultant at Drexel Burnham can structure a stock swap deal that will satisfy everyone. The goal we had to acquire the International hospitals is now too expensive and out of our reach. However, we would like to manage the group for you and would be happy to help you and Drexel prepare an offer. You do know that you are not exactly well seen in the AMI board room and this may be an easy way to achieve everyone's goals."

Pesch laughed out loud and voiced his contempt for what he alternatively called the "pathetic Weisman" or the "not-so-wise Weisman," Pesch then handed us our indemnity letters and asked us for details about our proposed employment contracts. He appeared much more rational and civilized than Wally or Lee Pierce, even though the latter was a shrewder businessman. The following day, while taking him to see the Zurich and Bern hospitals, it was obvious that an amateurish detective was following us. We even lost our tail while driving and then stopped to allow him to catch up with us.

When I got home, Wally called to say that Jean-Claude and I were to meet him at the Dolder Grand Hotel in Zurich. When our secretary made our reservations, the manager asked if we were having an AMI corporate meeting because eight other people were arriving from Los Angeles and London. I immediately understood that Wally, again, wanted to terminate us in front of a group. I asked André Kaploon to join us in Zurich.

My orders were to come to Wally's suite at 9:00 A.M. There I saw numerous executives from Beverly Hills, including in-house attorneys. Wally began the meeting with, "You both have behaved inexcusably by conspiring with an enemy of the company." Then he repeated his overused cliché, "We have to sever and sever forthwith."

Although I knew it was coming, the reality of being terminated from a career that had been much more than a job was more than a professional blow. The personal relationships I had developed, the business successes we had achieved, both in start-up situations and in turning around hospitals in difficult markets, had become a personal avocation as well as a job. For Jean-Claude, the moment of truth had arrived and he said, "Wally, you can save your salad. Since you are incapable of saying why, just tell us. Our attorney can confer with yours, but you are wasting our time—and yours. *How much?"*

We left estimating that this latest corporate mismanagement had cost shareholders another $100,000. I was shaken while Jean-Claude was thrilled he could finally walk away from Weisman. André negotiated with the in-house AMI lawyers and doubled the initial severance they offered in return for me signing twenty-seven resignations from various hospital boards and sub-sidiaries. Both the business disappointments and Tim's poor health wore me out.

When I returned to Lausanne, Wally had seized my company car and furniture, which I had *no* intention of keeping. I went straight to the hillside villa to tell Tim his good news, namely, we would shortly sail home on the last westbound crossing of the *QE2.* We packed and stored our belongings and then flew to London, from where we continued on to Southampton and col-lapsed in a Queen's Grill suite on the ship. Preferring to have a cold meal in the suite, we did not go to the dining room the first night. We exchanged gifts. I gave Tim a Swiss watch he always wanted and he gave me a Cartier money clip that matched my watch.

The presents commemorated our exit from Switzerland, the country of my childhood, a wonderful country with many distinc-tions, including having Europe's highest incidence of HIV, 7.6 cases for 100,000 residents.

Our restful six-day crossing was frenetically interrupted by Tim's newly developed coughing spells. When we reached New York we flew to Key West, where we planned to take an extended two-month vacation until after the Christmas holidays, then we would return to California and pursue trying to pick up our shat-tered careers.

Key West, Florida

I had a childhood friend who lived and worked in Key West as a real estate broker. Richard "Dickey" Glassen rented a house on a cute little lane off of Eaton Street, in the middle of Old Town Key West with his handsome young partner, Todd. On one side of their home lived an up-and-coming real estate developer, Pridam Singh, with whom, along with his charming wife, I would become close friends. Pridam had just bought the Truman Annex Navy Base and had a clever plan to turn it into Key West's premier residential community. On the other side of Dickey's house was a small cottage that belonged to the same landlord, and which Tim and I rented.

We had not been in Key West a full week when Tim's health started to deteriorate rapidly. One evening while watching television from our bed, Tim said, "René, get that cat off the TV." There was no cat in the house. Tim's face was pale and his nails were blue, signs of lack of oxygen to the brain. Since we had no car, I called a taxi and brought him to De Poo Hospital, where he was admitted and seen by a talented young pulmonologist, who had several HIV patients. Doctor John Calleja explained that Tim had Pneumocystis Carnii pneumonia and would be treated with the newly developed drug, Pentemidine. After the nurse had started the intravenous treatment and Tim began to dose off, I met Doctor Calleja at the nurse's station and thanked him for his late night care.

"I *think* he will be just fine in ten days or so," explained the physician.

"What do you mean 'think'?" I asked.

"Well, we have to be realistic, René. Tim's blood gases are very low and I have him on the maximum oxygen dose. I feel confident that the Pentemidine will work."

"But I don't understand," I said, bewildered. "Are you saying that Tim *could* die?"

"I'll give him better than a fifty-fifty chance of recovery," he said.

I sat down in a nearby chair and began to cry. Perhaps *because* we had more or less miraculously dealt with the issue of AIDS for several years, I was ill prepared to enter a new level of danger and despair. I walked home for an hour in the middle of the night and wondered what would become of us. This was Tim's second hospitalization for an opportunistic infection. I thought what Bob Davis had told me about two-and-a-half hospitalizations followed by death. That night I started to feel an annoying pain around my waist that rapidly flared up into a painful case of the shingles.

Tim's condition did gradually improve. Day after day I watched the level of prescribed oxygen diminish, but Tim's veins were collapsing and his IV's were becoming difficult to administer. Walking to and from the hospital, with carryout food for us both, was my only recreation and exercise. One day, after the long walk, I entered Tim's room to see a new intravenous located high up on his still very muscular arm, near his shoulder. The odd sight made a huge and frightening impression on me. Tim had another visitor, Jay Harkow, a volunteer from a group that was forming called "AIDS Help." She was the first person who had raised both his spirits and his hopes of survival. When she left the room, after giving us both much-needed down-to-earth advice, Tim said, "René, I happily followed you to Switzerland where I was treated like a leper. I feel comfortable here. Jay was so caring and helpful. Now I am asking you to please arrange for us to stay here in Key West."

"Okay," I reassured him. "I'll figure it out. We'll stay right here."

I walked home and called our landlord. "May I extend the lease for the cottage off of Eaton Street for six months," I asked.

"Of course," the owner answered, "but winter months are at a higher rate."

When that figure had been agreed upon, I wanted to clear with my landlord the issue of Tim's health. The last thing I needed was complications with the proprietor while an obviously ailing Tim lived in his house. To this end, I added, "I must tell you that my partner has AIDS and I will be caring for a very sick young man at your house, including professional home-health care."

"I am so sorry to hear that," he said. "In that case, the rent will be significantly higher."

I had no intention of complying with this demand or to altering Tim's positive experience in Key West, but I needed a friend to consult. I walked next door and, after telling Dickey how the pain in my sides was killing me, I revealed the news.

"Well, René, you have a few choices," my friend answered. "You can pay the bastard, you can sue him, or you can buy a home. I've known you all my life, so let's look at condominiums in the morning."

Within forty-eight hours I had an accepted offer to purchase a penthouse unit at Key West's recently completed Beach Club Condominium complex on Atlantic Boulevard. I proudly told Tim we would be homeowners and residents in Key West for as long as he liked. I balanced the good news I gave him with my request to get to know his parents. I suggested we explain to them that I was his life partner and that he was very ill. I bought a Mercedes convertible that Tim picked out and as soon as we moved into the condominium we launched into studying what new AIDS treatments were available. NIH (National Institute of Health) had set up an Office of

AIDS Research and Clinical Trials. We sent them Tim's records and asked to be advised if he qualified for any trials, but we never got a response.

While the FDA implemented new regulations designed to make promising therapies available sooner, we watched AIDS activists demonstrate at the FDA over the length of time new drug approvals were taking. The number of AIDS cases reported by the CDC had reached 86,000, half of whom had died. In November several new drugs were approved by the FDA for treating Kaposi's Sarcoma as well as CMV, the cause of blindness in HIV patients. While Tim did not have those particular opportunistic infections he began to rapidly lose weight and became increasingly disoriented. After he backed our car into a neighbor's car, we had a difficult discussion about his ability to drive and decided to monitor it carefully. One day, when I returned from Lighthouse Court's gym on my bicycle, I saw a lot of damage to the passenger side of the convertible. Tim admitted that he had hit a fence but had not stopped. After I found the house where the accident occurred and told the owner we would happily pay for the destroyed fence, I had to tell Tim he could not drive until his balance improved. It was a huge step for us both, but I emphasized how much more difficult our lives would be if "we" hurt or, worse, killed an innocent pedestrian.

We had bought Tim health insurance in Switzerland, but it was not valid in the U.S., which meant I had to pay for Tim's hospitalization, treatments, and medications. While I budgeted for this unexpected expense and the cost of furnishing the apartment, Tim's joy at decorating the Beach Club condominium was short-lived. His strength deteriorated daily, and there was little I could do to comfort, much less heal, him. When Hurricane Floyd was headed straight for Key West, my parents called. "There is a late season hurricane coming to the Keys; why don't you stay at our house here in Boca Raton until the storm has passed," my mother said.

The call was the catalyst for me to explain why I had not, and could not, see them. "Mother," I began, "you need to know why I have not been to visit you since we arrived in Florida. Tim is very sick and I do not want to leave him, even for two days."

After a nervous pause she continued. "Is it…. Is it AIDS?"

"Yes, Mother," I said. "I'm sorry to worry you. But I am okay," I lied.

"Dear God," she shouted. "How long will this last?"

"I have no idea," I said, ending the conversation.

It was a question they began asking every few days during phone calls until my hurt turned into anger. "Would you like me to go into the bedroom and put a pillow over his head?" I demanded sarcastically.

"Of course not," my mother said, "but your father and I cannot sleep. Is what killed Liberace the same pneumonia Tim has?"

"Yes, it was," I said as calmly as possible.

By late November, I had my second episode with shingles; Tim was passing out with some frequency and receiving regular blood transfusions at De Poo Hospital. With Tim's parents consent we decided to go to their home in Indiana rather than have them travel to Key West. I called my parents to advise them that I would be away for an extended period of time. My father took the phone from my mother's hand and began, "Do you know anything about these people?" he asked threateningly.

"Just that they are good parents—kind, generous, and worried. They prefer we go there to them because they live in a family compound in the country. Surrounded by relatives, they feel we are all better off caring for Tim in an environment with his family."

"Do they understand the gravity of the situation and exactly who you are? They have never even met you, correct?" he proceeded.

"No, Father, we have not met, and they only fear the gravity of *our* predicament." I said. "I intend to clarify this to Tim's father upon our arrival and to answer any questions he may have," I said, addressing the obligation I would soon have to undertake with great fear and trepidation.

"I urge you to go there with an attorney," he said, continuing to baffle me. Before I could answer he explained, "You are older and more fortunate then they. You brought their son to Switzerland and now are bringing him home to die. You need to protect yourself."

"It's out of the question, Father," I said emphatically. "I have no reason to believe that they are in any way hostile. The only emotion I have detected is overwhelming concern."

"And just when will this be over?" he demanded, repeating the absurd request for a time frame of the end of my partner's life.

"I have no idea," I answered coolly.

"If you do not go in the company of an attorney, you are on your own," he said as he hung up. We did not speak again until it was over.

Fort Wayne, Indiana

The day we flew to Fort Wayne, Tim had an early morning transfusion to give him the strength to travel. His extraordinary parents were at the airport when we arrived. Paul and Louise Hill were the perfect example of loving, wholesome, yet devastated parents. The look on these strangers' faces, when they saw the sad condition of their beloved son, was excruciating. They hugged and kissed Tim as they both cried. I stood some distance away allowing the horrible reunion to be uninterrupted by an outsider. Eventually, one by one, his parents came over and welcomed me. When we reached their family farm-like group of houses, Paul asked me to talk with him in another room. The dreaded conversation was beginning.

"I'll get right to the point," he said. "Is Tim dying?"

"I'm afraid so, Paul," I said.

"But we have read about new treatments and medicines. We thought lots of progress was being made."

"I fear they are too late for us," I said, with the same effect as if I plunged a knife into this large yet gentle man's heart. "I have all the available medications with us and I recommend we go to a doctor in Fort Wayne who has other AIDS cases, as well as the local agency for home health care and AIDS support groups." Paul winced as the word "AIDS" was pronounced for the first time.

"I don't think you understand how our family works," he said. "Of course we will consult our family doctor, but, other than you, there will be no non-family people cross that doorway."

"But, Paul," I tried to make my point. "The day will soon come when Tim is bedridden. He may need diapers…."

"My son will never wear diapers," he interrupted in a calm but determined voice. "Aunt Mary lives across the street. She'll be assigned laundry. If she has to wash one hundred sheets a day, she will. Grandma, down the road, will take turns with Louise staying by his side at night and Aunt Judy, over there, will run all errands and do the cooking."

And with that, except for two brief hospitalizations, he described how the following eight weeks would unfold. It was the silk lining in a very gloomy sow's ear. I stayed at a nearby motel and spent the days at the family homestead with Tim. As the troubled year drew to an ominous close, a strange peace settled into the Hill's warm house in the middle of a wind-blown, snow-covered farm field. I was as alien to my hosts as a Martian and yet we all got along well as we devoted ourselves to a common cause.

The family did not celebrate the holidays.

CHAPTER FOURTEEN

JANUARY 1-FEBRUARY 9, 1989

<u>Fort Wayne, Indiana</u>

Tim ate less and less while he grew steadily weaker. Gradually, all he would eat were special sugarcoated Popsicles that a family member would drive fifty miles to buy. He developed pneumonia in almost back-to-back episodes and was hospitalized in Downtown Fort Wayne. His last lucid experience was watching the Super Bowl with his father and me. I knew his dad was contrasting his dying son to when he was the captain of the local high school's basketball team only a decade earlier. Two pictures of Tim hung in the middle of the living room wall. In one Tim was wearing his basketball uniform; in the other, a cap and gown at his graduation from Indiana University.

His dad and I started carrying him to the bathroom and back to his bed because his parents did not want him to be in a wheelchair.

I returned to Key West every few weeks for a long weekend. There, I rarely left the condo. I ordered food to be delivered, and I sat on the balcony looking at the ocean in a trance.

In late January, Jean-Claude called to tell me that UBS had made a direct offer to AMI to acquire the Swiss hospitals for themselves. Our attorney recommended filing an immediate injunction to halt the transaction in what he believed would result in a pay-off to us. I was too weary and told Jean-Claude I was not interested in pursuing what I considered to be a long shot involving yet more stress and anxiety.

"My world has changed, Jean-Claude," I said, looking out the window at a bleak expanse of snow. "I am totally focused on helping Tim's parents the best I can and trying to add some quality and dignity to Tim's last days. Do whatever you like. I don't have it within me to focus on that right now. Please forgive me."

I was equally un-enthused, a few days later, when a former AMI executive called to tell me that Wally had been fired. It seems that several board members had become alert to the numerous errors in judgment their new chief executive had been making. They chartered a plane and flew to all AMI regional offices to investigate the many stories they had heard. Upon their return to L.A., they immediately terminated the "not-so-wise Weisman." My friend finished his conversation by saying, "If you live by the sword, you die by the sword." Unfortunately, I was thinking of a different type of death, the real thing. As much as I was there for Tim and held a stoic façade with his wonderful family, I could sense great melancholy and depression within me. I felt as if in a vortex, helpless and increasingly self-absorbed in my black space.

In mid-January, we moved Tim's bed into the small house's living room. He was the center of our attention and lives so why not locate him in the heart of the house? His conversation became more and more childish and his mother reassumed her earlier maternal role. Paul, Louise, and I developed a mutual affection, and I became very respectful of their basic instincts. The care Tim received during his gradual decline was reminiscent of the early days of pioneers when families surrounded aging loved ones as they gently faded away.

By early February, we placed morphine drops under his tongue whenever he moaned. On February 3, I read that the FDA had approved a treatment for the prevention of Pneumocystis Carinii pneumonia. It would be of no help to Tim, who had endured the debilitating lung disease three times in as many months.

Then, quietly, in the early evening of February 9, at the age of twenty-nine, Tim's breathing slowed, and he slipped away surrounded by his loved ones. My once 180-pound "big hunk" weighed 110 pounds.

We buried Tim two days later. The small funeral home was jammed full of family and friends. As I walked into the chapel where his coffin was placed, I noticed a small table carrying a phone that was off the hook. In front of it lay a sign that read "The Lord called." I found some humor in the charming rural ritual. The Hills had every attendee back to their house for a huge feast, which every female relative had begun to prepare the minute they were informed of Tim's death. Afterwards, in a blinding snowstorm, I returned to my motel for the last time. As I reflected on my time with Tim, I wondered if I had idealized our relationship and feared abandonment. Now that he was gone, I felt strangely liberated in my solitude. The following day I flew back to Key West in great physical pain as my third bout of shingles began.

For the next two days I stayed in bed, trying not to let my waist touch sheets or T-shirt, because the pain was so severe. Finally, I called my parents to tell them I was back and that "it was over."

"Well, you'd better return to doing what you know best," said my father.

"What's that, Father," I asked weakly.

"Making money," he replied.

"I am barely able to get out of bed," I tried to explain. "I have just returned from burying my partner. I'm sure you can understand that it will take some time for me to get back on my feet."

His answer underscored his lack of comprehension that two men could ever have shared a life and made plans for a future with developing careers and experiences. "No," he said, "we do not understand. We never did. But, if you need some time, I suggest you take a long ocean cruise and then get back to work. If you recall, I told you to put Tim in a nursing home last year. Had you followed my advice, you would not be in this position now."

This time, it was I who put down the phone first. I wondered how horrible it would be to live and die, if one had such an insensitive existence. I knew how he had lived and I'd find out how one dies with that attitude of detachment the following year. But, like Scarlet O'Hara, I'd worry about my parents another day. For now, I had to figure out how to survive alone, in a confused haze of mental and physical agony.

PART THREE

BOB
1989–1998

CHAPTER FIFTEEN

1989

As soon as I was able to get out of bed, I called Jay Harkow at AIDS Help to tell her about Tim. I asked if I could drop by to see her at the organization's temporary offices located in an old abandoned building in The Truman Annex. The once grand building had housed the base's administration when it was a vibrant deep-water navy harbor. The Administration Building was next to several other vacant structures, including The Truman White House, which was Harry and Bess Truman's home, both during and after his presidency. My new local friend, Pridam Singh, had recently bought the entire complex at auction.

Jay expressed her condolences, recommended that I attend a bereavement group at Key West's hospice, and invited me to a party to be held the following weekend on the grounds of the Truman White House.

I met many of the new organization's clients as well as a board member, Al McCarthy, and his partner, Ralph. Ralph was a radiology technician at Key West's hospital. We had met there previously, when I had taken Tim in for tests. I had been impressed with his kindness and compassion. At the gathering, the "late stage" condition of several of most guests was obvious and frightening. A few were wheelchair bound; some were covered from head to foot with Kaposi's Sarcoma lesions and most were emaciated. Al told me how the struggling organization was planning to survive and what services he dreamed of being able to provide for its many indigent members. I offered my assistance in any way possible.

That rapidly turned into a time-consuming positive and fulfilling job. I also signed up at Hospice to attend a six-week training program, which resulted in a Florida State license to make regular visits to AIDS patients who were registered for terminal care. There was no inpatient Hospice facility in town, so the dedicated staff worked with dying patients in their homes. In this way, I could work at both the "grass roots" level, by running errands for, and sitting with, bedridden patients as well as with AIDS Help Incorporated's Board of Directors on policy and financial issues. The combination gave me a will to get out of bed and be of some assistance to those much less fortunate than I.

I also started regular visits to my gym at the Light House Court guesthouse on Whitehead Street, across from the Hemingway House. The small gym, near the bed and breakfast's pool, had four regular morning clients, who quickly became friends as well as becoming my avenue for socialization. Mike Mulligan had a terrific sense of humor and would always cheer me up. He was also an aerobic instructor and excellent local amateur actor.

While we worked with weights and kidded around, we also commented on the various new tourists' faces we noticed coming and going every few days at the inn. Michael, another Hoosier, had gotten to know and like Tim during his brief stay in Key West. After Tim's funeral I had told Michael that I "would never look at another man" and would prefer to castrate myself rather than date.

"Well, I don't think I'd castrate myself if there was a chance I could have a date with that one," said Michael, pointing at a handsome, well-built blond sitting by the pool.

I looked through the window and agreed that the young man was amazingly good looking. "That's funny, Michael," I said "but I am too depressed to even think about it."

A few minutes later, Robert David Mann left his seat by the pool and entered both the gym and my life. As Michael left us alone in the small space, he sent me a look which said, "I guess you might reconsider."

Bob and I chatted. I learned that he had a Ph.D. in clinical psychology and lived in Malibu, California. He was in Key West on vacation to recuperate from a recent break-up with a boyfriend. He had just changed jobs and taken a position with the Radar Institute, a well-known group that treated severe eating disorder victims as in-patients, usually for a thirty-day stay.

"The Rader Institute!" I exclaimed. "Have you heard of AMI?"

"Well, yes, of course," answered Bob. "Didn't Rader just get kicked out of those hospitals?"

I explained what my position at AMI had been and that I was privy to discussions about the pros and cons of AMI's domestic hospitals housing eating disorder programs, which resulted in AMI not renewing the agreements or exercising an option to acquire the Rader Institute. We marveled at what a small world it was, as I became hypnotized by his strong yet sweet face, his soothing voice, and gentle demeanor. After telling him that I had just lost my partner, I gathered up all my courage and asked Bob if he would have dinner with me that night, which was my last night in Key West. Early the following day I was going to New York to meet with the Chief Executive Officer of one of AMI's competitors, NME (National Medical Enterprises).

"I'm really sorry," he answered, "but I am in town with two friends and we have already made plans."

The response did not surprise me, and I left the guesthouse unsure about whether or not I had been politely "blown off." Shortly after I returned to the Beach Club the phone rang and it was Bob, "I hope you don't mind, but I got your number from the front desk. I spoke with my buddies and they hoped that, perhaps, we could *all* have dinner together."

Quite nervous and not knowing why, I had begun the process. I picked up Bob and his friends in my two-seater convertible. It was a beautiful evening, the top was down, and Bob's friends sat on the trunk with their legs inside the car, while Bob sat next to me. He wore a pink and blue shirt and tight white pants, which showed off his beautiful figure and "bubble butt." We drove up and down Duval Street and ended up at Louie's Back Yard Restaurant, where we had an enthralling dinner outside by the ocean. The conversation was animated and Bob looked so handsome. He was obviously a genuinely kind and wise young man, with talents that were high on my list to find, given my recent experiences. After dinner, I took them all back to Lighthouse Court and went home mystified to realize that, so soon after losing Tim, I was falling in love with this man. I felt a deep connection within myself, paradoxically experiencing both pleasure and pain. I was unsure if I was totally crazy or the luckiest man alive. I soon understood that the latter case was the answer.

New York City

Richard "Dick" Eamer, NME's Chief Executive Officer, had contacted me and asked to meet. Although the company was located in Santa Monica, California, we got together at the Plaza Hotel in New York. There he explained that NME was pursuing the construction of a $75 million hospital in Paris and wondered if I would review the plan and help him quantify the expected outcome. His Chief Operating Officer, Michael Focht, was also present.

"Frankly, Mr. Eamer," I said after hearing his plans, "I think the venture is extremely risky. In spite of my French heritage and love for the country, I spent a fair amount of time getting AMI *out* of France at a break-even. Their reimbursement rates are not at levels which can justify the large capital costs of the first-class private hospitals which you want to create."

"We are thinking of operating totally independently from the government and charging any rates we like," he said.

"Again, I think that strategy is also very risky for any hospital other than a small, highly specialized facility, which is not what I understand you are contemplating. There simply are not enough French with adequate supplementary private health insurance to cover the rates you will have to charge."

When Mr. Eamer excused himself for a few minutes, Focht expanded, "If I were you, I'd not be so pessimistic. Dick loves France and has his thoroughbred racehorses there to compete in Deauville and Paris. He really wants this project."

"That's all well and good," I answered, "but I think that your shareholders would prefer you not lose many tens of millions of dollars because you want to have an excuse to travel to France. You can have a small activity there to justify some trips or just pay for the *private* activity *privately*."

I could tell that Mike Focht and I would never see eye-to-eye. When Dick returned to the living room, he offered to pay me a hefty per-diem fee to go to France and look over the hospital's drawings at the architect's office and meet several people, including a full-time representative, whom they had already housed in Paris. "I'd be happy to," I answered, "but again, it's not the drawings that worry me. It's the project's *cost* and its ability to command the necessary revenues to turn a profit."

"But, will you go?" he asked.

"If you insist and understand where my focus will be, yes, I'll go."

As the daylong meeting drew to a close, all I could think about was going back to my room and calling Bob, who was in Chicago on his first mission for Rader. I was nervous as the phone rang in his hotel room, hoping, in part, that he would not answer so that I could retreat into my shell. Luckily, I was spared.

"Hello." I heard that deep, masculine voice say.

"Um...hi, Bob! It's René. How is it going in Chicago?"

Bob never complained and only gave detailed answers, if specifically asked. "It's a new job and my first time as clinical director at this program. I have a lot to learn, but it is going well, thanks." After a short pause he said, "I really enjoyed meeting you and hope we can get to know each other better."

"Come back to Key West any time you like. But I guess that's not feasible, eh?"

"To the contrary," he said. "I will be in a different East Coast city every week for a few months. I can easily route my weekends through Key West."

"How about this weekend?" I asked somewhat recklessly, partly hoping he would say "no," so my nerves could return to normal.

"I'll make the plans and let you know when I'll be there."

On the local news that day, in late March, I watched three thousand protestors, organized by Act-Up, picket New York's City Hall in protest of Mayor Koch's lack of progress in providing assistance to AIDS patients. Two hundred activists were arrested.

Bob and I had a wonderful time that first weekend. When I took Bob's small bag into the guestroom, he appeared surprised and disappointed that I did not automatically put it in my room. We spent much of the weekend on my Boston Whaler, going to Sand Key at the reef six miles from Key West, during the day and cruising the harbor at sunset. As the sun slipped into the ocean, I cut the engine and took Bob's hand. "You know that Tim just died from complications caused by AIDS." I began. "As you may have imagined, I am HIV positive. I think we have to be clear on the situation and discuss the risks. What is your status?" I asked.

"Well," he answered, "first of all, I appreciate the candor. I was tested about a year ago and I was negative. My last boyfriend said he, too, was negative. However, I am planning on making sure and I want to test again soon."

"How about Monday morning before you leave town?" I asked.

"Sure, if you know where to go."

The rest of the weekend we flirted and kissed. Bob's likely being HIV negative perplexed me. I feared I could never relax sexually around someone I cared for and who was HIV negative. After his blood was drawn, I dropped him at the funky, little Key West airport. We agreed to meet at that same spot, in two weeks, after I returned from Paris.

Paris, France

Jean-Claude Salamin met me in Paris and, as in years past, we had a fun time. I had not seen him since Tim and I left Switzerland and his perspective on how I could get back on my feet after burying Tim was gratifying, "You need a new husband," he said. "And this time try to find a *husband*, not a wife." While Jean-Claude had been generous with Tim, they did not have affinity with one another. I told Jean-Claude that I recently met an interesting man, to which Jean-Claude responded, "Good. Bring my new sister-in-law to Switzerland for my inspection."

Jean-Claude had been hired by Roy Pesch to run his two Swiss hospitals. He promptly closed the worst one and transferred their business to the better hospital, The Clinique de Genolier, near Geneva. Historically, the facility had been a horrible financial blunder, built by the aging mother of a childhood friend, the Duchesse Serra de Cassano. After her death, the family had offered the hospital first to AMI and eventually found the gullible Doctor Pesch, who bought it. He did not fare much better than the Duchesse had until Jean-Claude took it over. It was hard for us to believe that, only six months before, we had frantically pursued the leveraged buy-out of AMI's International Division.

"Do you remember when that silly ass, Wally, tried to impose a thirty-mile zone around Lausanne where I could not work?" he giggled, reminding me of one of our many maneuvers during our termination process. Wally had told his lawyers to put a thirty-mile non-compete clause in Jean-Claude's termination package. We already knew he might run the Genolier Hospital, which was about that distance from Lausanne. We put a map on the bar at the Palace Hotel and drew a circle around Lausanne with a forty-eight kilometer (thirty mile) radius. Genolier was one kilometer *inside* the no-work zone. Taking that into account we instructed Kaploon, our attorney, to tell Wally's lawyer that you could not use "miles" in a binding Swiss agreement. The thirty miles was changed to an adequate number of kilometers that resulted in Genolier being one kilometer *outside* the forbidden zone. Jean-Claude assumed his new responsibilities, worry free of being sued by the very litigious Wally.

I informed Jean-Claude of NME's plan to build a major hospital in Paris and, no surprise to me, he agreed that it was pure folly. I told him about my visit to the proposed hospital's architect's office, to the selected site and my discussions with NME's American representative in Paris. "Oh, my God," he exclaimed. "Another American trying to impose a failed system on Europe! Let them build it, maybe we can sell it to Pesch." It was the first time I laughed in six months and we howled until we feared we were annoying the other guests at the Ritz bar.

I told Dick Eamer that I would report quickly, and in person, to him after my inspection of the proposed Paris project. On my flight to Los Angeles, I drafted my verbal presentation, but was distracted by a very chatty Joan Collins, sitting across the aisle, and my continuous thoughts about Bob, who I would meet in Florida the following weekend.

Santa Monica, California

It was very strange being back in the city where Tim and I had lived. I deliberately did not drive by my former home nor call Royce. My stay was planned to last one day and I pretended I was a businessman quickly passing through L.A. NME had built a beautiful building on Santa Monica Boulevard and, of course, Dick Eamer's office was a grand Hollywood-like setting.

"I am convinced that you will lose your shirt if you build the mega-hospital in Paris," I said. "I have marked up your overly optimistic pro-forma with reasonable revenue levels and occupancy rates based on my experience in France. Obviously it's your call, but I think you would be ill advised to move forward at this time in NME's history. How can you justify several years of certain losses in Paris when you are selling domestic facilities and while your growth has slowed significantly? Your shareholders will ask why are 'we' losing money in Paris while adding to reserves for malpractice suits in the US and uncollectible accounts in Saudi Arabia? It just seems like the wrong project at the wrong time."

"I guess we owe you a thank you," Eamer answered after a prolonged silence. "Would you consider working for me?"

"That is flattering," I answered, "but not right now. I have recently lost my partner and I have recurring debilitating bouts of shingles. This quick pop over to Paris was more tiring than my monthly round-the-world trips for AMI used to be. I would feel out of integrity to undertake an activity to which I cannot devote my full attention."

"That's the first time anyone has turned me down twice in one meeting," he said laughing. "You torpedoed my pet project and now you refuse to work for me. Can we call on you for specific time limited projects?"

"Of course," I replied. "I'd be honored."

By mid-year, the FDA had approved numerous new treatments and medications for HIV disease. Among these were an aerosol, Pentamidine, an initial treatment for CMV, the cause of blindness; a syrup form of AZT; as well as ddI, a substitute for AZT for use by patients who were intolerant of the toxic AZT. Most importantly, the FDA created an AIDS Clinical Trial Information Service, so that people suffering from the disease could be informed of drug trials using medications in the late stages of their development.

Act-Up continued their effective protests at strategic locations, including the New York Stock Exchange and Burroughs Wellcome's corporate headquarters. The latter compelled AZT's manufacturer to reduce the price of AZT by 20 percent. Three hundred protestors, organized by Act-Up, also demonstrated in Montreal, Canada, in late July. They achieved several major advances. Among these were putting a human HIV face on this and future AIDS conferences, promoting the slogan "Silence = Death," and drawing attention to the restrictive U.S. travel policies for HIV-positive visitors. All major news networks broadcast the dissidents which led to yet more displays of unrest at The Golden Gate Bridge and also led to announcing "A Day Without Art," which drew attention to the deaths of many artists, including Alvin Ailey, Robert Mapplethorpe and Amanda Blake, known as "Miss Kitty" from Gunsmoke.

Key West, Florida

Bob flew into Key West on Friday afternoon and we proceeded straight to the Public Health office where, anonymously, he had had his blood drawn ten days earlier. The receptionist told him that he would have to see a therapist before receiving the results. "But

I *am* a therapist," he said, hoping, in vain, to skip the step. While he was in an office with a psychologist, I walked around the block worried about what that requirement meant. Finally, strolling toward the building that housed the office, Bob emerged. Although I did not yet know him well, his face told the story. Bob, too, was HIV positive. We went back to the condominium and held each other for a very long time.

From that day on we spent every possible moment together in what became truly happy years. I was surrounded by both deep love and great competence, which I had never before experienced. I was forty years old. If life begins at forty, and in spite of HIV, I was all for the program!

The following day, we went to the Key West hospital to visit my friend Dicky, who was being treated for PCP. We did not tell Dicky about Bob's diagnosis, but rather focused on his own health and planned recovery. Dicky had two major problems to contend with, his first hospitalization with an opportunistic infection and the fact that his partner had left him. To add to his distress, Dicky was finding it increasingly difficult to keep his job at the new Truman Annex Real Estate Company. He asked Bob if he could consult him professionally—for free—on weekends, to which Bob generously agreed. I began to not only lust for, but also to admire this exceptional man with a surprisingly silent inner strength.

Bob and I spent every weekend together for the rest of the year. When he had to be in California for an extended period of time, I went there also. Otherwise, he came to Key West or we met somewhere on the East Coast. One weekend in September, we got together at The Pines on Fire Island. I had never been there with anyone I loved and I discovered that we had little desire to stay up late dancing. Instead, hand in hand, we took many hour-long walks along the beach to the neighboring towns and even ate several meals at restaurants in the "straight" villages on Fire Island. We walked around The Pines harbor, where *Les Beaux* had once been the venue for many wild parties. There, I learned that I was the only boat owner of the gay side of the harbor from the late 70s and early 80s who was known to be alive. Even the dock master had passed away.

On the seaplane returning to Manhattan, we both agreed that we would not go back to Fire Island. The many memories were too painful and represented the past. We would try other vacation spots instead. Bob wanted to meet my family and friends in Switzerland

Bob on the day he and the author met.

and we decided that we would sample Provincetown on Cape Cod. We would live life to the fullest. "Let's squeeze twenty years into five," I said as we parted company at LaGuardia airport.

Toward the end of the year we decided that Bob would move to Key West, so I went to Los Angles to help him pack up what he referred to as "his gear."

Bob had grown up in a therapeutic community in Malibu. While he was the product of his mother's first marriage, Bob spent most of his formative years with her second husband, Garry Troy. Garry was a tough but fair former military man, who, in the 60s, had allowed Bob and his brother to house their drug-addicted friends, providing that they underwent therapy and were drug-free while in his house. Over the following two decades, Garry bought several neighboring houses and, eventually, provided inpatient therapy for more than thirty recovering teenagers. The group was eventually

Bob boating with the author in Key West.

named "Teamm House" and had its own school, recreational projects, and therapists. Since it was located in Malibu, not far from the homes of many well-known Hollywood celebrities, donations kept the project alive. Bob explained that, as is often the case in similar environments, many of the graduates go on to become therapists themselves. He dreamed of running Teamm House as an adult, which he did after obtaining his Ph.D.

By the time we met, Garry was aging, the loyal supporters of the project were dwindling, and Los Angles County had built numerous facilities for troubled teens. So, the group decided to close Teamm House, which is what caused Bob to look for a job and go to work for another well-known Malibu physician/businessman, Bill Rader, the founder of the Rader Institute. Bob became their clinical director and traveled to all the hospital-based programs working with local psychiatrists to create a uniform standard of care. It was he who coined the still used phase, "It's not your fault, you are not alone, we care."

Even though Teamm House had closed by the time I got to know Garry and his wife, Nancy, their home was still run like a military academy. Approximately twenty remarkable former residents had remained fiercely loyal to the Troys and gathered in Malibu at least twice a week, both for ongoing group therapy sessions and family-style meals. Although everyone was cordial toward me, I was aware that I was responsible for Bob's move away from the tightly knit group and into a totally different environment and life. Bob was out to the understanding socially liberal group. But, as the only gay member, he felt a bit isolated and he welcomed both his professional and personal transition.

Teamm House had developed and practiced a unique psychological school called "Power of Mind" or "POM," which Bob taught me. This interesting version of mind control was very helpful in my recovery from Tim's death as well as in having a healthier attitude towards my union with Bob and life in general. It prepared me for the challenge of 1990.

That first Christmas in Key West, I was totally enamored and mesmerized by my talented and kind partner. For the first time in my life, the term "lover" was a word I was proud of and did not make me feel uncomfortable. We went to many Christmas parties given by the local gay set, and I watched everyone admire this newcomer to Key West society.

One evening when I returned from bringing food to Dicky, who was again hospitalized, Bob said, "There is a message on the answering machine you need to hear! Your fazzer called," imitating my dad's thick French accent.

I immediately returned the call. "René, I am sick and I demand your help at once. In fact, I need cardiac surgery. Set it up."

"Father," I said, "you don't just order cardiac surgery like carry out food. You need a complete cardiac work-up before you can determine if you need or even qualify for surgery. Then you speak to a cardiac surgeon."

"Then get me an appointment with a cardiologist," he ordered in typical fashion. "And be here when I see him!"

Before he hung up, I asked to speak with my mother. After repeating what I had told my father I added, "I speak with Tim's mother, Louise, every week. She has not mentioned receiving a condolence letter from you. Have you written her yet?"

"I would have no idea of what to say to her," my mother replied to my surprise.

"Mother," I continued, "you have written dozens of sympathy letters. Say the same thing to Louise that you would to anyone else. You may want to add something about the additional heartbreak a mother must feel when she looses a child."

"I cannot bring myself to do that," she said. "I'll send her a mass card."

The conversation troubled me for a long time until Bob helped me understand that my parents were only able to deal with their anxiety about the tragedy through denial. Placing one's personal handwriting on a letter made Tim's death too real for my mother to handle. Of course, she also would never benefit from the healing that proper grieving creates.

Bob encouraged me to make an appointment with a cardiologist in Boca Raton and to be present at the meeting the first week of January. Before that occurred, however, my parents' long-term family physician called. "René, I know your father is requesting cardiac surgery. You will find that is out of the question. I have ordered a CT scan. The results will be available right after New Year's. I recommend that you be here when we get the outcome. Please tell your brother to plan on a trip to the States." It was clear that Doctor Elkins already knew the prognosis. And it was not good.

During the closing days of 1989 I was overwhelmed at the knowledge that I had both buried a partner *and* found the big love of my life. Given my good fortune, I committed to be loyal to Bob, to support his career, and to care for both Dicky and my "fazzer."

On December 30, I received a call that my precious, ailing Nonnie had died. Bob held me on the balcony as I cried like never before. She was the same age as my father and had died peacefully in the very chair where she had sat as she told me her only concern for me being gay was who would cook and clean my house and where she always said I "was as good as gold." Her last words to me, two days earlier, were, "I am tired, René. I've led a good, long life and have children, including you, who are safe and educated. I really am ready to meet my maker." I would soon find out how rare, miraculous, and important it was to leave the planet with such a serene attitude.

CHAPTER SIXTEEN

═══════════════════

1990

Right after New Year's, Bob and I left Key West. I dropped him off at Miami airport for his usual weekly trip to an eating disorder clinic and I waited for my brother, Jack, to arrive from Switzerland. After his flight landed, we drove to Boca Raton where my father was hospitalized. Father had been one of the original founders of the local hospital thirty years previously, so he was given a suite at the end of a hall. My mother sat near his bed, holding his hand, as we awaited the family physician, Doctor Elkins.

"John," he began, "I have seen the results of all the tests we have run. I regret to inform you that you have cancer in every major organ. It is lung cancer that has metastasized to other areas of the body."

He paused to allow the news to sink in. Before he could continue, my father responded, "That cannot be. I am not in pain. All I feel is a shortness of breath. I have not smoked in decades."

"I'm very sorry," continued Elkins, "but it is true. Sometimes cancer is not painful and there are many incidences of lung cancer in non-smokers."

"Is this treatable?" I asked.

"No, René," answered the physician. "In this advanced stage, it would not be helpful."

"So what are we to do?" my mother asked, pleading for some direction.

"I recommend keeping Mr. Silvin as comfortable as possible at home."

───────────────

"Doctor," I asked, trying to get a handle on the future, "How do you see this will unfold?"

"I expect that your father will not last two months," he said, almost as if he and I were alone in the room. My mother gasped.

I walked around the bed and put my arms around her as she cried. "Do you promise you will keep him out of pain?" I asked, more to comfort my mother than anyone else.

"Of course! There is no reason for your father to experience pain. I'll sign the papers to discharge him in the morning and will add to his sleeping medication so that he gets some rest tonight."

With that, the brave physician left the room. The three of us sat silently by my father's bed for quite some time. When a nurse arrived with a dinner tray, she said, "I have your dinner, Mr. Silvin."

"I don't want it. Get out!" he said, in the tone that he would keep for the rest of his life.

After my brother and I had taken my mother back to her condominium, we sat on each side of her on a living room sofa. When she had stopped crying, she said in a weak voice, "I am so worn out, boys. Two months of his bad temper will kill me. I want you to both know that."

"Mother," I said. "I have a suggested solution."

My brother and she stared at me. "I'll set Father up in a facility nearby, where he will be well taken care of and you can be with him as many hours a day as you have energy for."

"Oh, René!" she answered, crying again. "You know your father. There is no way he will agree to that."

"Mother," I said. "Remember the French adage, 'Do not kill the living to help the dying.' If you truly feel there is no way to care for him, in spite of home health care nurses, I will put him in a nursing home."

We all discussed the option. It was my mother's clear wish, but one that she thought unavailable to her even in her declining health. She had been serious about fearing both their lives would end within two months. I left her and my brother and went into my father's office where I got on the phone to friends at NME in California. I got the name of the executive director of a skilled nursing facility in Boca Raton that, on occasion, took dying patients and worked with hospice. The lady was receptive to being called at home and asked me to meet her at the faculty the following morning at seven.

As we all retired for the evening, neither my mother nor my brother believed that the solution was possible. The following day, I discovered a pleasant, new, and well-run nursing home. The administrator and I made the financial arrangements and then I met the Director of Nursing and the floor nurses who worked on the wing where my father would be housed in a single bedroom. I had not seen my brother or my mother that morning. Both of them were completely unaware of the specifics of what I was arranging.

I explained to the staff that my father was a *difficult* man. "This is Boca Raton," answered a confident director of nursing. "We are used to spoiled and cranky people. We'll be able to deal with him."

"We'll see." I said, as I left to get my father.

When I entered his room at the hospital, my father was dressed and sat in an armchair waving his cane. "Where the hell have you been?" he demanded. "I have been waiting for you to take me home."

"I'm sorry I am late," I began taking a deep breath. "I was making arrangements for the best around-the-clock care I could find nearby, so that Mother can be with you as long as her energy allows."

"The hell with that!" he bellowed. "I'm going home—now!"

"I'm sorry to tell you, Father, that I do not believe Mother has the energy to supervise your care at home. I am taking you to a nursing facility where you will be well taken care of."

"That's bullshit" he screamed. "Home, now!"

"Father," I said, playing my trump card. "If you refuse, I will race home, grab Mother, and take her with me to Key West. You will never see either of us again. You know Jack has to return to Geneva. If you care anything about this woman who has been loyal to you for fifty-five years, you will go to the nursing home and be surrounded by competent people. Mother can come every day if she has the strength and I promise to be here half of each week."

I knew staying in Boca Raton full time would be an exhausting experience. Also, my childhood friend, Dicky, was in a nursing home as his own health worsened. It was the contrast of the two situations that made my uncharacteristic strong action with my father possible. Dicky was less than half my father's age and was in a dilapidated county nursing home in Key West. The luxurious surroundings, in a well-staffed facility in Boca, gave me the strength to make the case non-negotiable. I also decided to allocate some of my energy to be with Dicky, who had few friends, no money, and was as frightened of dying as my father.

I was both astounded and relieved that the approach had worked. I rode in the ambulance with my father as we went to his last new home. When he was set up in his room, and after receiving his order to "buy a decent bed for me to die in," I returned to my parent's condominium to tell a very curious family what I had done. Neither my brother nor my mother believed that my father would return home, unless my mother changed the arrangements after I left the area. To reinforce this I said to Mother, "I will come back here every week for three days to relieve you from going to see him. You must understand that he will ask you to remove him from the nursing home and bring him back here. You will have to be strong on that point. My guess is that his condition will worsen quickly and such a demand may only exist for a week or two."

Within a few days my brother and I had practiced our mother's driving to the nursing home to our satisfaction, and my father had accepted that he would not be returning to his apartment. On the second day he was at the nursing home he said, "René, go into my office, bring a gun, and shoot me."

"No, Father," I answered. "That will cause me problems for years. I'll tell you what I *can* do, however. I'll take you home for a lunch break and you can jump off the balcony." Thankfully that trick elicited his reaction to never once ask to go back to his condominium for lunch.

Before leaving, I received a call from the director of nursing. "René," she said, "we need to start around-the-clock private duty nurses for your father. The staff cannot handle him alone. Two nurses begged to be reassigned to other wings in the building. I have some names for you to call."

"I'm not surprised," I said. "I'll schedule the nursing coverage."

I explained to the nursing agency that my father was indeed a difficult and challenging patient. The reaction I received was similar to the initial retort I always got; "This is Palm Beach County. We are used to that."

The following day the first private duty nurse arrived. I was reading in my father's room.

"Good morning, John. I am your nurse," she said cheerfully.

"Who the hell told you that you could call me John?" he growled.

"Well, what would you prefer I call you?" she asked sitting down.

"Mr. Silvin! And who gave you permission to be seated in my presence?"

Still willing, the nurse inquired, "Where would you like me to stand, Mr. Silvin?"

"Take a chair into the hall and I'll call you if I need you."

I carried a large armchair into the hall for her. As the poor woman walked toward the door, my father said in a loud voice, "I told you she wouldn't give a damn."

"To the contrary," she responded, as she turned around. "I care very much. Can I not please give you a back rub?"

"Fine," he snarled. "But warm up the lotion! It's too cold."

As the nurse put some lotion into her hands, I hoped beyond hope that we may, in fact, have found a woman who had the patience and ability to handle him. I watched my father turn over as the lady rubbed her hands together to warm them. When she touched his back, he screamed, "Show me your hands!" The nurse complied.

"Just as I thought," said my father as if he were Sherlock Holmes. "You're a peasant!"

"No, Mr. Silvin!" the now clearly exasperated professional answered. "I am not a peasant, but what's wrong with *farmers*?"

"Nothing," he answered, "but I'll be God damned if one will rub my back."

Looking at me the nurse said, "Mr. Silvin, you were right. In fact, you understated the challenge. You'll have to find someone else to care for this man."

That was the first departure of a long stream of willing agency nurses.

The four-hour drive to Key West became my salvation. The beautiful blues of the ocean and the sky were so soothing and therapeutic. I drove slowly, with the top down, as I decompressed from the tension and readied myself to do what I could for Dicky, who was ending his life in a poorly furnished double room that smelled of urine, shared a bath, and had no television.

My work with AIDS Help had also been beneficial. Their temporary offices at the Truman Annex had relocated to a more permanent site in a building owned by the Catholic Church. Monsignor Eugene Quinlan had rapidly become a friend and accompanied me to see Dicky at least once a week. He always brought a gift for both my friend and any other ailing AIDS patients he saw there and at the adjacent hospital. On several occasions, I would meet him with food baskets to distribute. If we visited a dying patient at their home, "Padre," as we all affectionately called him, would slip a one hundred-dollar bill in with the food packages.

After one such visit, it was clear that Padre was having a bad day. I asked him to be my guest for dinner at Antonia's restaurant on Duval Street. Without asking what was bothering him, he began. "I am having problems dealing with the Toppinos, the leading Cuban Catholic family here. They all object to my asking 'who among you have reached out this week to an AIDS victim with assistance' at each of my sermons. But I am not going to stop," he insisted. "I spoke to one of the dying patients' mother in Ohio today," he went on. "I told her that if she wanted to see her young son again, it was time for her to come here. Do you know what she asked me?"

"No," I replied naturally.

"Did he repent yet?"

As I shrugged my shoulders, Padre continued. "Lady," I said. "I'm trying to give you advance notice. Your son is going to die very shortly. I'd like you to come and see him, but only if you can find it in your heart to be loving and drop the 'repent' crap. She said that was not possible, to which I told her not to bother to use her broomstick to fly down here!"

My next weeks settled into a routine. I would spend the first three days trying to ease my mother's anguish. The second half was working with Padre in Key West, visiting patients, and setting up new policies at AIDS Help. By Friday evenings, I was worn out. But standing by the chain link fence at the small airport as I watched my handsome, compassionate, and charming partner return to *our* home was an immediate tonic. Our weekends were as blissful as anyone could imagine and more than balanced out the horrors of the preceding week. One Sunday night, lying next to each other while we looked at the moonshine over the glittering ocean, Bob said, "René, you have to put an end to your father's abuse."

"And how do you suggest I do that?" I asked, laughing.

"Well, it is certain that he will say something cruel tomorrow. When that happens, just tell him that it's *not* acceptable."

"I'd love to have the power to do that, sweetheart. But I don't."

"Nonsense," said Bob. "Of course you do. If you feel too nervous at the moment of the insult just spit out a few sentences we will practice now. You'll be able to divorce yourself from the immediate tension and to end it forever. He'll never know the sentences were rehearsed. "

The following day, upon reaching the nursing home in Boca, my father demanded, "Go to my favorite restaurant, Marcel's, and get me oysters for lunch."

I left to go to the restaurant, relieved I had an errand that would take me out of his room. Upon my return, I greeted my mother and a nurse, who had earned the great privilege to sit in his presence. I said, "Father, Marcel had no oysters today. He did prepare a lovely tray of clams, which he said you also order frequently. He added that he would get fresh oysters at the market in Palm Beach for your lunch tomorrow."

As I placed the tray with ice and opened clams on the bed, my father threw them on me and the floor, spilling ice all over my shirt and giving me my golden opportunity to use Bob's brilliant sentences.

"That's the last time you will ever abuse me," I began my well-rehearsed lines.

"How dare you speak to me in that tone!" he yelled.

"Actually, Father, those were close to my next words."

Before I could continue, he looked at the two frightened women, my mother and the nurse, and yelled, "Get out! Both of you!"

As they scurried into the hall, and before he had a chance to say another word, I continued reciting the script. "I am very sorry that you are dying and that you are struggling with this. I have demonstrated that I am willing to put my life on its head to be here every week to help Mother and to care for you, but I will not be the brunt of your rage. I know there is a polite gentleman in there," I said pointing at his head. "If you show *that* man to me, I will keep coming here. If not, you will see my back for the very last time. It's up to you."

He never answered. I sat silently for what seemed like an eternity until I got up and went into the hall. My mother looked at me as if she were wondering who had been murdered in the duel.

"It's all right," I said, surprising myself. "Come back in now."

That Wednesday I had to return to the Keys, and as I reached the door, my father said, "René, did you notice I was polite? I was a gentleman!"

"Yes, Father," I said compassionately. "You were polite and a gentleman. It was a delight to be able to care for you this week. I'll see you next Monday."

Many emotions raced through my mind on the restorative drive south. There were so many useless questions about what life would have been like if anyone had held the ability to make my father realize he could not abuse those around him with abandon. Most importantly, I suddenly felt so secure that I lived with a wonderful man I deeply loved and being worthy of being loved. This was obviously the real thing—higher and better than ever before. I had finally found the one person who could understand me! I intuitively understood that he would have many more profound and helpful lessons for me over the years. I also *felt* loved and happy for the first time in my life. In a flash, I knew that the push-pull pattern I had always experienced with my father had been reversed. My father, who chronically had been so distant and so unavailable to me, thus damaging my self-esteem by reminding me of being unworthy, was now trying to gain my approval. Indeed, I was pushing and *he* was trying to pull me in.

Bob's insight, advice, and coaching were both brilliant and timely. He had given me the key to my liberation and, presto, my inner feelings of shame disappeared. Indeed, I measured up to my father.

Dicky died on February 19, an hour after I'd left him in his sad room. He was thirty-nine years old. My father followed the next day, February 20, in his nursing home with my mother by his side. With typical humor, Padre said that my childhood friend stopped off in Boca to pick up my father and take him to heaven. I had selected a white, cashmere sweater for Dicky to wear in his coffin. Dicky's mother asked Padre if "he was sure her son could *go* to heaven if he were not wearing a blue blazer." On February 21, after a mass at a crowded Mary, Star of the Sea Church on Truman Avenue, we buried him in a church plot donated by Padre.

When asked about titles for plays, Tennessee Williams once said, "There is a Catholic Church in Key West named 'Mary, Star of the Sea.' That would make a lovely title for a play." Dicky's life and death might have qualified as a great play had Tennessee Williams still been around.

From there I drove straight to Miami to meet the Swissair flight bringing my brother and his wife over from Geneva for our father's funeral.

When we got to my mother's condominium, she seemed weak yet relieved. I told her so when she said, "I still have one concern. Although he never went to church, you know your father was a Catholic. You remember, he made you and me swear we would not have any what he called 'Tibetan rituals' when we buried him? I am so conflicted because I believe he needs to have a Mass."

"Mother," I said, "we have discussed this concern before. I asked Padre about it, and he has a perfect solution. He will fly here tomorrow and will say some prayers at the funeral home. It is not technically a Mass and certainly not a Tibetan ritual. Padre assures me that Father will, in fact, go to heaven even though there is no Mass *and* a cremation."

I almost broke out laughing at how easy that was and how often Dicky and I had giggled over my father's words, Tibetan rituals and calcification, his term for cremation derived from his native French. I was not really sure about the going to Heaven part.

I met Padre at Fort Lauderdale airport and we drove to the funeral home in Boca. The only people present were my mother, my brother, his wife, and I. Padre put on a religious robe and read several prayers and passages from the Bible. He then produced a small plastic bottle like I had seen at the drug store and splashed holy water around the room and then on the coffin. There were no tears, just an odd sense of liberation. I had ordered a blanket of red roses to be placed on the casket. The only other flowers in the room were a huge arrangement from our friends, The Mérieux family, in Lyon, France. As we left the small room, the only sadness I experienced was realizing that my father had died as he lived— alone, angry, and frightened.

My brother left the building with my mother, ahead of Padre and me. As we reached the front door of the funeral home, not being well-versed in Catholic tradition, I said, "Oh, Padre, he never had his last rights. He was Catholic after all. Shall we go back upstairs and do that now?"

"I was rather heavy handed with the holy water," said Padre. "Let's go have a good lunch."

I was overjoyed that I could leave that entire nightmare nearly bent over in hysterical laughter.

In spite of the difficulties of the year's first seven weeks, my home life and my love life were thriving. It was hard for me to believe that the world could hold such happiness, especially after enduring two difficult deaths. In an odd way, the trauma of my father's and Dicky's illnesses and deaths were a catalyst to deepen my love for Bob. I was able to see firsthand how competent and supportive he was in the face of adversity.

I spent much of my time working with AIDS Help in Key West, which proved both productive and curative. My main project was to identify and it was hoped buy a housing unit for some of the less fortunate clients of our growing organization.

In April, the well-known Ryan White died at the young age of eighteen. His story and courage had done a great deal to bring awareness of the disease to a broader section of the American population. Ryan had become America's poster child for AIDS and suffered from both HIV disease and hemophilia. He and his mother had fought hard to not only keep him in school, but also active in school activities. Their valiant efforts became the vehicle to educate Middle America as to how HIV is–and is *not*–transmitted.

Shortly after Ryan died, Congress enacted The Ryan White Care Act, which still provides federal funds for the care of HIV-infected Americans. Seventeen years later, many have forgotten who this delightful young man was but still derive significant benefits from the results of the law that honors his name and commemorates his battle.

Bob and I decided that it was time for us to go to Switzerland to meet my great friends, Jean-Claude, Leo, and Pierre. Bob used his annual vacation to join me on a two-week trip. We stayed at The Palace Hotel in Gstaad and told our friends to schedule visits so that they and Bob could get to know each other.

At the first of many amusing dinners with Jean-Claude, it was clear that my former business associate was sizing up the man he knew I never wanted to be without. Jean-Claude loved to be provocative, using his humor to soften the points he was trying to make. During dinner at Gstaad's Olden Hotel in the middle of the village, Jean-Claude said, "You used to bring boys to Switzerland who had an ass. This one may have a brain."

Bob seized the moment to not only amuse everyone at the dinner but also to capture Jean-Claude's heart. He got up and turned around, showing his great physique from behind, and said, "Jean-Claude, I have both!"

We spent our days hiking up the Eggli Mountain and having wonderful mid-day meals at the restaurant beautifully situated at the top, where I had learned to ski over thirty years earlier. My brother left his two sons with us for a long weekend so they could get to know Bob, especially since they had both been traumatized by Tim's death. Tim had played with them for hours when they were younger, throwing them onto their beds in what he called a "body slam." We had all laughed and enjoyed each other in what became the subtle teaching to young boys that their gay uncle was really quite normal in many ways and that I could bring a fun addition to their lives. Early on, Bob earned the respect and affection of "our" nephews also.

To complete Bob's introduction to my Swiss life, he met Pierre and Michele Nussbaumer. In their typical generous, almost extravagant behavior, they invited Bob and me to join them at a luxurious Chateau Hotel in nearby France. There, they presented Bob and me with matching Hermes towels, which would forever symbolize our wedding gift. Pierre does not snap to hasty decisions but it was clear he, too, was impressed with Bob's quiet depth. I would soon learn that Pierre's support would come to mean a great deal to Bob.

As usual, Leo was both enlightening and entertaining. Bob quickly had added Leo to the list of people who admired him and were relieved to see me in the company of an exceptional partner. I knew how much Leo enjoyed good red wines and had brought a bottle of 1978 Vosne Romanee, one his favorites, to our room to drink before dinner.

"There are several new medications you both must become aware of," he said. "There is something called a reverse-transcriptase inhibitor, which is helping patients who have progressed to AIDS."

Ever the statistician and student, Bob asked, "What actually defines AIDS and differentiates it from HIV?"

"Each country defines AIDS differently," began the Professor. "It is no surprise that the Americans have the most conservative definition, thus delaying the availability of practically non-existent government-sponsored relief programs. Here in Europe, one is considered as suffering from AIDS if he or she has a CD4 count under 500 and has had one life threatening opportunistic infection. There is another yardstick in which I am most interested called viral load testing. Professor Chermann, who really is the man who isolated the virus at Pasteur eight years ago, has left Pasteur and opened an advanced research laboratory at the University of Luminy in Marseille, France. He is developing a measure of how present and active the virus is in its host. I assume that such a test will be extremely useful in treating the illness as soon as it is made widely available. Chermann will be speaking on national television this Friday. I suggest you watch the program and go see him before you return to the States."

That Friday Bob and I were glued to the television in our room. Switzerland carries Italian, German, and French networks as well as their own. We tuned into one of the French networks and listened to Chermann's illuminating description of how the HIV virus operates and mutates. A similar show on prime time in America would take another decade to air. After the program, I called my friend and pharmaceutical magnate, Doctor Alain Mérieux, to ask his opinion on what I had learned. The Mérieux Institute was the world's largest vaccine manufacturer in the 1990s and heavily involved in research. They had been kind enough for several years to supply me with their experimental HIV medication called DTC, without cumbersome bureaucratic procedures. I had spent many wonderful weekends with Alain's sister, my life-long friend Nicole, at her house on the Lake of Annecy near Geneva. We would all water ski from her beautifully varnished Chris Craft speedboat named *Virus*.

Alain confirmed that he knew Jean-Claude Chermann well and that his research was truly cutting edge. "But you must understand, René, Chermann is testing a medication and working on measuring the virus' activity. But this is no magic bullet. The world is many years away from adequate treatment, much less a vaccine. Your Anthony Fauci at NIH is also trying to formalize the process of clinical trials for patients to access experimental treatments."

"I really want to meet Chermann," I said. "Would you please call him in Marseille and ask him if he would receive me there next week?"

By the following Monday, Alain's efficient secretary, who had kindly provided me with many favors, called saying that I had an appointment in Marseille with the legendary Jean-Claude Chermann.

Bob's vacation was over and he returned to his eating disorder clinics in America. I took an extra few days to go to Marseille. Once I had found the research building at the university where

Chermann had set up his laboratory and was ushered into his office, I received the first of many harsh lectures followed by affection—Chermann's signature counter-balancing behavior.

"Before we begin," he said ominously, "I must tell you that I do not believe in medicine for the privileged. You did not have to ask a big shot like Mérieux to call for an appointment."

"I had no idea of who you do allow to visit and under what circumstances. I hope I did not offend you," I said sheepishly.

"No, you did not offend me, but you will be treated like any other person who walks through that door. Is that clear?"

Thus began a relationship that constantly deepened. Chermann's tone rapidly changed to include compassion and generous explanations. He confided that the weak link of his research was in compiling adequate statistics in a format acceptable to the scientific community. I volunteered Bob's services to help compile data, and we agreed to meet frequently to that end.

When I returned to America, I was amazed that none of the physicians I consulted knew anything about viral load testing or Chermann's other research in geno- and pheno-typing analysis to clearly determine what mutations an HIV patient had developed to the virus. I quickly stopped even mentioning these terms when my descriptions drew both blank faces that indicated others thought I was crazy!

I gave up my inadequate quest to draw attention to European HIV developments when a friend of mine in Washington, DC, had *his* friend call me. Chris Wallace was an up-and-coming investigative reporter at that time and the son of the well-known CBS newsman Mike Wallace. We had a long conversation about the advances in HIV treatment research the Europeans were making, especially in France and Belgium. While Chris said that he'd like to continue with follow-up conversations, it was apparent that *possible* future, scientific developments in HIV did not present a subject for broad discussion in America and was premature to retain his or his audience's attention.

As my emotion-charged year ended, it was clear that changes in the world of AIDS would be measured in baby steps resulting from hard work. There was no responsible promise of a cure or a vaccine. Unfortunately, progress was limited to providing assistance to the many victims of HIV disease who lost their life savings and their ability to remain productive components of society.

When Nelson Mandela was released from prison, one million South Africans had already been exposed to the virus, but the country's new liberal leader hardly talked about the crisis for the following five years. Other pressing issues kept his attention, as HIV gradually became South Africa's new Apartheid. AIDS would create the new under-class in Africa, dividing the more fortunate from those who could not afford treatment or comfortable surroundings in which to end their lives.

CHAPTER SEVENTEEN

1991

As our time living together began to pass, it was obvious that both Bob and I had each found a world of happiness we had not imagined existed. We told each other that often. During the workweek, I missed him terribly and kept busy at AIDS Help trying to raise enough money to acquire a housing unit for our clients. Having come from the for-profit health care industry, I had to adjust some of my thinking to adapt to a non-profit community organization. Even so, I became the sole voice of fiscal conservancy on the Board of Directors. This was driven by my obsession of being able to assure the long-term continuity of any new benefit we inaugurated.

Bob worked hard at each of Radar's eating disorder units. Our perfect and peaceful weekends were action packed with social activities in Key West, daily visits to the new gym at Duval Square, and romantic dinners, during which our non-stop conversation taught us more and more about each other. His descriptions of the patients he saw during the week, the gravity of their affliction, and his compassion for their plight was enlightening.

Shortly after the beginning of the year, we prepared a feasibility study to open an eating disorder clinic in Key West, but decided against the endeavor. During this period I got to know several of Bob's colleagues, all of whom respected his professional talent and personal charm. Bob's boss, the CEO of the company, believed there was opportunity for the Rader Institute to expand into Europe. As a result I made plans to spend the summer in

Switzerland, while Bob and I looked into the possibility and Bob traveled back and forth to existing clinics on the East Coast.

On the eve of one trip to Europe, I went to my safe deposit box at a bank in Old Town, Key West, to get my passport, some travel money, and a few other items, including a Cartier money clip that Tim had given me when we moved back to America from Europe. I had placed the objects in a travel clutch and left them in the convertible in front of Lighthouse Court while I went in to pick up my workout gloves. I was only inside for a few minutes, but when I emerged, I noticed my window had been broken and the small travel handbag was gone. I called the police, who said that there was little they could do other than fill out a crime report, which we did. When I got back to my condominium, I called an infamous city councilman who represented Bahama Village, the equivalent of a small inner city, situated on the blocks adjacent to Lighthouse Court. I knew Emory Majors because Padre and I wanted to set up an education program in the African-American churches about the risks of HIV. I was very surprised by the reluctance of the community leaders to acknowledge the problem and the relatively high incidence of bisexuality.

"Emory," I said, "my car was broken into in front of the Hemingway House less than an hour ago. I lost seven items of importance to me including an airplane ticket, my passport, a special pen, and a money clip. The police indicated a lack of enthusiasm and I wondered if you might help me recover them?"

"That's possible," he said.

"I'll offer $100 per item and will not ask any questions."

Fifteen minutes later, Emory called with good news. "I have six of your seven items. The money clip is not included."

That seemed obvious because my travel cash was attached. However, I had heard of a similar exchange when an acquaintance brought cash to retrieve a stolen car and got beaten up so badly he ended up in the emergency room. "I'll be right there with six hundred dollars to retrieve them. Will I be safe or do I need to bring some protection?"

"Ain't no one here who'll hurt you," he said, laughing. "But if you feel more comfortable, you can bring a cop."

Fifteen minutes later, and in the presence of a police officer, I had my six items that allowed me to make my trip the following day. Even though I went to every pawn shop over the next months looking for it, Tim's money clip–like Tim–was gone forever.

Gstaad, Switzerland

In Switzerland, I set up house in a rented chalet outside of Gstaad. I partnered the lease with a close friend, Smith Richardson. I had met Smith because Tim and he were in design school together and we all had become close friends. Smith's partner, Rick, was HIV positive and also one of the most fun people Bob and I knew. We loved being in their company and were thrilled that we would see a lot of them this summer. We also invited close friends from Key West to join us. Among them were Trip Hoffman and his partner, Alan Van Wieren. Both were active in the gay social set in Key West and had fallen on hard times with two failed business ventures; one in a start-up telephone company, the other a water filter product. We felt they needed the change of scenery and were happy to include them as our guests.

With Leo Eckmann's help, Bob and I interviewed hospital managers and owners, as well as psychiatrists, to determine if there was a need for a self-pay eating disorder clinic as all European insurance companies had refused to cover hospitalization for the disease. In addition, we had difficulty translating the term into German and French to create an understandable accurate description. While the incidence of eating orders is high, its acceptance is lower in this ultra conservative country. Most victims tried to treat the problem quietly in a psychiatrist's office. Hospitalization, if at all, was done under a different diagnosis, which further alienated the patients. At a decision-making meeting, we invited twenty well-to-do, local people who either had, or were closely related to, someone with an advanced eating disorder.

In the Palace Hotel's main lounge, one guest, a distant relative of Iran's deposed Shah, ordered pastries as we began the presentation. Trying to make his point, and sensing a bad omen, Bob interrupted, "I am sorry, Madam, but we will only be serving fruit juices."

Bob explained in advanced cases of eating disorders, one's very life was at stake and that in less acute conditions, psychological well-being was almost always impaired. During a question and answer period, a waiter circulated among the guest with a silver tray containing several types of beautifully colored fruit juices. As the questions began, we realized our concept of an American-style eating disorder clinic was premature. Bob tried to diplomatically answer questions like, "Can I bring my chef to your clinic?" or worse, "Do you have a well-maintained barn nearby? I'd come if I could bring my horse."

After the gathering, Leo, Bob, and I laughed at the naïveté of our plan. It had been a great learning experience in the cultural differences between continents, in relation to new medical thinking and beliefs.

"Don't you find it odd, Leo," I began, "that you are more advanced in discussing HIV in Europe than in America, but one still feels compelled to hide an eating disorder here?"

"It's actually easily understood," he answered. "AIDS is still considered a homosexual disease and you are much more homophobic in America. You can talk openly about alcoholism and psychiatric problems, but not homosexuality. Most Europeans have little or no problem with gay life, but have not reached an acceptance of psychiatric problems. We don't have an Oprah!

"This experience today proves my point. It is hoped, as more heterosexual stars like Magic Johnson admit having the virus, you may evolve. But you are still a highly religious–even righteous–people."

We discussed the bizarre contradiction in America and our conservative president's lack of having adequately addressed AIDS in the early days of the pandemic.

"Now, René, you need to start anti-retroviral treatment. There are several new medications, including a good one made by Bristol-Myers Squibb."

"Which one do you recommend?" I asked.

"Several," he said. "We need to box the virus in. It is a complex and intelligent little devil that mutates quickly. You need a cocktail of drugs, not just one."

It would be more than a year before the term cocktail was adapted in the States to describe the multi-drug regimen that benefits most HIV-positive patients.

"But I want you to see Chermann in Marseille before you start taking anything."

"Bob and I are going there next week," I said. "Won't you join us as our guest? There is a charming hotel on the coast in Cassis."

Cassis, France

All of us, including Smith and Rick, drove to the South of France the following week. It was their first meeting with the charismatic Professor Jean-Claude Chermann, who had the same first name as my friend and business partner in Switzerland. Leo fell in love with the hotel I had discovered and always offered to meet us there when we visited Chermann's laboratory. The five of us, including Mrs. Chermann, became very close friends as we worked and traveled together several times a year. Bob had taken over helping Jean-Claude put his statistics in an acceptable format for publication in medical journals and Leo balanced Jean-Claude's profound understanding of the virus with his own experience as a clinician and philosopher.

Like everyone else Bob met, Jean-Claude was wildly fond of my partner. Chermann spent hours describing how the virus operates and how best for people in general, as well as us in particular, to deal with it. In typical French tradition, he felt that we had gone overboard in America with an obsession for controlling the so-called "co-factors."

"Don't get hysterical about diet and exercise," he advised. "Of course, a good balance is mandatory. But Americans are so extreme and you need to have fun in life. Relax! Even *if* you are faced with a life threatening illness. It will soon become manageable rather than a death sentence. Viral load testing will help clinicians recommend the timing of medications. There again, I fear Americans will be overzealous in prescribing these very toxic drugs. And geno-typing will help competent physicians determine when a patient's virus has mutated so that medications can be altered as new drugs, and even new classes of drugs, are developed."

"We are going to Belgium when we leave here," Bob said, "to see the new lab there which processes the geno- and pheno-typing of HIV blood samples."

"Please call me when you have seen it," said Jean-Claude. "It is the wave of the future."

"Why is it," I began with a question that had tormented me for nearly a decade, "that I frequented all the places and had sexual relations with many HIV-positive people who are all dead. Why am I here and relatively healthy?"

"You either were infected with a weak strain of the virus or, more likely, your system has the ability to plateau. It finds a level at which your immune system can contain the virus from further damaging it. That's why viral load testing is an important component. But I go much further than simple viral load measurements. I measure the mood of the virus in a co-culture that takes thirty days, and the types of antibodies the host produces are identified. In your cases, at this point, I do not recommend treatment and I believe that you, René, may not benefit from traditional antiviral treatment over long periods. It's odd but there is also a mutant gene, called Delta 32, which *prevents* infection! So, while you are lucky so far, there is an even more fortunate smaller minority who cannot *become* infected in the first place. I want to study them more in order to look into the possibility of a vaccine. Isn't it amazing that a genetic mistake can be life saving?

"Now," continued Chermann, "I want you to be interviewed on French television tomorrow. They will be in my office and I need you to explain your case."

"But I am not French," I said.

"That's why I need you," he answered. "It would be of help to me and will show French people that, if some folks come from America for my tests, that more French should take advantage of what is at their disposal, especially non-progressors like you. We may even be able to locate some people with Delta 32."

"It's a good thing your father is dead, René," said Bob. "I don't think he'd be overjoyed to hear from his French relatives that you were coming out on national television."

The amusing comment made me realize how fortunate I was to not have those kinds of concerns any longer and how much I hoped we could help others reach a similar position of freedom, whether or not they had disapproving relatives.

Before the television interview, Chermann brought Bob, Rick, Leo and me into his office. "We have received the results of your blood work and I have several pieces of news," he began. "Bob, you and René have a protective antibody called R7V. Your counts are better than René's, so I definitely do not recommend you be treated at this time. Rick and René do require medication, but not with antivirals yet. I am convinced that the thymus is a key element in boosting the immune system. It is where CD4 T-Cells are made. I want you both to begin daily injections of a thymus extract, which I believe is the best available immune modulator. What do you think, Leo?"

"I have always maintained that strengthening the host is better than fighting the virus while the patient still has an immune system to protect," answered Leo. "So I wholeheartedly endorse the injectable thymus booster. I'll teach you both how to administer inter-muscular shots. You'll see that it is no big deal and will become comfortable with it within a few days."

For the following two years, Rick and I would have to go to Marseille every other month to get our two-month dose of the experimental medication and to be monitored at Chermann's laboratory. We always hated coming through customs in Atlanta or New York with syringes and an unknown medication packaged in unmarked containers. Except for a few minor problems when we were brought into a room to be questioned, letters explaining our condition and the medication sufficed to get us back into the country. All my and Rick's blood counts improved significantly while we used the thymus extract.

Unfortunately, the product was purchased by Upjohn Pharmaceutical, which promptly discontinued it and did not honor the protocol agreements that had been entered into with all the voluntary experimental patients in France and the U.S. They refused to give us any explanation of their upsetting decision or to allow Professor Chermann and me to speak to their lead scientists or executives at my expense.

This was my second experimental medication, along with the Mérieux Institute's DTC, which had helped build my immune system and which was cancelled before it became readily available to the public or to the trial patients. The experience, while devastating when it occurred, taught me the absolute need for flexibility and balance in dealing with the ever-changing world of HIV treatment. I learned that I had to control the usually brief euphoria associated with good medical news so that the contrasting bad news was tolerable.

Vevey, Switzerland

Bob flew home from France and I returned to Switzerland to admit my mother to a facility to address a prescription drug problem that had gradually worsened. Switzerland has always had various private specialty clinics where numerous conditions are discretely treated. Jean-Claude Salamin had recommended a clinic in Vevey, a charming flower-filled lakeside city where Charlie Chaplin had lived and died and Nestlé has its world headquarters.

This particular clinic was located in one of the town's best hotels. Each patient enjoyed a lakefront room, no different from the others but located on different floors in the hotel. A psychiatrist and psychologist were assigned to the case to wean my mother off of tranquilizers, anti-depressants, and sleeping pills.

My mother was a willing patient because she had developed what is known as a paradoxical reaction to the tranquilizers. The more one takes, the more jitters one experiences, which is followed by yet more pills, and so on. Her physician in Boca Raton was dispensing five hundred pills at a time. Bob called the doctor when we discovered the problem. "Doctor, this is Doctor Mann speaking. I am calling on behalf of Mrs. Silvin and her son, René," he said. "We are both very concerned about her extreme agitation caused by excessive use of tranquilizers and anti-depressants."

"I wouldn't be overly disturbed about that," her physician answered.

"But we are, Doctor," he said in his calm yet determined manner. "In fact, we are taking Mrs. Silvin to a sanatorium overseas. The purpose of my call is to tell you that we fully expect you to only prescribe acceptable doses of such medication to her when she returns and *only* in consultation with me."

"Is that a threat?" he asked.

"No, Doctor," continued Bob. "I merely want you to know that if we find that you have allowed Mrs. Silvin to overuse prescription drugs again, I will call you up in front of a panel of your peers for review."

Unfortunately, Bob had to have a similar conversation with several physicians who preyed on elderly, lonely widows in Palm Beach County for the rest of my mother's life.

By the end of the year, several of my past associates had encountered serious legal problems. At National Medical Enterprises a class action suit against the company, and the two senior officers I had been dealing with, began. Dick Eamer and Mike Focht were accused of a breach of fiduciary responsibility in handling company money and business.

Roy Pesch's Swiss hospital company was entering bankruptcy. To round out highly publicized legal problems brought against acquaintances, Emory Majors was sent to prison when federal officers came to Key West and arrested several well-known local politicians.

All this news was overshadowed, and almost rendered irrelevant, by the fact that ten million people had been infected with HIV worldwide as 1991 drew to a close. I had lost hundreds of acquaintances, scores of friends, and my partner, Tim. But I had a great life with Bob and we were well on our way to squeezing twenty years into five.

The author with Bob and nephew in Gstaad.

Above, Bob emerges from a swim while working with J.C. Chermann in France; below the author and Bob with the Cassis cliff in the background.

CHAPTER EIGHTEEN

═══════════════════════

1992

Stability and happiness would be the best way to describe 1992. While both Bob and I knew we had a life threatening illness, we believed we were fortunate in being advised by both a great infectious disease immunologist and the world's most advanced retrovirologist. Bob loved working on Jean-Claude Chermann's statistics, and we managed to make our frequent visits to France exciting rather than focusing on the often confusing medical news and the somewhat dehumanizing time spent at the public health hospital in Marseille every time I needed two more months of the experimental thymus injectable product Chermann had recommended.

Our friends, Trip and Alain, had a Jack Russell named Spanky, and Bob said he was the type of dog he would like. When Alain said that they had bred Spanky and would be happy to sell us one of his offspring, I was ecstatic and could hardly wait for the puppy to be old enough to adopt. We spent many fun moments thinking of an appropriate name and decided we wanted a female who would be called "T-Cell." That way, we could make light of the endless and tiresome conversations about "how many T-Cells you have" and, after all, Jack Russells are strong, energetic, and healthy, just like a real T-Cell should be.

My T-Cell count had begun to decline from four hundred to three hundred, and Bob said, "Think about it, René, we will always have at least one T-Cell!" Since I was the oldest, as well as the longest HIV-positive part of our duo, we both assumed I'd be the first to go.

───────────────

During the winter, I made two patches for the popular AIDS quilt project in San Francisco; one for Tim, the other for Dicky. I tried to design each one to match the character of the person it was meant to memorialize. Tim's quilt was a long distance, joint venture because I included several of his childhood friends in the work. We wanted it to be trendy, young, colorful, and fun. We incorporated Tim's red high school basketball jersey and some mementos from his all too brief career in interior design. Sadly, in Dicky's case, there was no one whom I could enlist to assist me. I had several of Dicky's early dramatic black and white modeling photographs, which had been shot in New York, made into fabric patches. With them I created a quilt that was dramatic, handsome, and stylish. The process was cathartic and necessary. I worked on the patches every day and, upon completion of the second quilt, decided I would never make another but would continue to support the project financially. I felt that part of my healing process was over and I was ready to move on.

Working with Al McCarthy in Key West, we identified several possible sites for a housing unit for the most deserving AIDS Help clients. The sites we could afford with the monies raised by the very diligent fund raising committee were either inadequate or required so much additional money to bring up to acceptable standards that the project appeared doomed. We finally found a compound on Bertha Street, near to where Bob and I lived, which was ideal. Once again, the price was out of our reach. One evening Al and I met with Jerry Hermann, the well-known songwriter and lyricist, to tell him of our progress. Jerry had recently lost his partner, Marty Finkelstein, with whom I'd worked out at the gym. I had elected him "The Best Chest," which we all admired, and I was crushed when his illness got out of control and he rapidly deteriorated and died.

"I'm afraid we will be abandoning the dream of having our own housing unit–at least for now." I began.

"What was the best one you saw?" asked Jerry.

"It is over near B's Restaurant and would be perfect for our needs, but we need $750,000 more than we can raise. Remember, Jerry, we have had over fifteen local fundraisers. The locals are pretty well tapped out."

Jerry asked for a few more details, got up, went into his study, and came back with a check for the required $750,000. While Al and I sat speechless, Jerry said, "I have two requirements you must agree to in accepting this donation. The first is that you not cash the check for ten days."

"That's hardly a problem," said Al, as we all chuckled.

"The second," continued Jerry "is that the project be named after Marty."

Al explained that we would bring the issue of the name to the full Board but that, again, the huge gift which would enable Key West to be a leader in housing for otherwise displaced AIDS patients would render his request moot. Within months the compound was acquired, several units were renovated, food was being routinely delivered each day from well-known local restaurants, and a beautiful gold and green sign sat at the entrance to the compound that reads, "Marty's Place."

France

For my midwinter trip to France to collect my experimental medication, and to take a few extra days' vacation, Bob was able to accompany me. He had never seen the great castles of the Loire Valley, which I had passionately told him about. In typical fashion, Bob researched several of them, and we planned our holiday around visiting the Chateaux with the most riveting histories and stayed in quaint local inns near each one.

Not surprisingly, my favorite, the Chateau de Chenonceau, also became Bob's. It was built over the river Cher, near the town of the same name, by Henry the Second for his mistress Diane de Poitiers, reputedly the most striking and inspiring woman of her time. We lingered in the perfectly planned gardens and absorbed every detail of the tour guide's explanations of the Chateau. That night we saw a stunning production of *son et lumière* (sound and light) detailing the castle's history. Bob and I lay on a blanket and watched the dramatic show like two children in love seeing the Nutcracker at Christmas for the first time.

Highlands, North Carolina

During the summer, together with our friends, Smith and Rick, we rented a house in Highlands, North Carolina. Smith and Rick lived in Atlanta and could easily escape the hot city to reach the resort that, at five thousand feet, was almost always cool. I did not want to be away from Bob in Europe, so the solution sounded perfect, especially since neighbors at the Key West Beach Club also rented mountain cabins in the area.

Since my years of working in Washington, DC, I had owned a cabin near Charlottesville, Virginia, in the neighboring county of Louisa. Bob pointed out that as we never used the little house, I should look for a similar property in the Highlands area and swap the Virginia cabin for something that we could all frequently use during summers. I was invariably very excited when I picked up Bob at the Asheville airport. On our way back up the mountain, Bob would tell me about his fascinating, nameless eating disorder patients, and I'd show Bob the cabins I had seen. We would also drive around various other neighborhoods. One evening we drove past a contemporary home, built across a stream.

Bob had never before expressed a passion for any material item and surprised me when he said he thought the house was "the most beautiful home" he had ever seen and wanted us "to live and die there."

"It's hardly a cabin, Bob," I said, "but I have seen this house listed for sale in a real estate broker's window in Highlands. Let's go speak with him tomorrow."

The following day we went into the John Shiffli office on Main Street. My thoughts that the realtor's name was Swiss were confirmed by the décor in the office, which included several Swiss artifacts like a cowbell and yoke. However, any resemblance to a Swiss *personality* vanished when we met the gentleman. From the start, dealing with Mr. Shiffli was strained and increased when he was reluctant to show us the listed property. Day after day, I would return to the office trying to schedule a showing. Each time there was another excuse. Finally, the standoffish broker gave me a key and told me to "go see it on your own."

I drove the eight miles to the property only to find that the key did not work. After a repeated experience, I concluded that Mr. Shiffli, decidedly, did not want to show me the property. Undeterred, I wrote the owner and eventually received a call from a sweet elderly lady who was surprised by my letter and the information it contained.

"I have been away, but I am here now and you may come by any time you like," said Mrs. Asbury.

After our second meeting, she and I sat on the deck overlooking the scenic private pond. We had an immediate affinity for one another, which was proven by her statement, "Mr. Silvin, I am sorry you had such a difficult time with Old Shiffli."

"Do you know why he would not show me the house when he has the listing?" I asked.

"It is embarrassing," she began, "but he told me that he was a friend of my late husband's and Jack would 'roll over in his grave' if he knew I might sell the house to 'two fags.' You must know that, if you do move here, there will be others who are stupid old big-ots—even in this neighborhood—and who may try to make life unpleasant for you."

"That won't bother Bob and me," I replied naively. "The world is changing. Imagine! An AIDS victim named Mary Fischer even spoke at the Republican National Convention! Also, the gay world has hopes that if Bill Clinton is elected in November, we'll enter a period of greater acceptance, understanding, and medical research."

"I want you to have this house, which brought Jack and me great happiness, but I want to warn you that there are other Shifflis around here."

That Saturday, when Bob returned for the weekend, we spent over an hour touring the house and the property. Even though the house had been badly maintained and needed extensive renova-tion, Bob's delight at the thought of moving there was apparent. "Let's make this our retirement home, René," he said. "There are 200,000 HIV infected people in America, one and a half million worldwide. Who knows how long *we* have?"

"Since it crosses a river, let's name it something to do with Chenonceau," I added, as our excitement turned into exuberance. "Instead of Henry the Second building it for the most beautiful woman in the world, I'll *remodel* it for the most handsome *man* in the world."

Within a few days we were under contract to buy the house of our dreams, which we would name "Chenoncette" (baby Chenonceau) and close the transaction nine months later. This would allow Mrs. Asbury the time she wanted and also offer us time to sell our condominium in Key West. We pledged to each other to make it into a small island of tranquility and love and for us to end our days there.

Key West, Florida

Bob never ceased to amaze me with his unwavering devotion, absolute emotional presence, and authentic attention to my feelings. It was a common occurrence that gay men would blatantly cruise Bob, on occasion even placing their telephone numbers in his hand or trying to lure him into another room to talk, hoping I would not notice. Invariably, Bob would say, "Excuse me, but I guess you have not met my partner, René," and he would put his arm around my shoulder and smile at me.

That fall, I developed pains in my esophagus and went to see one of the local Key West physicians. He told me that it was indigestion, which could be handled with antacids. When the problem persisted, I decided to call Leo Eckmann. "What is your current T-Cell count?" he asked.

"Two hundred," I replied.

"Tell your local doctor you want a prescription for an anti-fungal. I recommend one hundred milligrams of Diflucan per day. You will see that the symptoms will end in a week."

"But he is sure it is indigestion."

"Tell him two things. The first is that he must start reading the *New England Journal of Medicine,* and the second is that you need another doctor!" concluded Leo with his usual clever humor.

By the end of the year, Bill Clinton had been elected president and hopes for a more liberal and understanding life in America flourished among most of our friends. His wife, Hillary, had pledged to overhaul the nation's healthcare system as soon as they took office, and there were rumblings that life for gay military men and women might also, finally, be able to be undertaken without fear of reprisals and dishonorable discharge.

As Leo predicted, other anti-viral drugs were in various phases of research. The FDA approved ddC or Hivid, the first one to be used in combination with AZT, and began efforts to accelerate the approval process of similar medications to reach HIV/AIDS patients faster.

There definitely was reason for optimism to fuel my hopes to live many healthy years with Bob at "the house of his dreams."

Johnny and Bob on the wall in front of the Chateau de Chenonceau, which became "the inspiration to build the house we would live and die in." Below, Chenoncette (Baby Chenonceau), home to Bob and the author in North Carolina.

CHAPTER NINETEEN

1993

The year began with great excitement about moving to North Carolina and possible significant improvements for the AIDS community. Bob and I enjoyed Key West, but we both felt the gay set was limiting and somewhat self-serving. Wearing a new silk shirt to an AIDS fundraiser at a local restaurant became trite, and we both preferred to actually do something. Our communication with Professor Chermann increased even as his ability to spend full time in his research laboratory at the University was made more difficult.

Marseille, a major French city on the Mediterranean, had both a liberal and an extreme right political element. The National Front (Le Front National) was led by Jean-Marie Le Pen, France's equivalent of Jerry Falwell. The opposition was led by the liberal senator (Deputé) Bernard Tapie, who had been under intense pressure from his political opponent and was forced to resign amid charges of improprieties while running his sports apparel giant, Adidas. Under the French system, a senator who resigns is allowed to pick his or her successor to serve during the balance of the elected term. Bernard Tapie selected Jean-Claude Chermann to be his replacement (Suppléant).

Both Jean-Claude and his intelligent activist wife, Dani, sprang into action to combat Le Pen's extremist views of cracking down on immigration, encouraging women to stay home and have babies and reinstituting the death penalty. It was a strange political movement in an otherwise socially liberal France and one the

Chermanns were determined to combat. We were all particularly outraged at Le Pen's pronouncements that the Nazi gas chambers were a "detail of history" and that his position was "neither left nor right"—a slogan he used in his repeated efforts to be elected to the French Presidency.

We had also become close friends with an unusual couple who had recently bought President Eisenhower's former house, a historic building in the Truman Annex in Key West. Their names were Duane Rath and Fredrick (Ted) Hurdman. Pridam Singh, the neighborhood's developer, needed a strong vote of confidence to prove that the property could indeed become the exclusive area he had in mind. Several abandoned former Navy buildings were scattered throughout the nineteen acres. These included a hospital, an administration building, two red brick foundry buildings, some admiral quarters, Harry Truman's Little White House and President Eisenhower's former home.

Duane Rath bought 51 Front Street and beautifully landscaped and remodeled it in a style consistent with the home's design and reminiscent of where a vacationing president would relax. Fifty-foot tall Royal palms were brought in as this largest single piece of property in the area was professionally landscaped. The abandoned and dilapidated house, overlooking the harbor, was rebuilt and splendidly decorated and furnished. The living room featured one of the island's few beautiful fire places in front of which sat a tea table, one of two. The other belongs to Elizabeth Taylor. A huge Venetian glass chandelier hung above a contemporary custom-made dining room table, chairs, and rug. Adjacent to the living room was a warm, elegant library decorated with rare Indian chief pictures that Duane acquired from the Curtis Elephant portfolio. The library furniture was upholstered with Clarence House fabric, with additional rolls stored nearby in case the dog soiled a seat. This expensive endeavor gave the Truman Annex the vote of confidence it indeed needed. The remaining lots along Front Street sold in rapid succession, and new large duplications of historic homes in Old Town were planned and erected.

Duane and Ted had been together for fifteen years and were envied among the gay set because Duane had great wealth and added a totally new and superior dimension to the level of possible charitable contributions. It was odd to us that their arrival in town did not create a sense of comfort amongst our friends but rather jealously and envy. I suppose that Duane and Ted spent more and more time with Bob and me because those negative feelings were obviously not present when we were together. We felt lucky to be able to offer our thoughts on how Duane could position himself as a true gay philanthropist, even if we were not able to match his large contributions. The more good that Duane did, including offering friends like Trip and Alan a much needed mortgage on their home at 313 William Street, the more slightly veiled resentment from the gay set grew.

Duane was a true entrepreneur, even at a very young age. At four years old, he bought candy bars from a local store in his hometown of Council Bluffs, Iowa, and sold them from his little red wagon for a profitable ten cents each. Later, after graduating from the University of Wisconsin, Duane went to work for his father, who manufactured stainless steel tubing. When Duane eventually took over the company, he developed the business and the technology that brought the newly named Rath Corporation to international fame for superior quality stainless steel tubing for the food industry. Their development of a mirror-finish greatly reduced, to the point of virtually eliminating, the possibility for bacteria to form and contaminate food, especially in industrial kitchens. I had seen his products installed in hospitals in Europe.

Duane had recently sold the business and created a charitable foundation with the bulk of his vast fortune. While the initial charter of the foundation was to fund education, Duane had a plan in motion to change both the Rath Foundation's charter and its mission to focus on gay issues, notably education for under-privileged inner city gay adolescents, whose suicide rate was ten times higher than that of their straight peers.

Duane took a shine to us, especially to Bob. In working with Pridam Singh, a plan was conceived to carry out Duane's dream on a national scale. Pridam was also interested in Psychology. Therefore, he attended several seminars with Bob and Duane to refine a plan to bring to fruition the ambitious project. Initially, Bob and Duane worked with police departments in both small and large American cities to develop an information database on crime and suicide, especially in the gay sub-culture. In later phases of the master plan, a staff of teachers and psychologists would operate at each site to promote self-esteem and pride to the targeted group. Duane would also start an all-gay television network, as well as radio stations.

Duane spoke with Bob about turning the passionate part-time activity into a full-time project and began plans to do so as we prepared to leave Key West. The four of us became inseparable friends. Since we all rarely gave large parties or even attended the constant, shallow cocktail gatherings of the set, the four of us became both an oddity and a subject of considerable gossip and invented intrigue. This would quickly magnify.

Ted was a sexy, handsome former Green Beret and defined the expression tall, dark, and handsome. He had been Duane's loyal partner during the years of Duane's hard work and had assisted him in their rise to fame and fortune as the company expanded. When Duane sold the Rath Corporation, he had allowed Ted to indulge his several hobbies, including automobiles, horses, and fox hunting. Ted bought world class horses and hunted with all the well-known fox hunting clubs. He had his beautiful hunting clothes made on Savile Row in London and generously gave many sets of pinks, saddles, bridles, and other expensive equipment to friends, including Trip, who fancied himself as a great hunter but did not have the means to indulge in the expensive sport. The adage of "No good deed goes unpunished" became evident as Ted's generosity was accepted by increasingly jealous sycophants.

I resigned from the AIDS Help board. Bob and I sold our condominium and we moved to Cashiers, North Carolina. I loved working with Jim Fox, the architect who had originally designed Chenoncette, to remove a poorly added wing and restore the house to its original design. Smith and I went to many furniture stores in Atlanta to try to find furniture that would match the Frank Lloyd Wright design of the house, but we finally decided that I should ask Jim if he would design our home's furniture. Thinking that my request was a parallel to asking Michelangelo to paint my bathroom ceiling, I put the request to Jim, who was delighted to comply in what would be a two-year project.

My brother owned a small house in the new Truman Annex, near the mansion at 51 Front Street, which he agreed to sell us the following winter. This would allow us the affordable luxury of spending winters in Key West, albeit much less of the year than previously, and to be near Duane.

This became all the more logical and achievable because The Rader Institute had been experiencing financial difficulties; was restructuring; and Doctor Rader's son, Jonathan, assumed Bob's position. His unemployment coincided with our move to North

Carolina and our first months there were spent both renovating the house; searching for a new position for Bob; and deciding if his working for a friend, Duane, at the Rath Foundation, was responsible and wise.

By late summer, I was experiencing intestinal discomfort, which steadily continued to worsen. In consultation with Leo and Jean-Claude, I began my first combination therapy using the available anti-viral drugs of AZT and Hivid. I found these medications extremely hard to tolerate and assumed that they were greatly responsible for my stomach problems, preferring instead to believe that the developing side effects of the strong medications were exclusively responsible for my discomfort. One night, after dinner, while reading with Bob in our den, I felt as if I had been shot in the stomach. Bob had to help me to bed. Against his advice, I spent the next two days in near agony in our bed, terrified to go to a hospital.

"René, we have to get you to a hospital," he said.

"It will be better in the morning," I replied, preferring to die in my own bed than be treated in a hospital.

Bob was so surprised that, for someone who had spent his entire career in hospitals, I was terrified to access one. I explained to him that it was *because* I had worked and lived in many hospitals, some the most famous in the world, that I was anxious. On the third day I began passing out when Bob tried to help me to the bathroom, and he decided to take matters in his own hands, regardless of my protests. He asked a neighbor to help him carry me to the car and take me to Atlanta. They reclined the passenger seat to the maximum and padded it with several comforters, as even the slightest movement was agonizing. As we drove out of our property, two of our many curious neighbors, who wondered about the mysterious gay couple, happened to be walking by. Michael Jackson had just been accused in his first child molestation case. As I waved at the nosy neighbors from my apparently absurdly luxurious car-bed I said, "You know, Bob, these people may think this is how we go to the supermarket every day and that we are as nutty as Michael Jackson."

The humor ended there because after an examination and a CT scan at Emory Hospital, in Atlanta, I was told that my intestines had ruptured. "You are a very lucky man," began a surgical intern, "most people die within a few hours of an intestinal rupture. Your body was able to wall off the area by encapsulating it. We will operate in the morning."

I was exceedingly anxious that night in the typically austere hospital room. Bob stayed by my bed the entire time. When I had anxiety attacks, and felt as if I could not breathe, he would gently put his hand on my chest and speak in his soothing voice. "Take deep, slow breaths, René. You'll be fine, this is just anxiety. Everything will be fine."

The following morning, a team of surgical students, parading behind the chief of surgery, all crowded into my room. I was expecting to be prepped and brought to an operating room, but instead, after a lengthy discussion in my presence, they felt that I should be treated with intravenous antibiotics in the hope of reducing the infection before an operation. Could the HIV issue complicate the decision and the operation, they asked one another? An infectious disease specialist was brought in for consultation—a delay that left Bob and me baffled.

Day after day, similar "classes" on walled-off HIV-related ruptured intestines took place in my room. Day after day surgery was postponed. I had been given no food, of course, and the weakness that created, combined with a morphine drip, began to cause bizarre hallucinations. Thankfully, each time I awakened, Bob and either Smith or Rick were in my room, ready to comfort and orient me. During the daily medical team discussion on the fifth day, Bob said, "Look, Doctor, René has had no food in six days. He is shaking from weakness. Either you operate today or feed him, but I will not stand by and see him starve to death."

The team still considered surgery too risky, so I was given some soft foods. After several days, the chief of surgery said that the infection was reduced, but that it would be best to operate in six to eight weeks, during which time more antibiotics would further reduce the threat of a possibly fatal sepsis infection during surgery.

The day I was released from the hospital, we stayed at Smith and Rick's lovely home in Atlanta's residential neighborhood of Buckhead. Bob sat on the floor next to the couch on which I was lying while we had dinner. Even though surgery would eventually follow, the relief I experienced was enormous. I was never happier than the following day when we were back in our home in Cashiers. The joy of spreading out in our bed, with Bob by my side, and in relative comfort, was equivalent to the greatest feeling of relaxation I had ever experienced, but in the middle of the night, the phone rang.

"This is Sophie," began my mother's companion. "Your mother is lying on the floor, and I cannot revive her."

"Call 911, go to the hospital in the ambulance, and call me back when a physician has been assigned," I said.

Bob and I noticed that I could make sane health decisions for others but not for myself.

We had several conversations that night with the staff at the Boca Raton hospital. My mother had suffered a stroke, fallen, and ruptured her spleen, which had to be removed. It seemed so odd that our two medical crises had converged. Unfortunately, my mother appeared to have had another stroke on the operating table and then lingered, for ten days, on a ventilator in a state called "conscious but non-responsive." After two weeks of being in this condition, a decision had to be made, and I decided to ask my surgeon at Emory if I could travel to Florida to follow my mother's situation and expected decline.

"It's a bit risky," he said, "but as long as you do not exercise, lift anything, or strain yourself in any way, it should be safe. We will need to operate in a month though."

Bob and I drove the eight hundred miles to South Florida. I was so happy to have him with me to help with this otherwise over-whelming predicament. We even spoke about how fortunate the timing of his being unemployed was. Otherwise, he might not have been able to be with me full time during the two concurrent life-threatening medical emergencies. I wondered how hard-working single people could cope with numerous disasters alone, and we pledged that, regardless of cost or employment, we would never leave the other when similar catastrophes occurred.

Bob and I met with the primary doctor caring for my mother in an office at the Boca Raton Hospital, near where I had spoken to the hospital's administrator in previous years. The physician rec-ommended removing my mother from the ventilator. Since she had both a living will and a DNR (or "do not resuscitate"), he explained that she would probably die within a few hours. We called my brother in Switzerland and told him he had to come back to Florida immediately. We decided that, upon his arrival, we would do as the physician recommended.

My brother, his wife, Bob, and I sat with her for three days, not hours, after the respirator was removed and watched her slip away. Several nurses asked me why I clutched my stomach constantly, but I pretended that my pain was not worsening. Following my mother's death and funeral in late December, we decided to go to Key West for a few days to recuperate, after which my brother would return to Switzerland and I would be operated in Atlanta.

Bob and I discussed what a sad life my mother had experienced, living with a tyrant and not having been appreciated, and always putting on a good face to outsiders, regardless of humiliating psychological pain. She was the sad victim of a generation of women who were raised to believe that they had to obey their husbands, regardless of how illogical or even cruel the situation became.

On New Year's Eve, Bob and I dined alone with Duane and Ted in the recently completed former home of President Eisenhower. Instead of a formal meal in the dining room, we ate in a family area off the kitchen, so we could feel at ease. We marveled at the beautiful landscaping and furnishings, which included elaborate Chihuly chandeliers. At midnight we drank a bottle of Champagne and all retired, after making ambitious and exciting plans for the gay mission of the transformed Rath Foundation. The New Year held so much promise. Duane had met with President-elect Clinton to discuss his dream, and other meetings were scheduled with the new administration. Duane had pledged to fund a gay wing of the holocaust museum on the Mall in Washington, DC, and wanted Bob to serve on the museum's board. The possibilities of great progress for AIDS patients and for the greater gay world seemed endless. Although it embarrassed Duane, we told him that, finally, there was the possibility for the American gay community to have its own Martin Luther King. Duane laughed modestly.

We spoke of the many friends we had lost during the year as well as the famous AIDS-related deaths of tennis star Arthur Ashe and ballet legend Rudolf Nureyev. Duane relied heavily on our knowledge of HIV because he had not been exposed to the virus. He planned to send Ted to visit Jean-Claude Chermann and express his intent to support Chermann's vaccine research. I was impressed to hear how delighted Duane was that the CDC had revised its definition of AIDS. He hoped that would result in greater benefits being provided to organizations, like our local AIDS Help, and that the issue of opportunistic infections was now included in CDC language relating to HIV disease. Duane believed strongly in Key West and wanted to upgrade the town. To this end he offered details of his generous donations to create a park adjacent to the historic Key West library and build a kidney dialysis unit.

I followed one sad story in the closing days of 1993, namely that Jacqueline Kennedy Onassis was diagnosed with large cell Non-Hodgkin's lymphoma. Since I admired her and had seen her several times in both Paris and Gstaad, I felt particular compassion and concern for what the distant idol must be enduring. I would soon learn more about her suffering than I had planned or wanted.

CHAPTER TWENTY

1994

My Swiss friends, the Nussbaumers, visited Key West in the opening days of January. Pierre was alarmed about my posture, always clutching my stomach, and said I looked terrible. I was scheduled to return to Atlanta a few days after Pierre left town, but my plans were abruptly aborted. After returning from taking Pierre to the airport, I told Bob I felt like going to bed. I took one call from France telling me about Alain Mérieux's brother, Jean, who had been killed in a car accident, ate some soup, and tried to sleep.

Around 2:00 A.M., the same acute and agonizing stomach pain I had experienced five weeks earlier reoccurred. There was no doubt that my intestines had ruptured a second time. Stupidly, I tried to stay still and let Bob sleep. At 6:00 A.M., I told him we had to go to the hospital.

The Key West hospital is not where one wants to be treated for any serious condition. It is badly maintained, dirtier than most hospitals in developing countries, and overcrowded. It was designed to treat less acute patients than it currently serves, which results in congested corridors, sloppy storage areas and stressed staff. To make things worse, there are no medical teaching programs or up-to-date medical committees, which results in egomaniacal physicians who practice bad medicine.

An emergency room physician, who was not only asleep on a cot but also reeked of alcohol, met us. We begged "Doctor" Bermudez to examine me gently, as even the slightest pressure on my abdomen was excruciating. After his initial palpation, which was more like a punch, Bob told him that he was discharged and that we required another physician. The new doctor ordered a CT scan. Bob stayed by my gurney hour after hour. When he asked why it was taking so long to get me to radiology, he was told, "They have an emergency case there."

"What would you call ruptured intestines?" Bob asked.

It was mid-afternoon when I was scanned and received the conformation that my intestines had, indeed, ruptured and needed immediate surgery. I waved at Bob to avoid his commenting on the immediacy issue as I had already been lying around for eight hours. At 6:00 P.M., I was rolled into surgery after having met the surgeon, Michael Klitnick. He asked me to sign a release for a possible colostomy, which I did. As the anesthetic was about to be administered, Roger Mills, a nurse I knew well and who was to assist the surgeon, said, "You know who is going to perform the operation, don't you?"

"Yes, Doctor Klitnick," I said.

"No, I'll perform the surgery."

With that horrible joke, the lights went out.

When I woke up in the middle of the night, Bob was sitting by my bedside in the recovery area. "Did I have a colostomy?" were my first words.

"No," he answered. Later he confessed that he had wanted to add that I would not need "new shoes to match my bag."

Around midday, Klitnick came into our dirty room. I had been listening to a patient moan across the hall and screaming for a nurse while Bob was dozing in a chair. The only time he ever left me was to walk our dog, T-Cell. "Well, I have good news and bad news," began the surgeon, inappropriately. "I have cleaned up the abdomen. It was a mess! As you may know, I have not sutured you, as there is a risk of infection. But, if all goes well, I will do so in two days. You really are lucky you did not die from peritonitis."

"So what's the bad news?" asked Bob.

"The pathology indicates René has lymphoma. Given his HIV status, there is no way he can survive chemotherapy. Dan Gill will be here shortly to tell you the same thing."

Dan Gill was the hospital's pathologist, chief of staff, and a close friend.

Bob cried for the second time in our lives together, which hurt me as much as the news we had received. Dan also delivered the same prognosis along with his partner, Fran, another close friend. Fran sat on my bed and held my hand as the death sentence was delivered.

"Large cell non-Hodgkin's lymphoma. No hope for treatment given the diminished strength of the immune system—four months." The same diagnosis as Jackie Onassis but, it was hoped, she had been given a more humane prognosis and delivery.

A prolonged silence mercifully came to an end when Bob said, "René, these clowns are not oncologists. Let's get on the phone and do some research."

I tried to ignore both the physical and psychological pain and retain some element of humor that always energized Bob. "If, in the future, I croak in an ambulance going to Miami," I began, "I will not damn you. But, if I *ever* wake up in this dump again, I WILL damn you!"

Bob called several oncologists over the subsequent two days. The first one essentially confirmed what we had heard from the local staff. Undaunted, Bob found a young oncologist at the University of Miami who said there was a 10 percent chance of survival, but the next year would be rough and I would have to start chemotherapy in two weeks regardless of how I felt. "Can you both accept these rules?" asked Doctor Levy.

I listened through a morphine haze.

"Doctor, you are telling us that René will be shot at dawn. But, there is a 10 percent chance he can escape. Of course we will try to escape."

My friend, Pierre, called from Geneva to express his surprise and alarm. He had told my brother we had eaten together in Florida the previous day. "He had surgery and is in the hospital," my brother answered. After we told Pierre our interim prognosis, he related several stories about friends who had been given death notices only to go on to a lead a normal life. His strong words added power to our belief that I could survive HIV, cancer, and *even* the Key West hospital.

The worst part of the next days was cleaning my open wound. It was simply agonizing. No matter how careful the nurse, the previous bandages were stuck to the raw flesh and had to be pulled off. I screamed and bit my sheets to not overly disturb other patients. The day Klitnick told me I would be discharged, I reminded him I needed to be closed up.

"Mr. Silvin," he said in his detached way, "I have told you. You will be dead in four months. Why not just go home and get your affairs in order?"

Bob responded, uncharacteristically, showing his anger. "Doctor, even if René will die in four months, we want him sutured. By the way, René's 'affairs' *are* in order. And, may I suggest you temper your emotions when you address your patients?"

Klitnick was "too busy" to close my open abdomen and I left the hospital never having been sutured, stapled, or even taped. Bob changed my dressings every two hours to avoid the pain of removing a bandage stuck to coagulating blood and flesh. He gave me courage to persevere and stayed on our bed, with T-Cell nestled between us, most of the day. When Jean-Claude saw my scar several months later he said, "That idiot did not operate, he gave you an autopsy!"

Ten days later we went to Miami to meet our oncologist and have a marrow tap. There was a Boston Chicken restaurant nearby, which became our usual stop before chemotherapy treatments. To this day, I get nauseous if I think of Boston Kitchen, as the chain was later renamed.

As always, Bob insisted on staying by my side for the unpleasant marrow exam. At the start of my first chemotherapy session, I had one of my panic attacks and started gasping for air. Again, Bob calmed me down and told the nurse not to be alarmed. He patiently dealt with my fears and bad humor, buying books like *How to Survive Chemotherapy* and carefully editing medical news relevant to my condition, so as to deliver any available small piece of optimism. He had read that my hair would fall out about ten days after my first round and brought me to a barber before then to shave my head. "This will be less traumatic than seeing large patches of hair on your pillow or in your hands. Anyway, bald is in vogue and stylish now," he said.

Every three weeks we would return to Miami for treatment and I gradually grew thinner and weaker. We had discussed my having the second half of my treatments at or near home in North Carolina with Doctor Levy. Young Isaac had become a friend and did not typify the hardened attitude of many oncologists. He was very grateful when Bob bought his office a case of each of the most informative and positive books on chemotherapy to distribute to other patients. Eventually, to my great delight, I was allowed to return to North Carolina. The last evening in Key West, accompanied only by Duane, because Ted was out of town, we ate at our favorite restaurant, Antonia's. Bob joined us later because he had been working at the Key West Police Department collecting data for use as a baseline when Duane implemented their inner city self-esteem program for adolescent gays.

It was obvious that the many friendly waiters and the owners, Antonia and Philip, all expected not to see me return the following season. Who could blame them? I was gray, wore a wool beret, and begged to have the temperature repeatedly moved higher.

Before Bob arrived, Duane urged me to verbalize my greatest fears. I looked around at the charming space and focused on the Dade County pine woodwork, adorned with art from local artist friends, to collect my thoughts. I stared at the kitsch and fun bust of Caesar by the front door, grateful for the opportunity to delve deeply into my heart and reveal the thoughts most lovers have when facing possible death.

"I worry about Bob," I said. "If I die, I wonder how he will be able to manage Chenoncette. And I wonder what his future will be. He wants to work and is so good at what he does."

"Let's hope that will not happen," Duane answered instantly, understanding the specifics of my general statements. "But, if it does, I promise I will have my handyman at the property the next day and I will assume all expenses immediately."

While I tried to formulate words of appreciation, Duane continued, "René, I care deeply for Bob. I want to work with him and build the new foundation with him. Are you aware of local gossip about an inappropriate relationship between Bob and me?"

"Yes, Duane," I said. In an attempt to lighten the moment, I added, "Some well-meaning jerks have already given me their condolences. In fact, I was naughty and said something to Luccio which may have fueled the gossip." Luccio was an unhappy, overweight, former looker who was partnered with a wealthy and educated man, a descendant of the Weyerhouser Company's founder. Instead of enjoying his position, Luccio was bitterly jealous of Duane, like so many other so-called leaders of the gay community in Key West.

"What did you say?"

"Understand, I was angry when Lou pretended to be doing me a great favor. I told him I would give him the real inside story. I whispered in his ear that we could not afford our two homes, trips to Europe on the Concorde, and nice cars. So I had an arrangement with you to give me $10,000 every time you popped Bob. Lou swallowed it, swore to never repeat my confidence, and probably told the whole town by nightfall."

"You are wonderfully wicked," Duane said, smiling briefly. His jovial look quickly disappeared and Duane returned to serious words, which were his trademark. "You know that Ted and I have had some problems and I won't deny lusting for Bob, but I swear to you, Bob has never given me the slightest encouragement and nothing unfaithful to you has ever happened."

"Duane, I questioned Bob when the first 'friend' brought the cheery rumor back to me. You will learn that Bob is incapable of lying. His denial was enough for me. Anyway we know you are more of a prude than a predator!"

"Would I have your blessing to pursue Bob *if* he was left alone without you?"

Some people may have been offended at such a question posed during a perilous, life-threatening time. But I was flattered and even honored to be so close to such a profound gentleman.

"Duane, you don't need my permission," I said pleasantly. "I love Bob and want the very best for him. I'm realistic about my chances. If, as the French say, I 'break my pipe,' I can't imagine a better life for Bob than being with a man of your kindness, generosity and talents. Speaking of generosity, I know you will be very generous to Ted."

Duane affirmed that he had given thoughts to the specifics of a separation agreement with Ted and that, indeed, Ted would remain very comfortable, with horses, cars, and houses. "He'll be happier than with a boring workaholic like me," he added.

The following day Bob and I drove out of Key West for what I knew might well be my last time. I was greatly relieved by my extraordinary conversation with Duane as well as how amusing we must look with an intravenous drip pinned to the convertible top of the car while Bob drove and T-Cell sat on my lap.

I told Bob about my conversation with Duane and Bob rephrased the question, "What are you most frightened of?"

"Dying alone and being cold," I said. "I have heard that brain cells remain alive for ten minutes after the last breath is taken. I have a huge fear of being thrown into a morgue's refrigerator before then and being cold."

Cashiers, North Carolina

It was a great relief to be back in our home. The serenity and beauty was like a tonic to me even as my strength deteriorated. Bob had told me that I had to walk one hour each day, even if that was the only time I got off the couch. I believe that daily walk was an important element in my mental and physical well-being. Adjacent to Chenoncette there is a park with paths that wander through hills that are thick with old oak trees, wild azaleas, and native rhododendrons. The only annoying experience I encountered during these pensive walks was running into Doug Smith, a deacon in the local Episcopal Church and an hysterical homophobe. He had called me a liar by saying that there was no way I could have worked for the Washington National Cathedral in Washington, DC, because I was going to hell. As my appearance worsened he added, "The only thing that can save you now is to repent and pray."

The rest of my days consisted of lying on a couch in our den, often with a roaring fire even during that summer, as I could not get warm. When Bob traveled with Duane, I missed him terribly and did my best to keep my mind off of my likely plight.

Two neighbors started bringing me food on a regular basis. It taught me that food, especially when delivered in disposable containers, is the very best gift a caring neighbor could give. Virginia Smith, the hypocritical doomsday announcer's wife, was one generous provider of meals. She would have to sneak into my property when her husband was away and asked me to not let "Doug know that we have a relationship."

In sharp contrast, the other angel was Bennie Addison. She and her husband, Ed, had retired to the neighborhood after a brilliant career which had culminated in Ed's tenure as Chief Executive Officer of the Southern Company, one of the world's largest utility companies and the largest investor-owned electric utility holding company in the United States. They were considered the neighborhood's "royalty" and Bennie's endorsement of Bob and me provided us with a protective shield from the homophobes. If Bennie accepted us, the rest had "better watch out" was clearly how she positioned her affection for, and attention on, us. Bennie was one of those ladies who did everything perfectly and, like Jackie Onassis, with style and beauty. Her posture was erect; her hazel green eyes always sparkled and revealed her loving nature.

She delivered her meals on beautiful trays and included pretty linen napkins and, usually, a sweet note. I always admired her unique yet tasteful clothes during her brief but frequent visits, which became all I longed for aside from Bob's return. On one visit she said, "Ed and I never knew that a gay couple could be responsible neighbors, lead a constructive life in a well-run home, and love each other deeply. I hope you will forgive me for my ignorance." That day we sobbed in each other's arms.

My eyesight was affected by the chemotherapy, and I found reading very difficult, even painful. So I indulged into mindless television and watched every word of the OJ Simpson pre-trial hearings. It even provided me with some humor when the testimony of OJ's house guest, Kato Kaelin, was like a comedy soap opera. My only subjects of serious news interest were Jackie Onassis' progress with her treatments for the same type of cancer I had and searching out single mothers in chemotherapy. Some days when I hardly had the energy to make a sandwich, my thoughts turned to single moms with cancer. Within this outlook, my condition took on a different perspective and was relatively easy. The only responsibility I had, which required any physical effort, was to open the door for T-Cell. How could a mother prepare food; clean house; work; and cope with similar aches, pains, and fears, I wondered? I found an organization that worked with women living such nightmares and became a contributor.

In May, on my birthday, I heard that Jackie O had been taken to a hospital in New York. I left the television news networks on all day, hoping for some information. I thought of her amazing life as First Lady and later as Mrs. Onassis. I recalled with affection the few times I had laid eyes on her. I always marveled at how graceful she was, and I chuckled remembering how she had said that she never wanted to be called "First Lady" because it "sounded like a saddle horse." She had also made many profound statements that stuck in my mind, notably, "I want to live my life—not record it."

Her death on May 19 hit me harder than my own diagnosis, probably because it brought to the fore the very real possibility that I would soon follow her. When her son, John, addressed reporters in front of her Fifth Avenue home the following morning, he used words which meant a lot to me. He said something like, "My mother died last night around 10:00 P.M. surrounded by her friends, family, and books." He went on to utter a phrase I will never forget: "She did it on her own terms." I took this as a clear signal that she had decided not to pursue treatment for her relapsed lymphoma and chose to end her life. I admired that decision. If I relapsed immediately after treatment, as Jackie did, Duane would take care of Bob, his handyman would care for T-Cell, and I would do things "on my own terms," rather than being tortured by aggressive treatments in dehumanizing hospitals.

My treatments ended in September. Both Jean-Claude Chermann and Leo had urged me to come to Europe right after my last chemotherapy treatment so that they could take baseline statistics and prescribe paramedical immune system boosters. Bob walked beside me in my wheelchair as we boarded a Swissair flight. I had lost thirty pounds and shook like a Parkinson patient. In the middle of the overnight flight, I overheard a flight attendant say to her colleague, "I sure hope he does not die before we get to Zurich." I was acutely aware of my appearance, so the comment was more amusing than offensive. My T-cell count had dropped to single digits and Bob and I joked that we could now assign names to each of them. Our medical team decided I should begin Bristol-Meyers Squibb's new drug, d4T, as soon as I got home.

When we returned to the States, Bob had to catch up on his work with Duane's foundation, which had become a passionate, full-time activity. While they traveled to inner city projects in New York and California, Bob kept close tabs on my condition while Duane worried about his mother, Marjorie, who was in poor health with congestive heart failure. Bob was alarmed that the World Health Organization had reduced its staff assigned to the AIDS desk to four. He lamented that, only three years earlier, more than two hundred people worked on the crisis. Perhaps this was something that Duane would ask President Clinton to review along with the loss of a strong voice to the cause of pediatric AIDS as a result of the death of Elizabeth Glaser.

On October 4, Bob called with the news that they were shortening their trip to San Francisco, because Marjorie's condition had worsened and Duane wanted to be with her. He flew to his home in Janesville, Wisconsin, and I picked up Bob in Asheville, as I had just begun feeling comfortable driving again. On October 5, we both spoke with Ted and Duane at their farmhouse outside Janesville, mostly about Marjorie. Duane repeated his offer that his new chef in Key West, Michael Pelke, would be bringing food each day and looking after me until I was stronger and urged me to return to the island as soon as possible. He also spoke of his new project of creating another residential community with Pridam at the Key West Golf Course, concluding with specifics about the progress on three units he was building in the Truman Annex's historic foundry building. His intention was to give one to Ted, one to his parents, and the other to us. Ted gave me details concerning what he was preparing for them to eat that evening and our only concern as we spoke with them for the last time was Duane's mother. Ted and Duane appeared to be entering a new and mature space even while a friendly separation was being considered.

In Bob's home office the following morning, as I was reading and Bob was working, David Mixner called. David was a Washington, DC, insider who had been a key fundraiser for the Clinton campaign and had become an advisor to Duane and the president. We had all sat together by the pool in Key West lamenting over President Clinton's compromise concerning gays in the military—the unacceptable "don't ask, don't tell" solution.

Shortly after Bob had greeted David, I heard a huge crash and saw that Bob had fainted. After checking on Bob and reviving him, David, still on the phone, continued relating early reports of the devastating news. Both Ted and Duane were dead! Duane was found in their bed with multiple knife wounds while Ted had been asphyxiated in their garage with two car engines running. "It appears to be a murder-suicide," said David.

"Who found the bodies?" I asked.

"Schultz, the handyman," he answered.

"Did he stay until the police arrived?"

"Actually, he called Jim Sanger, a foundation trustee, not the police," concluded David with a statement that was more like a lingering question.

A few moments later I spoke with Duane's exceptional sister, Beverly, who confirmed the disaster as clearly as possible through her grief. To compound her misery, her mother had passed away the same morning and a dual funeral was being planned for Duane and his mother. Ted's body would not be honored along with them, she explained. She asked us to meet her in Janesville as soon as possible. Bob and I were as close to being physically numb as I can recall. Not only had we lost our dearest friends, but also the dreams of bringing significant benefits to underprivileged adolescent gay men and huge supplemental relief programs to AIDS organizations had vanished. Although the paperwork for changing the foundation's charter had been prepared, it was unsigned, as

Duane had not yet given the bad news to his existing trustees, who were to be replaced. We spent much of the rest of that sad day taking calls from gossip seekers in Key West as the news spread like wildfire.

"I guess we'll see you at the funeral," I told several recipients of Duane's largesse. I was repeatedly disappointed at their negative response, hearing statements such as "We are too busy" or "There is nothing we can do to help anyone."

Janesville, Wisconsin

On October 7, Beverly met us at Duane's office on the top floor of what had been the Parker Pen Company building in Janesville before Duane bought it. She was controlled but clearly devastated with compounded grief. Duane's flair for design, which had been executed by the best interior decorators, had produced a large, comfortable, and dramatic suite of offices. One of Duane's trustees, Jim Dodson, was sitting behind Duane's desk. Dodson's wife was there also and the both of them were smoking and had their feet propped up on the furniture. Two shredders were humming and numerous large, full, black plastic trash bags were being stuffed and placed in the foyer. A copy of *The Janesville Gazette* was on a coffee table and read in part, "Rath's body was lying face-up on his bed in a front bedroom on the main floor. Rath had suffered 12 stab wounds or a few more and he had put up a fight." The article made reference to a suicide note left by Ted. I asked if a handwriting analysis was being performed on the note. I never had a reply. Another article read, "Rath was stabbed to death after an argument that police surmise was over either Rath's new lover or money." Bob and I read the articles in astonishment as we knew beyond a doubt that there was no new lover, that the environment in the farm house on the night of the deaths was cordial, and that Ted had no reason to be suicidal.

Between outbursts of tears, Beverly and Bob drafted Duane's obituary and I overheard Bob tell Beverly that Duane had frequently referred to her as "his best friend."

"There are several people in Key West who you do not know and who Duane was caring for," I said to Dodson. "I'm sure you will want to honor Duane's wishes and treat them compassionately."

180

As Dodson looked at me with skeptical eyes, I removed a piece of paper from my pocket and proceeded to describe the various charity cases.

"Jeremy, the gardener, is uninsured and has AIDS. Duane has sent him to our physician in Switzerland and pays for all his medications in Key West. I'd like to tell him that you will continue that commitment."

"What do other indigent AIDS patients do in Key West?" he asked.

"There is an organization called AIDS Help which tries their best to provide necessary benefits but...."

"Tell Jeremy to go there," he interrupted.

Initially, I thought the man had a personal vendetta against poor Jeremy, so I persisted as more documents were put in the shredder. "There is a young medical student who Duane has committed to send through school. Duane pays the tuition from a small personal account in Key West. I'd like to tell him that the foundation will pay his last year's tuition."

"Tell him to get a grant somewhere else," I heard and wondered if I was confused.

I had to finish my list, regardless of the unreasonable responses. "Duane hired a cook away from a gay friend. His name is Pelke. Duane sent him to Italy for a vacation before he would begin working at the Front Street home. The poor chap will soon discover that his job does not exist. He may find getting back on his feet difficult. Can we give him a very generous severance?"

"But he has not begun his duties and Duane bought him a house and was ripped off by his brother, Walter."

"Jim, I am talking about incidental expenses which a responsible trustee will surely want brought to his attention. I urge you to carry through with what Duane would have asked us to do."

"They can all screw themselves. The party is over and you can tell them that."

I wondered if I was dreaming, living through an outlandish hallucination. As I sat by Duane's desk, now occupied by a silly tyrant trying to exercise newly found power, I heard Jim take a call regarding Ted's horses.

"Tell Mrs. Hurdman that she must move the horses, which now belong to her. We want them moved by tomorrow or we will turn them out of the barn. That's what she gets for having them registered to Ted."

"Jim, I beg of you! Be human!" I said, raising my voice. "These poor animals are innocent. I'm sure Ted's mother will sell them as soon as she can. I think it's cruel of you to further offend her in her grief. You can charge her board for the horses until she figures out what to do with them." That was the only "concession" I was granted that rainy Sunday afternoon on the top floor of a once vibrant and forward looking foundation office.

The following day, the day of the funerals, *The Janesville Gazette* wrote, "Police said Thursday that the deaths are suspicious and are being investigated as homicides."

Beverly, Bob, and I drove to the funeral home with Patches, Duane's Jack Russell terrier. We both fanaticized about what the sweet little dog would say if she could speak. Beverly told us that as long as Patches lived, as long as her little heart beat, she would feel Duane's heart beating. What happened in that house on October 5, we wondered? I was certain it was either a dual murder or a "hit" on Duane which had gone wrong so that Ted had to be killed also. Continuing the surreal experience, another trustee, the man Schultz had called before calling the police, met us at the door of the funeral home and said, "Be sure to look at Duane's neck. They did a good job, but you can see the slash. And, fear not, we will take that platinum Patek Philippe watch off Duane before we close the casket."

I looked around the room and noticed we were the only gay people there—not one friend or beneficiary of Duane's largess from Key West had bothered to come. Several Pinkerton security guards were making themselves very obvious. Who had ordered them and why had that person not protected Duane while he was alive, I wondered? Two identical silver open caskets were placed near each other forming a "V" in the far end of the room. I glanced over at Marjorie's coffin and stood by Duane's for a very long time. They looked more like brother and sister than mother and son. Eventually someone led Bob and me to seats where I started to shiver and did not stop for several days.

On our way to the airport, we studied yet another baffling article that read, "Recently, Rath found a new lover," and "Rath had become so afraid of Hurdman that he discussed the possibility of hiring a bodyguard with a friend."

"Did Duane mention anything to you about hiring a bodyguard?" I asked Bob.

"No!" he replied empathically. "This is so bizarre and makes no sense whatsoever."

Key West, Florida

A month later, Bob and I returned to the Truman Annex, once a residential paradise which Duane had been so instrumental in creating. It was among the dreariest days of my life, and I spent most of the time on a couch. I got up only to walk T-Cell and our new rescue dog, Silly. All Duane's properties were for sale. Walking the dogs past any of them was too difficult and I deliberately went the other way, regardless of the inconvenience.

Bob recommended that I start an antidepressant, which deadened my feelings. I wanted them deadened, I so liked the effect. Our sadness was worsened because no other acquaintances showed much, if any, grief or sadness at our community's indescribable loss. The more Duane had given to people, the less they wanted to express sorrow at his disappearance or discuss the murders. No one had called to offer condolences to Beverly or Duane's father, Virgil—not *one* the beneficiaries of Duane's great generosity in Key West or the foundation trustees.

I kept one of our cars in Duane's garage, next to one of Ted's classic antique Mercedes. They gradually lost tire pressure and eventually went flat—just like our emotions in the last days of the horrific year.

Chapter Twenty-one

1995

If staying in bed for excessive periods of time is a symptom of depression, Bob and I certainly were depressed at the beginning of the year. We amused ourselves by scheduling some redecorating of our Truman Annex house and by going to the local gym. Chemotherapy had taken all my strength away, so I also hired a trainer at the gym who carefully and diligently worked with me to gain some weight and energy. He treated me like an octogenarian who had just begun to visit a gym. He started me off with walking on a treadmill, and he persuaded me to drink protein shakes nearly all day long. Gradually, some weight and vigor began to return.

Numerous nasty rumors swarmed around town. One explained the murders as a murder-suicide, claiming that Ted could not accept that Bob and Duane were lovers. An even more hurtful rumor, promoted by Pelke—the very man we had tried to help—actually accused Bob of doing the killings. He nicknamed Bob "the Murderess," which we overheard on several occasions. I loved Bob more than I could ever have previously imagined and hearing such cruelty focused on him, while he was grieving the loss of our friends, was excruciating. The result was that we completely disassociated from society in town and became rather reclusive. I even retreated from social gatherings with former fellow board members of AIDS Help.

The popular gay magazine *The Advocate* had a cover story written by Jorge Morales called "Sleeping with the Enemy, The Life and Death of Duane Rath" with a drawing of a jagged, bloody knife on the cover.

Referring to this article, *The Janesville Gazette* wrote "Janesville businessman and philanthropist Duane Rath donated millions to gay rights and AIDS-related charities in the last few years, and his death is a loss of profound proportions to the national gay community. This is according to an article that appeared in *The Advocate*." That article in *The Advocate* said, "He (Rath) was a gay man who had it all; money, power, influence, a friendship with Elizabeth Taylor, and ties to England's royal family. He gave millions to gay organizations and even put the children of his company's employees through college. But a tempestuous love triangle changed everything."

The gossip among the phonies in the Key West gay set went wild and the very sight of several people we used to associate with became distasteful and counterproductive to my physical rehabilitation. We deliberately accelerated our isolation from the hypocrites.

Since there were still many vacant lots in the Truman Annex, I amused myself by throwing tennis balls for my dogs and taking them swimming in the harbor. Gradually, after accepting no more invitations to the nightly, purely social cocktail parties, the calls mercifully stopped. On several occasions when we ate at Square One or Antonia's, people would point at us and whisper. As a result, we even stopped frequenting our former preferred restaurants. These experiences were some of the worst I had ever endured and I challenged myself to not pay too much attention and to them and to focus on recovering from chemotherapy.

It had been futile to even ask Duane's trustees about Bob's plight with the foundation. We assumed he had seen his last paycheck the second Duane died, so we knew he needed to find a new career. The foundation's trustees discontinued any donations to gay charities almost immediately and continued a shockingly aggressive attitude toward anyone Duane had previously assisted, including his dear sister, Beverly. They refused to allow her to keep a car that Duane had provided her or for her children to receive sentimental gifts of relatively little value, such as Duane's leather jacket collection. It was a dark, sad period.

We converted a bedroom in our house into an office and added matching, side by side desks made of distressed pine. We then spent a lot of time exploring what job opportunities existed. As our furniture was, we too were indeed distressed as we searched for a new life away from the painful memories of Duane and how Key West dealt with it.

Our physician was an infectious disease doctor in Miami named Corky Steinhardt. Corky had recently sold his practice to a clever hard-charging entrepreneur named Ray Mira. Ray embarked on a buying spree of HIV-related physician practices in a new industry called PPM, or physician practice management. The national going rate per physician varied greatly, but went as high as two million dollars per doctor as Ray gradually acquired some seventy doctors on both coasts.

We were fond of Corky Steinhardt, who had recently gone through a costly and messy divorce. By selling his practice to Ray, he hoped to get back on his financial feet. He was also considering other options, including moving to Europe. We explained that, even if appropriate permits could be obtained and the language barrier properly addressed, physicians in most West European countries made even less than their well-known American counterparts.

To prove the point, we invited Corky and his new wife to accompany us to France on one of our regularly scheduled trips to visit and work with Jean-Claude Chermann. Corky was eager to hear Jean-Claude's explanations and theories. We also scheduled several meetings with physicians I had remained in contact with since my days with AMI. During the trip, we learned more about Ray Mira and his clever business strategy to become a major player, on a national level, in HIV medicine. It became clear to us and, eventually, to Corky that Ray's deal was as good as it was going to get in a medical specialty field in which it was becoming increasingly difficult to earn a living consistent with what physicians had become accustomed to. Furthermore, it was obvious that Corky, and especially his typical American wife, would never be able to adapt culturally in France or Switzerland. Bob and I would roll our eyes when Mrs. Steinhardt would screech, "I want my American coffee!" after each great French meal.

Bob and I returned to the States aboard the *QE2* accompanied by Jean-Claude Salamin, his girlfriend, and the Nussbaumers. We had planned the celebratory trip a year in advance and booked the Queen Elizabeth suite for us and, across the hall, the Queen Mary suite, the two nicest accommodations on the ship. Crossing the Atlantic by ship was my passion, and Bob and the others had never done it. So I decided to splurge and treat Bob to an extravagant trip. It was the only time Bob questioned any expense I undertook. "Are you sure we can afford this?" he asked.

"No, we can't," I replied, "but we are going to do it anyway. I want you to experience this the right way."

One night after a great dinner, Jean-Claude and I stopped at the Cunard travel bureau on the ship and asked the agent when our suites would both be available at the same time again. The agent told us that it would be several years but that another Cunard ship, the *Sagafjord,* had recently added similar suites and those two were available the following spring in Southeast Asia. Since Bob had never been to Asia we recklessly booked both apartments for what we hoped would be Bob's introduction to the Orient.

HIV medicine was changing quickly. President Clinton conducted a first conference on HIV/AIDS. The treatments, albeit costly and replete with side effects, were improving. Medicare reimbursement rates were based on the number of minutes a physician spent with their patients, often regardless of their specialty. Naturally, the vast majority of insurance carriers followed Medicare's rate structures and many physicians were reimbursed on a ten minute, per patient visit. While that amount of time with a patient is restrictive in most specialties, it is absurd for HIV. Most AIDS patients cannot even describe their numerous symptoms in ten minutes, much less get any feedback and information from their doctor. Infectious disease physicians, in turn, were becoming specialists in all disciplines because long term survivors were developing problems in dermatology, cardiology, orthopedics, neurology, and ear-nose-throat, in addition to the original AIDS problems of oncology and pulmonology. Patients began expecting these dedicated, often overworked men and women to be pharmacist, researcher, psychologist, and physician.

The FDA approved the new category of anti-retroviral medications called protease inhibitors as Glaxo Wellcome's Epivir became widely prescribed. Swiss pharmaceutical giant Roche was also given permission to sell their equally expensive PI, called Saquinivir. Since many of the newly approved medications, or others still in trials, ended with "vir" (Sequinivir, Epivir, Ritonavir, and Norvir), the joke was that the next breakthrough would be called "Save-a-queer."

We shortened our winter in Key West and decided that Chenoncette, our little paradise in the mountains, was preferable, even in the cold. At least that cold was physical and not psychological.

By the end of the year, AIDS was still mainly thought of as a gay disease, even though the incidence of the illness was spreading rapidly into the heterosexual community, mainly in poorer inner city neighborhoods. Numerous well-known gay celebrities' disclosure of their positive HIV status fueled the unfortunate view in the broader American public's eye. The admission by Greg Louganis, Olympic gold medal winner, that he had been diagnosed prior to the 1988 Olympic Games in Seoul, Korea, was a case in point.

Bob said he wanted to have a traditional Christmas and he launched into a major plan to decorate the house. We bought floating lighted stars, like the ones we had seen at Mangoes in Key West, and placed them all along our balconies. Before long, tourists and residents were driving by the house just to see the wonderful decorations at night. Bob went into the woods and chopped down a twenty-five-foot-tall spruce tree, which we placed in the living room and decorated beautifully. Visiting gay friends watched him cut down the tree, marveling, "My God! He is so butch!"

Each night we lay on the floor in front of a roaring fire in one room or another, happy to have each other and to have survived Duane's tragic murder as we began to plan for a world without the gay community's most qualified, and quantified, philanthropist to date.

CHAPTER TWENTY-TWO

1996

We hardly went to Key West during the winter. After our wonderful Christmas at home in North Carolina, Bob suggested we further improve Chenoncette by buying an adjacent cabin and adding a fireplace to the master bedroom. The owner of the cabin was reluctant to sell and this began a several year discussion with him. As much as Bob loved nesting, he was a worker and his need to be actively employed became our priority. We decided to meet Ray Mira, the man we had heard so much about from Corky.

Ray was a fascinating man who embodied a series of interesting contradictions. He was bright and street-wise, but not organizationally trained or motivated. He was short but had a sweetness about him that made him handsome. He was kind but subject to fairly violent outbreaks of rage. Finally, he was frugal in many aspects, but lived in grand residences in New York's Columbus Circle and on the beach in Fort Lauderdale. His sexy and beautiful long-term partner, Gigi, was equally bright and hard charging. Together they conceived the clever, and legal, plan to own HIV physician practices, as well as regional reference laboratories and a mail order pharmacy. While the physicians could not encourage, much less compel, patients to use these sister businesses, one arm of the business eventually fed the others. The result was that the lucrative laboratories and pharmacies more than compensated for the relatively unprofitable physician practices.

Since Bob and I had met the owners of the patents for both HIV viral load testing and geno/phenol HIV typing in Europe, we recommended that Ray acquire as many of these rights as possible. While he ultimately declined to do so, the due diligence undertaken to reach that decision led to a mutual respect and friendship.

Ray hired Bob to become his company's C.O.O., in charge of the physician practice side of the emerging empire. He also asked me to advise him on preparing the joint company to study the possibilities of going public through an initial public offering, or IPO. Bob was very effective at understanding the ins-and-outs of the various physician offices and, through his determined yet non-threatening manner, was able to maximize any possible efficiencies. He traveled weekly, as before when he had been working for the Radar Institute or the Rath Foundation, but mostly to doctor's offices in South Florida and throughout California.

The new company was named Quest Medical and by the end of the year it "owned" physicians as famous as Joel Weisman and Robert Smith in California. Both men had been pioneers in the initial discovery and treatment of HIV fourteen years previously. Bob also recruited and hired several younger physicians to assist the lead doctors in the South Florida offices. Among these recruits was Donna Jacobsen for Steinhardt's group at Mercy Hospital in Miami and Peter Englehard in Fort Lauderdale.

One day, shortly before we were due to leaving for our vacation—which was to be Bob's introduction to the Orient—I received a call from our travel agent. She told us that the *Sagafjord,* which we were to have boarded a week later, had burned up the previous day in the South China Sea. Bob was relieved because he had just started working with Quest and even though we had told Ray about our previously reserved trip, Bob was uncomfortable taking ten days off so close to having begun a new job. Cunard offered us two identical suites aboard the sister ship, the *Vistafjord,* the following year.

"How about we celebrate your fortieth birthday next year and take advantage of Cunard's offer?" I asked him.

With that, we happily booked the suggested trip. In addition, Jean-Claude and his new girlfriend planned on joining us. We now had another entire year to look forward to a grand adventure.

In July, we read that Roy Pesch, the "physician who would be a billionaire" and had tried, in vane, to acquire AMI, was arrested for fraud. In a rarely used accord between the U.S. and

Switzerland, he was extradited in August, under guard, to Switzerland, where he was imprisoned.

Nineteen ninety-six saw a huge increase in the use of the new class of anti-retroviral medications, the Protease Inhibitors. Among these were Viramune from Roxane Labs, Norvir from Abbott Labs, and Crixivan from Merck. All three medications received their FDA approvals during the year. As a result, a C ("huge fundamental") change emerged in the HIV/AIDS community, which had far reaching implications. The new combination of drugs instantly became known as "the cocktail," a term Professor Eckmann had coined in 1991, years before the drugs were invented. Interestingly, many severely ill patients began to improve and return to some sort of normal energy levels. This development was not without great costs, however, both literally and figuratively. The new cocktails typically cost in excess of twelve hundred dollars a month. As one could imagine, many HIV patients could not afford these expensive breakthroughs. Some others, like me, found the cocktails very hard to tolerate, while yet other group developed what became known as "the Lazarus complex."

Lazarus was the biblical figure who returned from the dead. The new term referred to relatively young, ill patients who had, they hoped, budgeted their resources to carry them through a short-ened life to a premature death. Suddenly, many found themselves financially and emotionally challenged with aborted careers. At the same time, AIDS organizations scrambled to address both the financial and psychological repercussions of the changing times. The New York Times Sunday Magazine offered the first insights to this on November 10, in the article "When AIDS Ends" by Andrew Sullivan. It discussed the unprecedented experience of the end of a plague, during which victims would have contemplated their deaths and adjusted their lives accordingly, but would then, later, have to reassess their possible survival. Fifty years ago in his book, La Peste (The Plague), the father of Existentialism, Albert Camus, brilliantly described the mindset as a population evolves to face death. Now, Sullivan had studied what occurs when that condition is, at least partially, reversed.

Patients' adherence to the new "cocktails" was also an interesting sociological study. Some became excessively focused on the strict protocols and resulting daily schedules, while others were unable or unwilling to comply.

My "triple-therapy" cocktail included both Crixivan and Norvir. The former had to be taken three times a day on an empty stomach or two hours after eating, and one hour before a meal. This rigid program led those of us using this very popular medication to get up in the night and to adjust our mealtimes to a strict routine. The physical side effects of Crixivan are also significant, as illustrated by the new term "Crix belly"—to accompany "AZT butt," because many patients on Crixivan develop abnormally large stomachs while AZT users tend to lose muscle in the rear ends. The worst physical side effect for me was from Norvir, which led to the rebirth of the term "lypodystrophy," which means a redistribution of fat, usually from the face to the upper neck. The hollow, sunken cheeks became a sign, like a scarlet letter arm band, to many HIV patients, as did the "buffalo bump" on their necks.

Personally, I managed to adjust to the daily routine surrounding the use of Crixivan, even during travels to France, but I hated the advent of the physical side effects, which also included constant stomach discomfort, indigestion, headaches, and reduced energy levels.

In his profound book, *Dry Bones Breathe*, the late Eric Rofes analyses these conditions in a chapter titled "The Protease Moment Takes Hold." He points out how, suddenly, national marketing campaigns for the new medications showed very healthy smiling faces boasting which drug they were using. Fortunately, yet not without some physiological and psychological side effects, many AIDS patients were facing and planning for a life "beyond AIDS," a life that was no longer solely defined by *having* AIDS. Rofes concludes his chapter on PI's with, "As men construct new identities for themselves in a post-AIDS period, finding new language that captures our experience will be a critically important activity." It was clear that these people also had to add new behaviors and thinking to the "new language."

Although my lymphoma diagnosis was, even by the most conservative definitions, an AIDS-defining diagnosis, I was learning how to cope with "the cocktail," Bob and I were not significantly affected by these problems. Bob was too healthy mentally to allow either of us to wallow in self-pity or senseless blame. Bob was more focused on getting to know the major players in American HIV treatment and research, including HIV researcher David Ho, who became *Time Magazine*'s 1996 Man of the Year, as well as the head of the World Health Organization's HIV team, Doctor

Jonathan Mann, who was often confused with Bob due to the similarity of their names.

Bob's new career during an era of evolving HIV medicine and science was our avenue to maintain a balanced, somewhat positive and productive outlook.

CHAPTER TWENTY-THREE

1997

Since Quest had several large HIV physician practices in California, Bob traveled there regularly. On most trips he made time to visit his stepfather, Gary Troy, who had been so instrumental in bringing life to Bob's career in psychology. Gary had recently been diagnosed with cancer and his prognosis was poor. In midwinter, both Bob and I went to Gary's home in Malibu to see him for what we knew would be the last time. Many of Teamm House's "graduates" had gone on to become clinical psychologists and many of those loving and devoted former protégés surrounded Gary and his lovely wife, Nancy, while Gary deteriorated in his own bed. Although I had seen numerous friends die, my presence at Gary's bedside was a new, constructive experience that would serve me well during my biggest challenge, which would happen the following year–the saddest period of my life.

Later, the same midwinter, Bob developed a severe headache, which gradually worsened over several days. When we went to the emergency room, a spinal tap revealed that he had meningitis and was hospitalized. During the week he spent at the Key West hospital, we discovered that Bob's blood counts had deteriorated significantly and, after consultation with Jean-Claude Chermann and Corky Steinhardt, Bob began his first HIV cocktail.

In early April, Bob and I met with Ray and Gigi in Fort Lauderdale. Ray had recently acquired a beautiful piece of property on the beach in Lauderdale and had remodeled the previously unassuming house into what Bob and I called "Miami Vice." During the meetings, we made progress on the plans to launch the IPO the following year. One of the decisions to maximize the chances of success was to move Quest's headquarters from Ray's building in Philadelphia to a yet to be determined office in Lauderdale. That evening I told Bob it seemed silly for us to have a house in Key West from which Bob would have to travel weekly only to stay in a hotel in Lauderdale. We decided that our Key West experience would end and we would sell the little house in the Truman Annex and buy a home in Fort Lauderdale. This was an easy decision for several reasons, the most fundamental being that Duane's murder had definitely changed our pleasure of being in "The Conch Republic."

Jean-Claude Salamin and his girlfriend *du jour* joined us in Florida for our scheduled crossing on the *Vistafjord,* which had been in the planning stages for two years and had been aborted a year earlier due to the fire aboard its sister ship, the *Sagfjord.* The trip was to be a crossing of the Atlantic from Fort Lauderdale with several stops, and ultimately ending in Malta fourteen days later. Ray and Gigi gave us an old-fashioned *bon voyage* party at their beautiful beach front home, and we all proceeded to a grand finale on the ship. The two adjacent suites' living rooms could be opened into one large room facing forward, looking out over the ship's bow. An impressive semicircular bar dominated the back of the room while picture windows surrounded the front. One of the guests who came to the party was the head of the U.S. Coast Guard for South Florida.

We sailed at dusk on April 5 and, after a great dinner, we four sat out on the large terrace in front of our suite. Tired from flying over to the States, our shipmates retired and Bob and I enjoyed a Jacuzzi outside our bedroom under a clear sky full of brilliant stars. Shortly after midnight, I awoke aware that the usual vibrations from the ship's engines had stopped. I went up our private stairs to the living room above and went out on the balcony. The ship had definitely stopped and, as I looked aft at the great funnel, I saw sparks and a flame flying out. Looking down, almost at the same time, I saw several sailors frantically unwrapping tarpaulins from life boats.

I ran into our bedroom and told Bob to grab his passport and wallet just as the fire alarms began ringing. Then I crossed the hall to wake up Jean-Claude and told him the same thing. "It's not a joke," I added, since we habitually teased each other with elaborate plots.

"Oh, I fully realize that," he said as we all preceded to our assigned evacuation spots adjacent to life boats. The life boats were lowered, ready for us to board and we all stayed in that position, wearing life jackets, for five hours as the ship's staff fought the fire in an attempt to save her. Before long, U.S. Coast Guard planes were over-flying the ship and my new Coast Guard friend, from the previous evening's party, later told me that he personally supervised the possible rescue at sea if the fire worsened during the night. Bob comforted several elderly passengers who were visibly nearly panicked, using his soothing voice and smart psychology to reassure as many as possible. Seeing a few of our fellow life boat colleagues needed medical attention, he found a doctor and assisted him in attending to them.

By dawn, huddled together under blankets, we were told that we would not have to abandon ship. Instead we would be towed into Freeport in the Bahamas where we would disembark and be flown either back to Lauderdale or to London, England. Sadly, we learned that one young sailor had been killed in the fire. So during the day that we stayed aboard in Freeport awaiting charter flights to arrive, Jean-Claude and I raised a relief fund for the poor German sailor's family.

We listed our house in Key West for sale at a high price that Trip Hoffman said we would never get. When it sold at full asking price in a week, we decided to stay at Chenoncette through the end of the year, after which we would go to Fort Lauderdale. The plan was for Bob to open the new Quest office and for me to identify and buy a home nearby.

In mid-December, we went to New York. We stayed at the Waldof Astoria and were to attend a dinner-dance party atop Rockefeller Center. Gigi and Ray had recently sold their company's home health care division to a New York Stock Exchange medical conglomerate, Integrated Health Services, Inc. IHS's well-known flamboyant chairman, Doctor Robert Elkins, a psychiatrist, had founded the company a decade earlier. He led a successful IPO in 1991 as he aggressively bought up nursing homes in a strategy of "bigger is better" in sub-acute inpatient care. I had seen this strategy, or rather lack thereof, fail during my career in publicly traded hospital companies as it related to chemical dependency and psychiatric hospitals and was very skeptical about IHS's long-term future even though its revenues had gone from $195 million to $3 billion in just five years.

I begged Ray to bail out of the company stock as quickly as possible. This advice proved helpful as IHS's stock plummeted from $40 a share to just pennies eighteen months later when the company defaulted on loans and was de-listed from the stock exchange along with numerous lawsuits initiated by patients' family members alleging inadequate care. The now infamous Richard Scrushy was on IHS's board of directors along with several of his questionably ethical cronies at Health South years before their own somewhat parallel scandal.

Elkins had contributed some $600,000 to the 1996 Clinton-Gore reelection committee in the hope of adjusting Medicare's reimbursement system in IHS's favor. At that moment, he was still viewed as the very successful creator of a strategy to increase his company's stock price through the leveraged buying of numerous nursing homes and related businesses. His rapid rise to wealth and fame would be short-lived. But for now, he was determined to host *the* Christmas party for important company executives.

Bob had never seen New York at Christmas time, so we walked up and down Fifth and Madison Avenues admiring all the dazzling windows. The night of the black tie event, I brought out the two dinner jackets I had packed before we left North Carolina. To my shock, and Bob's disappointment, I had correctly packed mine but had mistakenly included an old one that Bob had outgrown as his chest and shoulder muscles had developed as a result of our workouts. We only had a few hours before the party and we decided to go to the concierge to ask where we might be able to rent a tuxedo at the last minute. When the elevator door opened and we entered, Imelda Marcos, the former Philippines First Lady, was inside, accompanied by several male companions. I had met her in Manila some twenty years earlier.

"Good evening, Mrs. Marcos," I said. "You may not remember me but I was standing near you at the opening of the Philippine Heart Center when you endured that unpleasant experience many years ago." In fact, she had been stabbed while we stood on the receiving line with several world famous cardiologists and cardiac surgeons. Using quick reaction, Mrs. Marcos had raised her hand and deflected the would-be assassin's knife, which only badly cut her hand. I never heard about the aggressor's fate.

"Of course, I remember you," she said rather unconvincingly but with charm. "What are you up to?"

After introducing Bob, I continued. "We are going to a black tie event tonight and I did not bring the correct one for Bob. So we are in a panic looking for a substitute."

Mercifully, one of her associates gave us directions to a place where they rented tuxedoes for last minute dress events. As we walked away, Bob whispered, "Why didn't you ask for some shoes while you were at it?" making reference to Imelda's well-publicized huge shoe collection.

"I didn't think they would fit you now that you have such big tits," I joked back.

Bob looked so very handsome as we walked past the great Christmas tree at Rockefeller Center and passed the long line at the public elevator to ride a private one to the rooftop restaurant. There we noticed a large collection of Chuhuly glass placed along the top of the walls. Bob and I had met Dale Chuhuly with Duane when he ordered a chandelier and garden sculptures for the Key West house, and I saw a flash of sadness on Bob's face as we were reminded of our loss.

I could not help but compare IHS's executives to AMI's domestic staff under Wally Weisman. They were a similar group of over-confident, under-experienced upstarts. The only difference was that Wally's herd emulated their boss' total lack of style, while this group, one decade later, obviously overly indulged in expensive clothes consistent with their leader's nouveau riche style. They looked uncomfortable in their newly found arrogance and it was evident that a shock was soon to come as thousands were fired when the company collapsed.

The only rewarding part of mixing with them was how very clear it was just how respected and admired Bob had quickly become among a group of people with which he had little in common.

After the exciting weekend, we returned to Chenoncette where Bob put on his usual big Christmas decorating showcase.

By year end, it was discovered that HIV both "hides" in reservoirs of the body and learns how to mutate in order to render parts of the cocktail inefficient to many patients. These discoveries underscored the need for geno/phenol HIV testing to specifically define which medications had become useless. Unfortunately, those patents had been acquired by LabCorp after Quest had rejected them a year earlier.

The triple-therapy cocktails had reduced HIV-related deaths in the United States by 40 percent, which gave us some hope that our mutual relative health could be sustained. Globally the HIV news was not good as the virus thrived with the advent of globalization and the collapse of the Soviet Union. It was estimated by year end that thirty million people had been infected with the HIV virus worldwide.

During the last ten days of the year there were several mountain storms, including a serious ice storm. We built large fires, played with our dogs, and enjoyed each other's company. We also invited several couples to spend a few days each with us during that very festive last Christmas we had together.

Boarding *The Vistafjord* with Jean-Claude Salamin and his "girlfriend du jour" on the day of the fire.

CHAPTER TWENTY-FOUR

1998

In the opening days of January, Bob and I loaded up two cars and, along with the dogs, Silly and T-Cell, drove to Fort Lauderdale. I had rented a house for six weeks in the hope that we would be under contract for our own home by then. The first night we were there, Bob had some indigestion that reoccurred every day for a week.

After consulting both Corky Steinhardt and Peter Engelhard, we made an appointment with a gastro-enterologist to scope Bob's stomach. While I waited in a room nearby, I watched breaking news on television about Linda Tripp and Monica Lewinsky—as the most famous blow job in history began to be discussed world-wide.

The first investigations revealed nothing, so a CT scan was performed. Since the report said that a certain mass in the pancreas was "consistent with lymphoma," Corky scheduled a biopsy to be performed, in surgery, at Mercy Hospital in Miami. When Bob was rolled into the operating room at 3:00 P.M., the surgeon told me that the procedure would take thirty minutes and that he would speak with me as soon as it was over. I waited in a huge crowded waiting room, which, I fantasized, was what a boarding area for an overbooked 747 flight to Havana might be like. Mercy Hospital is predominantly Cuban, and English is definitely the second language. It appeared that each patient had his entire family waiting. I sat alone trying my best to stay calm. Family after family was called up for news of their loved one. I heard calls for the Sanchez,

Ramirez, Gutierrez, and Garcia families as the room gradually emptied out. My inquiries at the information desk were met with "we have not heard anything yet." At around 6:00 P.M., the lights were dimmed and the cleaning crew arrived.

Corky had not answered my calls, so I phoned Bob Smith in San Diego and begged him to help me. Within a few minutes, after speaking with people in the OR, he returned my call. "René, it's unbelievable," he said "but the surgeon left without speaking with you and left no word for anyone else either. Bob is in recovery and you can see him there." Trying to control my anger, I spoke with a resident in the recovery area who said that the tissue "looked like lymphoma," but that it needed to be confirmed by pathology the following day.

Dejected, I returned to our rental house and cuddled with our dogs. When I went to Bob's room at Mercy Hospital the following morning, Donna Jacobsen, a physician Bob had recruited to work in Corky's office, was sitting in his room. When I entered they stopped speaking and Bob tapped the sheets next to him, indicating that I should sit on his bed. He then took my hand and gave me the news with the same compassion as if it were I who had the cancer diagnosis. He had large cell non-Hodgkin's lymphoma, just like I had had four years before. Donna explained that Bob would have a bone marrow tap to determine the staging, but that it was doubtful they would find marrow involvement. By late afternoon, after the marrow exam and an initial consultation with Corky's recommended oncologist, Manuel Guerra, we returned to our house and dogs.

"Bob," I began sincerely, "I beat this and you are stronger and younger than I am. We will get through this together. Consider the next nine months as pay back for all you did for me. And you will, once again, be the biggest ox back at the gym in a year."

Early the following morning, Corky called to say that, contrary to what they had assumed, the marrow, too, was positive for lymphoma and that we needed to meet as quickly as possible. Two hours later, Bob and I sat in his office along with Donna.

"I don't like it at all," began Corky, in a surprisingly negative tone. "All the choices will be bad."

"Neither do we like it, Corky," I said, holding Bob's hand, "but we need to define where we go from here?"

"You'll have to speak to Manny again, but the treatment you discussed yesterday will not be adequate. I have no idea what he'll say."

Manny was much more compassionate and professional. He explained that Bob would have the same chemotherapy regimen as I had received, called CHOP, in addition to three chemo injections directly into the spine. Those treatments would have to take place as an inpatient and begin as soon as possible.'

When we got back to Lauderdale, I returned numerous phone calls from concerned friends and loved ones, including Jean-Claude Salamin in Switzerland. "Bob has lymphoma," I said.

"Where was it discovered?" asked Jean-Claude.

"In the pancreas," I answered.

"René," he said, "you'd better ready yourself. Pancreatic cancer is always fatal."

We then called Ray with the news. After reassuring Bob that we could work around his treatments, Ray spoke with me. "What are you going to do?" he asked.

"I guess I'll see if we can extend our lease here and stay all winter."

"Don't do that, René," said Ray. "We won't be using our house this year so just move in there."

"Why won't you be using Miami Vice this winter? There is much to be done here and it's miserable in New York."

"I, too, received a cancer diagnosis this week," he said to my shock. "Mine is in the thyroid and will require several operations in Boston. Gigi and I feel more comfortable not wandering far from Boston and New York. You and the dogs are most welcome at our house. Just do it."

"What will this mean for the IPO?" I asked.

"I'll decide in a few days, but with both Bob and me laid up most of the time, I think we will alter course."

On the first day of Bob' s initial hospitalization, Ray informed us that he had made a deal with IHS to sell some additional ancillary units of his company and that he had decided to shut down the physician practices. There would be no IPO. I was on an extension, so the conversation was three way.

"How do you want to handle the docs?" asked Bob.

"You know that most of them are goofballs," said Ray. "I gave them a ton of money and now they'll be whining about small shit.

Just do the best you can, but dump them all. As far as I'm concerned they can buy the office equipment for peanuts."

"Ray," I interjected, "the fight will be over the receivables."

Medicare and the insurance companies take up to ninety days to reimburse physicians. I knew that all the doctors would not be able to self-finance ninety days of operations under their ownership and would want Ray to concede the delayed revenues from their practices while they were salaried by Ray.

"Do the very best you can," he said.

Unfortunately, we had to interact once again with Corky's surgeon to place a port in Bob's chest for safer administration of the chemotherapy. This time he kept Bob waiting on a stretcher in front of the operating room for six hours and then did not implant the device properly. It had to be replaced by another surgeon two days later, so Bob and I made sure to report the arrogant quack to every possible agency and review board. He did not practice surgery for long, but no apologies were forthcoming.

Our lives set into a new routine. When Bob was at home, we played in the surf in front of Miami Vice with the dogs, and I cooked dinners at home every night. When Bob felt well, we negotiated separate deals with each physician, and when he did not feel up to it, I'd field the calls. Only two doctors were intolerant of Bob's bad days, and Corky was one of them. On one occasion, Corky came to Bob's room in the hospital after a painful spinal treatment. He wanted to discuss shaving a bit more out of the deal to help him cover the ninety days of new receivables in the pipeline. When he ignored my plea to defer his concerns until Bob felt better, I literally took his arm, escorted him to the door, and pushed him out of our room.

We started to rely more on Peter Engelhard when we were in Lauderdale and exclusively on Donna when we were hospitalized in Miami. Both were professional and compassionate and they always made themselves available to us. Peter came to our rescue when, after a failed spinal injection, Bob developed a debilitating and painful spinal leak. On his day off, Peter concocted and administered a blood patch made from Bob's blood, which sealed the leak and ended the pain.

Miami Vice's housekeeper also cleaned several of the local physician offices. I spread the numerous syringes, medications, and assorted paraphernalia I used to boost both Bob's red and white blood cell count out on a table in Gigi's dressing room and explained what they were to her. When she did not come to work the next scheduled day, I called to inquire why and she said that her religion would not allow her to work in a house where there was AIDS.

"But you clean Doctor Engelhard's office," I said confused.

"That's a business and it's different. This ain't right," she replied.

When one is under the type of stress as I was going through then, a small slap in the face can take on huge proportions. The discussion with the cleaning lady broke my dam of tears and I dreaded telling Ray as much as I dreaded speaking with Corky about "all the bad choices."

I knew I loved Ray when, after composing myself, I called him to explain. "Do you think Bob might limp out to the pool and cough on the pool man," he said. "Gigi hates him, too. So maybe he will quit as well. Also, Gigi hopes you will not wear out any of her pretty clothes in her closet!"

"Not a chance," I said, so relieved. "They don't fit either of us."

Cashiers, North Carolina

Immediately after Bob's last hospitalized five-day chemotherapy infusion, we folded camp at Miami Vice, loaded the cars and dogs, and drove back to North Carolina. A friend drove one car, as Bob was not able to drive safely. During the previous weeks, we made arrangements with a home health care agency recommended by IHS to handle Bob's next three chemotherapy sessions and to liaise with Doctor Manny in Miami.

In very much the same way as when I had returned to Chenoncette to complete my treatments, we were nearly ecstatic to be going home to our island of peace and hope. The typical lymphoma treatment of CHOP had advanced in the years since I had endured it, mostly because a gradual continuous five-day infusion had been determined as less toxic and more effective. Bob wore a belt containing a pump that delivered the mixture twenty-four hours a day. He was able to work, take walks, and even accompany me on errands, where only a few people wondered what the waist belt was. I'd lay awake at night trying to keep him as comfortable as possible, in spite of the tubing and the noise from the pump.

One day, I received a call from my friend Pierre Nussbaumer, from Switzerland. "What are you both doing this Saturday and Sunday?" he asked.

"As you know, Pierre, we are pretty well homebound now."

"We were wondering if we may come by for the weekend."

"I know Bob would be delighted, Pierre. Where in the States are you coming from or traveling to?"

"Nowhere," he said. "We'd like to come over just to spend an evening with Bob."

This extraordinary gesture from a busy friend who, with his wife, was prepared to fly round trip across the ocean and then drive three more hours to the North Carolina mountains meant so much to us both. Bob lit up and enjoyed the evening. He even cooked his famous chocolate soufflé desert. I will never forget it.

We routinely saw our internist, Doctor Patti Wheeler, at the nearby Highlands-Cashiers hospital. She also prescribed medication for nausea, pain, and anxiety, if needed. For my fiftieth birthday, in mid-May, Bob gave me some lovely Frank Lloyd Wright items to match the décor of the house as well as a wonderful, adoring letter—expressing his appreciation for my care and his never-ending love.

Shortly before Bob's last treatment, I asked him what he wanted to do immediately afterwards to celebrate. His response was, "Go to Switzerland and take walks up the Eggli Mountain for lunch." Happy to oblige, I made the necessary reservations. The only open issue was when he should have the subcutaneous port removed. Bob wanted it out the first day after his last treatment and for us to leave for Europe immediately afterwards. We compromised on waiting ten days.

Just prior to the end of treatment, he had a CT scan that was e-mailed to our friend, Doctor Manny, in Miami. Upon receiving it, he called immediately. "Congratulations," he began in his jovial voice; "you both deserve Champagne. Bob's scan was clear and you are good to go to Switzerland."

On June 13, we said good-bye to the home health care agency, which removed all the equipment and supplies from our bedroom, returning it to a more intimate and less therapeutic atmosphere, and we eagerly looked forward to being in Gstaad. When Bob started complaining of stomach pains the following day, I was certain it was only the destructive effects of the chemotherapy. But I became alarmed the day after that, when his stomach appeared distended. We went directly to Doctor Wheeler, who palpated his abdomen and said, "I think you need a CT scan."

"He just had one last week," I interjected in her examination room.

"I think he needs another," she repeated.

"When?" I asked.

"Right now. Let's walk across to the hospital now."

The small town local hospital was well equipped and, without any wait, Bob was on a table having a scan while Patti and I were in the control room with a technician.

'René, it's everywhere," said the alarmed physician.

"What do you mean?" I said, hoping for a miracle in her next statement.

"There is tumor in every organ I am looking at. This is serious."

In retrospect, I realized that I almost broke Patti's arm as I squeezed it during her brave delivery of that horrific news. We told Bob right there in the radiology department, and then we walked back to Patti's office, where she made an appointment for us to see an oncologist in Asheville the following day.

The overcrowded oncology office had grudgingly decided to squeeze us in. As a result, we sat for two and a half hours waiting to see the oncologist, a tough lady with a thick East European accent. "There is nothing I can do other than to prescribe morphine and refer you to hospice," she said after examining Bob and looking at several frames from the CT scan. She filled out the prescriptions and added nonchalantly, "He will be dead in ten days."

In total silence, we got back in our car to drive the hour and a half to Cashiers.

"Doctor Milosevic is not the last word," I said after a prolonged period, making reference to Slobodan Milosevic, Serbia's tyrannical strongman. "Let's call Doctor Levine.

Alexandra Levine was a revered, self-described "lymphomaniac" who practiced at The Kenneth Norris Cancer Research Center at the University of Southern California. We had tried to see her when I was diagnosed with lymphoma and again, six months earlier, when Bob received the same news. I had never even been able to speak with anyone other than her secretarial staff and both earlier attempts at being treated by her had been unsuccessful. This time, however, I reached her.

"I will take Bob as a patient," she began, in her long stream of confidence building statements. "But if, and only if, he is here in L. A.

tomorrow. The ten-day prognosis you received is generous. That tumor is likely doubling in size daily, and Bob will not live out the week unless we begin some aggressive experimental drugs immediately."

"We'll be there," I said.

We made all the necessary calls from the car in the following hour. We scheduled flights for the following day from Asheville to Los Angeles and begged a sweet lady, whom we had previously hired, to sit with our dogs while we were gone. As we drove into Stillmont, the residential community where Chenoncette was located, Ed Addison was collecting his mail at a community mailbox that we had erected for the neighborhood at a pull off on our property. Ed's miraculous wife, Bennie, had been monitoring the crisis with several calls each day and delivered her loving signature frequent nightly meals. Ed took one look at us both and, without either of us uttering a single word, burst into tears.

After a restless and, for Bob, painful night, when we cuddled together in bed with our dogs, I packed a few things, including cash and passports as I had no idea of what to expect or how long we would be gone. While I was running around doing these chores, Bob sat outside on our deck, overlooking the pond we had rebuilt. It was dried up when we had bought the house, as the retaining dam had been broken. The new pond was totally lined and symbolized the peacefulness of our home, as did the large Koi living in it. The Koi swam around the lily pads, seemingly in a dancing circle, whenever we played music outside on the deck.

I knew what Bob was thinking, and watching his ashen bald head look over the railing at the fish was heartbreaking.

USC Medical Center, Los Angeles, California

Bob nearly died in the plane from Atlanta to L.A. He began throwing up and we stayed huddled in a bathroom for most of the last half of the flight. Although Bob's real and adopted families live in the Los Angeles area, we had not asked, nor expected, anyone to pick us up at the airport. I almost carried Bob to a taxi and we made the long ride to East L.A. where the USC medical center is located. Though I had lived in L.A. for several years, I had never been to this part of town. While doing field work, during his Ph.D. in psychology, Bob had worked at a juvenile detention center located adjacent to the medical complex. Otherwise there would be no reason to visit this area. The compound itself was pleasant and, during the day, full of busy students and family members, who walked between the several hospital buildings, dormitories, and classrooms. The area surrounding the medical center, however, is one of the worst and most dangerous parts of the city. At night it was empty, dark, dangerous, and austere.

Doctor Levine and several of her colleagues received us immediately. She was eccentric yet stylish in her dress and appearance, a tall, brilliant, compassionate lady, full of energy and enthusiasm. We both adored her from the second we laid our tired, frightened eyes on her. A group of six of us was cramped into a windowless room, sitting around a central square table. An easel and flip chart were tightly squeezed into a corner. Alexandra wrote out, and drew, her assessment and recommendations. She reconfirmed that a rapid relapse after the regimen Bob had received was usually immediately fatal. The tumor, which now looked like the worst Crix belly we had ever seen, was crowding his organs and creating the pain and the dry heaving. She explained several experimental procedures and medications she had access to and carefully reviewed all pertinent details. There was little room for questions because we had no options. We were traumatized and terrified. Furthermore, the experts' explanations were so complete that there was little room for queries. Finally, I only asked, "When do we start and do you really believe we have a chance of success?"

Alexandra went back to the easel and, with a red magic marker, wrote, "Now and *YES*."

We had experienced so many ups and downs, beginning with the initial cancer diagnosis. We then had to go through Corky's pessimism, when the marrow test results were unfavorable, then a successful clean scan at the end of the treatments that was rapidly followed by a relapse. Now, contrary to what Doctor Milosevic had told us, this legendary lady, whom we had so recently met, was telling us that Bob would live and she would personally see to it. I could see in Bob's eyes that he not only believed her but that he was fearless about the medications she was proposing.

Alexandra's team was equally impressive. One physician's assistant, Lisa, knew more about oncology than ten physicians combined, as did her physician associates. The floor nurses were competent and efficient. What a difference from Mercy Hospital, much less the pesthole in Key West, we thought.

Although I took a room at a nearby Omni Hotel, I stayed at the hospital all day and many nights. Bob's mother, sister, and brother visited, as did the exceptional graduates from Teamm House—with whom Bob had worked in clinical practice for years. The summer was a hot one in Los Angeles, with temperatures hovering at 100 degrees most days. The students ate at a nearby cafeteria, located in the main medical center, which had been acquired by NME, and endowed by my former client, Richard Eamer, NME's C.E.O. I passed by a huge painting of him, which hung in the lobby, on my way to one of the cafeterias that I frequented daily. I brought Bob our breakfast and lunches. At four o'clock each day, I bought ten iced cappuccinos and handed them out to hot tired employees in the hospital. I also bought our dinners at that time, as the cafeterias and the entire neighborhood all shut down in the late afternoon.

Days turned into weeks and there was significant hope during an entire month. After our first week at Norris, Alexandra flew to Geneva to lecture at The World AIDS Conference. Jean-Claude Salamin put a chauffeur-driven Mercedes at her disposal and met her at the airport with one of his typically classic and blatant statements. "If you can save our Bob, we will all be forever in your debt."

Some weekends we were allowed to leave the hospital and stay in the area. Even though Bob was weak and we never left our room except to get carryout food, we enjoyed these furloughs. Several of them were spent in a hotel on Ocean Avenue in Santa Monica, three blocks from where Tim and I had lived, and several others at our friend Smith Richardson's guest cottage in Venice. One of Bob's former Teamm House associates, Melanie Kassman, a beautiful, competent woman, was a production assistant at a movie studio. She brought us a large suitcase full of videos containing all the films that had been nominated for academy awards in 1998.

Even with an ever-increasing number of intravenous pumps on his rolling pole, I walked Bob around the hospital's' floor several times a day. A second double access IV port was surgically placed to allow for more and more medications. To amuse Bob, I would talk about the design flaws that we had mastered during my hospital planning days and the managerial discrepancies between American and private European hospitals. On our frequent daily walks, we saw many patients and some family come and leave. Some patients left alive. Eventually, every nurse and hospital worker knew us and marveled at our dedication to each other. The more fortunate patients had visitors for a few hours a day but I lived there and was not about to change that. Some sad cases had few or no family and friends sitting by their beds. In "our" room, Bob used his new laptop computer and watched the business channel on television. We talked about the various interviews and companies' performance, focusing on several IPO's while Bob drew on all he had learned during Ray's planned public offering.

Bob monitored the beginnings of discussions regarding human trials for an AIDS vaccine on the Internet and tried to educate me in how to surf the web. He reminded me that we had all been told fifteen years earlier that vaccine trials would begin within two years and a cure would be available within five years. We learned that, for the first time since the beginning of the pandemic, the crisis in Africa was beginning to be discussed in some progressive circles, thanks in part to Congresswoman Maxine Waters. We were interested that a few European pharmaceutical companies were making generic anti-retrovirals to distribute in Africa's most devastated areas, in defiance of American patent law.

I did not want Bob to wear a hospital gown and, for most of his stay, he was allowed to wear a sweat suit. There was no laundromat nearby, but I noticed one in the basement of a locked dormitory. I would gather up our clothes and take a small paper cup used for salad dressing from the cafeteria. Then I would go to the only bathroom that had liquid soap and fill my makeshift detergent container. Necessity definitely became the mother of invention and, shamelessly, I managed to jimmy a basement window in the dorm in order to get inside and wash our clothes there every few days. The only time I recall leaving East L.A. was to have a Sunday lunch with my childhood friend, Ahmed, and his family at their country club on the West Side of town. His lovely wife, Laurie, made sure the club packed a beautiful dinner for Bob.

Gradually, the sense of optimism began to disappear as one experimental drug after yet another was tried. After five weeks, I told Bob's father that he had better come from Minnesota. We spent that weekend aboard the *Queen Mary* in Long Beach, but Bob was barely able to get out of bed. The following week, Bob began having two IV poles with three and then four pumps on each. Finally, I could see despair on the faces of all the doctors— except Alexandra's. I attended a meeting with her entire team to assess what should be done, and we decided to tell Bob that everything possible had been tried but that, now, they recommended discontinuing treatments. Five of us walked into his room as he watched the business channel. For some reason, everyone lined up on one side of his bed—except Alexandra, who stood along the opposite wall. I stood at the foot of the bed. Before anyone had a chance to speak, Bob did. "You all are the bears," he said, pointing at the team and making reference to business analysts who took a negative view of the economy. "You, Alexandra are the only bull. I'm sticking with the bull."

We all walked out of the room without having delivered our prepared speech. "I just couldn't say it, René," said Alexandra. "I'll try one more experimental drug but it is highly toxic and is not well tested. I just can't tell that man I'm done. I just cannot."

For that new regimen, during the seventh week of our stay at Norris, Bob was moved into the bone marrow transplant (BMT) unit that is equivalent to a super-sterile intensive care unit. Everything deteriorated, from the nurse's abilities and compassion to Bob's condition. We clearly were just another hopeless case versus the friendly survivors who had become friends with the staff on the regular hospital's floor. Bob began sleeping more and more in a state of semi-consciousness.

One day, the phone rang. It was our neighbor in Cashiers who owned the cottage we had tried to buy for two years. He offered to meet our last price. I responded with "I am not in a position to respond or to think clearly. Thank you anyway," and I hung up.

"Who was that?" mumbled Bob.

"Letchworth. He wants to meet our last offer."

"And you said no? Call him right back and say you will buy it. If something happens to me, you will put a caretaker in there that can maintain the property and make your life easier. Do it, René!" Bob's wish became my command.

After a long day, August 5th, I decided to go to the hotel to sleep. As I left Bob's room a physician who worked in the BMT said, "You know we are at the edge of physiology."

"Doctor, if you mean that Bob is dying, yes, I know."

I turned to the nurse's station and told them to call me if there was any change in Bob's condition during the night.

When I returned at 7:00 A.M. the following morning, Bob was confused, gasping for air, and not alert. I raced back to the nurse's station to tell them.

"It's shift change time and you'll have to wait until the new team gets up to speed. We are reviewing all the charts now," said a nurse, who looked amazingly like a human pig.

I had remained controlled for as long as possible. My nerves were frayed and my patience was exhausted. With one huge sweep of my arm, I threw all the charts on the floor. I yelled, "You come in there with me now!" pointing at the doctor who had said, "He is on the edge of physiology." The pig-like nurse franticly picked up the phone and asked for hospital security as I returned to Bob's room with the physician.

After the doctor examined Bob, I said, "Remove everything and let this man be in peace." I pointed to eight IV's with an air of disgust as a security guard came into the room. The doctor shoved the officer back into the hall.

"That is the right decision," he said looking at me, "but you need to leave one line in for morphine."

"Thank you, Doctor," I said, "but do it now! No crap about shift changes."

Five minutes later I climbed into the bed and up next to Bob, who had one remaining IV tube going into his body. I called Melanie and told her that she had to come to the hospital immediately, as did any other Teamm House member who wanted to be with Bob on his last day.

"I have a very full day," she said.

"That's fine," I said, "just remember I called."

The phone was not back in its cradle for even a full minute before Melanie called back. "I've told my associates I have to leave and I'll also call everyone else. We'll all be there as quickly as possible."

I lay next to Bob whispering sweet words into his ear. I told him many things including that he imagine that we were in bed at Chenoncette, looking out at the lake with our dog, T-Cell, tucked in beside his tummy. I also told him how valiantly he had fought, that our partnership had brought out the best in me so that I felt anchored in myself, how much I loved him, and that it was "okay to let go now."

When Melanie and many friends arrived, I got out of the bed and went out into the hall.

"This is how we are going to do this," I said, with a strength that appeared from some unknown source deep inside me. "You all wait in the family room over there. Then, one at a time, you come into the room for five minutes each. You are to say nice things in a gentle voice. This is not a time for unfinished business. It is to help Bob leave us peacefully. Okay?"

For the next two hours, Bob's friends and loving colleagues did exactly that. Nancy Troy, Garry's widow, sang a song. Others rubbed Bob's feet or freshened a wash cloth and put it on his head. I stayed in bed with him, hugging him. As I embraced him, I sensed within me a new level of emotional sensitivity and depth that Bob helped me reach.

At 10:25 A.M. Pacific Time on August 6, alone with Bob in bed, he drew his last breath and died in my arms. I respected our "ten minute rule" and chose to hold him for twenty more minutes and until I was certain his brain waves had ceased. This was my way of staying with the deeply felt connection between us, purposefully transferring Bob's essence as we merged into one.

I have a spotty recollection of signing papers and speaking with Alexandra afterwards, and there are differing reports about how I got to LAX airport. I left everything I had brought to the hotel and somehow, in complete darkness, I flew to Asheville via Atlanta. I have boarding passes to prove that I changed planes but all I remember is waking up in the Asheville airport parking lot looking for a car I had left there weeks earlier.

Chenoncette, Cashiers, North Carolina

For the first month after Bob died, I rarely left the house. Bennie delivered my meals. Donny, the same friend who drove one car back from Fort Lauderdale, came for a few days. He was a clever former insurance actuary and he worked on reversing the sale of Bob's life insurance. Shortly before, in an effort to cover some of the expenses of the previous months, Bob had sold his policy to a viatical company. I could not go near Bob's dressing area in our bedroom and only went into his office to help Donny find documents.

Ten days after I had returned from California, our neighborhood held its annual property owner's meeting. It was a custom to stand and pay respects to dead owners and even previous proprietors. Ed called and urged me to "emerge from my hole" and attend the meeting. Doug Smith, the self-righteous Christian, who would not pay for his cancer stricken wife's medications, presided. Not a word was mentioned about Bob, his struggle, or how much the neighborhood had lost. As a result, I retreated further into the secure darkness of Chenoncette.

At the end of August, I went to the same lawyer's office where Bob and I had signed the papers to close on the purchase of the house five and half years earlier. The attorney had two sets of documents ready for execution. One set opened Bob's estate so we could process his will and the other set was to acquire the small house adjacent to Chenoncette, which we had tried so hard to own together. I only recall the attorney explaining that there would be taxes to be paid on our home.

"That can't be," I said naively. "We own it as joint-tenants with right of survivorship."

"Sadly that applies only to husband and wife in North Carolina," she began. "The tax will be less than if you had not recorded the deed in that manner, but there still will be a tax liability. With right of survivor there is no tax for a spouse, a small tax for a blood relative, and a higher rate for joint tenants who are not related."

One day Bennie arrived carrying a small box. The lady post office manager had called her to let her know that Bob's ashes had arrived and that she hoped a friend could pick them up and bring them to me, rather than for me to find them in the mail. That generous, perhaps even illegal gesture more than made up for the news of the estate tax law. I would have to work hard to overcome my emerging revulsion for the few neighborhood homophobes who had used my weakened condition to make nasty statements. I recalled my first and only real boss, Royce Diener, saying that "the oppressed become the oppressors and can kick you when you are down."

On September 3, I heard that Swissair Flight 111, traveling from New York to Geneva, had crashed the previous evening near Halifax, Nova Scotia, killing everyone aboard. I had taken that same flight literally dozens of times and had three acquaintances aboard that day, including Doctor Jonathan Mann, who Bob and I had met on several occasions.

Bennie called me that afternoon to inquire what plans I had for Bob's memorial service. "I have not even thought about it," I replied. "Nothing I guess."

"I think that's a mistake, René," she said in her gentle voice. "Think about it and let's discuss it again tomorrow."

Together, we decided to have a small non-religious commemorative on Chenoncette's deck and place Bob's ashes in the pond he so loved. "Just a few intimate, local friends," I said.

In the ensuing few days, several friends who lived in different parts of the country called to inquire about me. To my surprise, when I mentioned the emergence of a plan for a ceremony, one after the other asked for dates and offered to travel in order to be included. Gradually, the group grew and, while still intimate, was made up of many life-long friends.

One sunny September day, we all sat around in a circle on the deck. I had placed a special item of Bob's on each chair, along with a card I had printed to send to acknowledge the huge number of sympathy letters I was receiving each day. The front of the card had a black and white picture of our house in the snow with the pond frozen over. The back read, "Winter came early to Chenoncette. Please keep Bob alive in your hearts." I delivered a brief acknowledgement of my appreciation for the attendee's presence and asked each guest to read a statement received from friends of Bob's who could not be with us. I had placed them in a deliberate sequence that resulted in a history of Bob's forty-two years, beginning with his kindergarten teacher and ending with recent friends' accounts of his incredible character. When the testimonials were read, each guest put some of Bob's ashes in "his lake." Bob and I had been told that the Koi would never reproduce in our pond and, in the five years we watched them grow, they had not. Mysteriously, however, the following spring there were literally several hundred baby Koi swimming around in the lake.

One guest had catered a beautiful lunch to be held at their cliff-side house nearby. There, a few poems were read and each guest threw a rose over the cliff. Local guests then drove the out-of-town friends to airports. As I left, Ed said, "In all my experience, reading the statement was the hardest thing I ever did and that was the most beautiful memorial service I ever attended."

By the end of the year AIDS had killed an estimated twenty million people worldwide. Twenty years before, there were only vague hints of a killer virus brewing and little attention had been attributed to this gay plague. By December 1998, one quarter of African Americans in some inner city communities were HIV positive while black churches still resisted confronting the crisis, much less hosting open discussions on safe sex and HIV transmission. This was in spite of the new statistics that showed that 80 percent of new American infections were among minorities.

"When someone you love dies, a part of you dies with them
and a part of them lives on in you."

PART FOUR

THE ARC TO TRIUMPH

CHAPTER TWENTY-FIVE

In the months after Bob's death, I existed in a numb trance. I later understood that this condition was my body's defense mechanism, which came into play when emotional survival seemed incomprehensible to me. Gradually, a level of awareness began to surface as my conscious mind wakened. Although I felt injured, angry, frightened, and compromised, I began to notice behavior that more closely resembled the thinking patterns and actions that Bob habitually exhibited in contrast to my more emotional responses. Initially, I thought that I was trying to emulate him, but then I understood, at a deeper level, that a part of Bob was alive within me. Authentically integrating his more admirable behavior not only immortalized him, it simultaneously fueled my transformation. The earliest clue that this miracle was occurring was when I genuinely laughed for the first time in many months. I noticed that my laugh sounded more like a blend of Bob's and mine.

My numbness gradually wore off during the first year I was alone, which taught me, that, at least in my case, the first year of recovery being left alone is not the chronological first year. I developed the expression that "the first year is really the second year," meaning that the first year of living and experiencing growth comes later—when the acute phase of grief lessens. In her brilliant study on grief, Elizabeth Kubler Ross discusses the various phases of anguish. However, these must be put in the context of each individual. They may become merged, accelerated, or experienced out of sequence. While I would have loved to speed up the clock,

I knew this was impossible and, more importantly, it would be counter-productive.

There is a place and a personal space for grieving which, when understood, becomes beneficial—almost in direct proportion to the degree of pain. In dealing with depression, I understood that, if you fight the waves of sadness and anger, the daily existence is more difficult. Instead, like a boat in rough seas, turning around and carefully riding the waves consumes much less fuel. With hope, you may even identify a goal and chart a path to more efficiently reach it.

As I went through my version of this process, I experienced recurring flashbacks of holding Bob in my arms as he was expiring. I had this unexpected feeling of satisfaction— not to be confused with relief. I felt genuinely proud that I was able to support Bob during his final struggle. I felt deeply and vividly connected to my life partner! Somehow, he had transferred his deep sense of calm to me. To this day, I remain in awe of his capacity to function and make decisions, even as his curtain was falling. Almost a decade later, I still try to discover his secret. I will never forget that he was the one who showed me the path to constructively confronting my father.

Webster's Dictionary defines survival as the "ability to remain alive." However, it has to mean more than just breathing if life is to be worth living. That brings one to ponder a second *Webster* definition: "To carry on *despite* hardships and trauma." In order to practice that definition of "survive," one has to come to terms with the hardships and trauma and then identify a source of strength and gradual growth. For me, that began with going back to primitive basics. First, I spent all my time with my dogs and doing outside work while isolating myself at Chenoncette. I could vent my anger out while chopping wood or working out in a gym and rediscover primal love in the eyes of my animals. I would eat and sleep to survive for them and, later, develop more complex thought patterns and behavior. At first, any effort seemed impossible—even painful. Eventually, the pain is actually worsened by the inertia, as tiny morsels of satisfaction are born out of progress. But what defines progress? For me, it was the realization that it was acceptable to die of fatigue and illness, but *not* of grief and anger. I was more upset, frightened, and angry than tired—so it was *not* yet *my* time.

Shortly before my Nonnie died, she told me, "René, I have lived a good life. I have raised good children, including you. I am tired and ready to go." More accurately, in my case, I had the will to survive. I remembered those wise words and understood that I was not "ready to go."

I am agnostic. Thus, the typical comforting thoughts and phrases religious people hear mean nothing to me. I formulated the idea for my own self that one dies like one lives. In fact, those last brief moments are my version of heaven or hell. I had seen my father die angry, alone, and fighting with everyone around him. That same season, my dear Nonnie had slipped away tired but comfortable, at ease in her rocking chair. A religious person would say that one went to hell and the other to heaven *because* of their worldly behavior. I choose to believe that one's mood during the last flashes of consciousness, formulated by their cumulative behavior, is of equal importance to the decades spent on Earth. Our duty then becomes trying to develop the mechanisms to leave life in the most positive way. Although Tim died emaciated at twenty-nine, he was surrounded by a generous and loving family as he became childishly content. Since I had always referred to Bob as "my angel," due to the angelic life he had led, I know that he died an angel's death, and I was lucky to have been able to assist him.

Opposites define each other

No recovery is a straight line out of darkness. During my first chronological year, I experienced pronounced mood swings that, I learned, were symptoms of my recovery. As such, they were not to be feared. One can always apologize later and anyone worth being associated with has to have the ability to tolerate erratic behavior during deep despair and pain. When someone annoyed me with well-meaning, yet superficial, phrases such as, "I know how you feel," or "you'll be just fine shortly," I simply ignored them. I have always believed that opposites define each other; namely, one cannot truly appreciate a good day without experiencing a bad day nor enjoy a profound friend without having been exposed to superficial relationships.

Applying that simple doctrine has made me search out people who uttered words and emitted behavior that made me feel opposite to what I felt when I heard what seemed like silliness or, worse, unsympathetic toxic comments. Had my neighbor not been insensitive and, possibly, deliberately cruel at my first emergence from my house after Bob died, I may not have fully appreciated how meaningful and curative Bennie's regular delivery of food and her gentle insistence on planning a memorial was.

What are the opposites of homophobia, ill health, anxiety due to confusing medical opinions, loneliness, jealousy, and anger at politicians and ignorance? The answers are available, and, if focused on, will produce the *feelings* that follow from the thoughts that there *are* accepting people, good health days, some peace when a medical regimen is identified, companionship, enlightened politicians, and moments of significant clairvoyance. When the feelings produced by fear and isolation raised their ugly heads, I slowly forced myself to recall opposite experiences—to consider how those experiences felt and where and with whom I experienced them.

But where had humor gone? It, too, reappeared one day. I had received repeated calls from both realtors wanting to list our home to "help" me and from certain opportunists wanting to replace Bob. The first time I laughed was when I concocted the double *entendre* that what they had in common was that both groups wanted to "screw" me and I laughed—like Bob would have. It sounded like him and it was him. I felt a bit better.

I tried to frame the nightmare of the last seven weeks of Bob's life while at USC in an effort to identify the positive elements. Had I not seen people die alone and frightened in Key West, I would not have known how to help Bob experience peace and companionship. Had I not witnessed people's inability to provide support to the dying, I would not have survived on automatic pilot and been there for Bob during those weeks. Instead of feeling sorry for myself, I gradually felt sorry for those who could not offer that gift to their loved ones. Deepening this thought process, I focused on the *quality* of my actions and feelings again by defining those qualities by their opposites. Had AMI's short-tenured chief executive officer not said, "All any fag waiter has to do is spit in my soup and I'll get AIDS," I would never appreciate the gift of *feeling* prejudice and creating an environment which allowed Bob to die unencumbered by homophobia and ignorance.

Survival vs. Survive

The word "survival" is defined as "living or continuing longer than another person." To that one *must add* "with quality or purpose." My new life, alone and without my soul mate, had to gradually identify some purpose and elements of quality. This can be as simple as F. Scott Fitzgerald's expression that "living well is the best revenge," focusing on one's personal health; planting a new garden; or defining a goal like working, being involved with worthy charities or writing a book. Sadly, if one wallows in sorrow, what Louise Hay termed as using the "pity pot," which she would pass around during her meetings, it becomes very difficult to help oneself. The old adage that "the universe helps those who help themselves" has to become the credo.

This became patently clear during my work with AIDS "victims." Interestingly, even the nomenclature of long-term HIV cases has changed from "AIDS victims" to "living with AIDS" to "surviving with AIDS" and, now, "thriving with AIDS." In order to *live* those changes, and not merely use of new words to describe a life with purpose and quality, one must be able to find some meaningful, interpersonal relationships and to disconnect from the daily expression of the crisis. AIDS patients experience regular wide swings in information relative to their longevity, medications, and finances. While this material has to be processed and acted upon, if these constantly reappearing calamities are not eventually put in the back of one's mind, one may "survive" but not experience "survival with quality."

My biggest concern for AIDS (and other) assistance programs is to identify ways to help their clients make the transition from self-pity to a responsible life partially led with, and guided by, higher thoughts, motives, and activities. Some people may find that through a church or support group, but I believe those avenues provide more of a temporary—ergo dangerous—fix than a cure.

Many well-meaning assistance programs tend to reinforce the negative downward cycle. Since the vast majority of people surviving with AIDS have to seek some mix of local, state, and federal assistance, they quickly learn that these benefits will evaporate if the recipient "thrives" and goes back to work. While volunteer work can be very comforting, it never equals earning one's own living over the longer term.

I challenge individual assistance programs to bridge this gap on a person-by-person plan, after ability and psychological make-ups are assessed. The result can define the difference between AIDS "victims" and people "taking responsibility for" an ailment or "handicap."

The dangers of handing out benefits, be they medical, financial, or emotional, is to over-comfort the recipient and allow them to use the "pity pot."

In time, this inevitably leads to a sense of entitlement and claiming rights that have not been earned. This has the perverse effect of diminishing self-esteem and restraining freedom. Equally dangerous is to hide behind the disability and avoid taking on, and living up to, responsibilities. *One simply can't have it both ways.* Even the most mentally and physically healthy people have to force themselves to persevere in times of setbacks and adversity. Even the most self-assured and directed of us will, on occasion, doubts those convictions.

The danger for the beneficiaries of assistance programs is that they are allowed, indeed often encouraged, to give in to a bad day or piece of problematic news that, rapidly, will reduce and eventually kill the survival instinct.

"There must be a pony!" —Kurt Vonnegut

In one of Kurt Vonnegut's book's, he tenderly describes an optimistic child who, upon entering a barn full of manure, exclaims, "There must be a pony!"

Given the extremely slow and dispassionate response to the early American *and* global response to HIV, one might only see a large pile of political manure. It is only if we experience the *feeling* of the tragedy that we can then overcome the anger and frustration.

And, by definition, the catastrophe must have existed to experience it. On a smaller scale you, as reader, would likely not be especially interested in this conclusion, this arc, if you will, had you not read the previous sections of the book.

In a crisis, one's true personality and abilities emerge. The primal core becomes apparent and can be nurtured. I saw many late stage AIDS patients experience various forms of dementia. Some became excessively angry and combative, while others exhibited kindness, the ability to love and to become an innocent child again. Each retreated to their core.

In *The New York Times,* on September 5, 2006, Doctor Elissa Ely, an expert on dementia, wrote, "Dementia releases the essential self. We wander backward uncontrollably and become more of what we already were."

I maintain that crisis and grief also allow us to understand our essence. From that understanding there can be progress, growth, and ultimately peace. Just as during my thirty years of living with AIDS, there were many times when overwhelming anger could have become my main motivator, a search for meaning and peace became essential to survive.

From the late 1970s, it was obvious that something was very wrong with many of my friends. In the early days, the majority of Americans felt that this was a homosexual virus and turned their backs on education and research. Again, when it took Ronald Regan six years into his presidency to utter the word "AIDS," one could have translated those very real insults into all consuming anger. But, had the history of AIDS been different, it is axiomatic that the huge contribution of the Bill and Melinda Gates Foundation and the teaming up with Warren Buffet would not have occurred. So, in a very real way, Reagan's refusal to deal with AIDS in the early days was merely the barn full of manure waiting for the Gates/Buffet pony.

Before these gigantic philanthropic efforts could be identified, the crisis they were to address had to exist. There had to be 500,000 newborns infected with HIV every year and twelve million orphans worldwide for the Gates Foundation to know where and how to direct the future of charitable contributions.

In no way can any sane person imply that the catastrophe of the AIDS pandemic is a positive aspect of our era. But one has to search for the pony! Had AIDS not caused twenty-five million deaths, there would be no Clinton Global Initiative (CGI) to address the needs of the forty million citizens of the world who need assistance from the world's two wealthiest people and from a committed two-term past American president. Seen from a broader context, the Gates Foundation may be the catalyst necessary to empower women, in general, and not just as it relates to contraception and safe sex.

I've had enough vs. I have enough

Going back to my individual story during the history of the crisis, I have to recognize that AIDS was certainly not the worst thing that happened to me. Without it, I'd have not pulled back from the business world and met the many interesting and evolved people I have come to know. Most importantly, I'd have never met Bob Mann and experienced the happiest decade in my life—by far.

Tennyson's famous line "it's better to have loved and lost than never to have loved at all" is true. In my sadder moments, I feel that, in order to be accurate, he should have added "provided you croak first." Nevertheless, the idea is valid and implies that all we humans can do is *to live.* Everything we experience during our tenure on Earth is all we have. If we allow it to overwhelm us, then we lose, and when we have had enough, we quit in one form or another.

I loved Tim with my libido and Bob with my brain and my heart. Yet both were necessary to create my experience. Tim allowed me to create a persona, to come out, to be comfortable in who I was. Bob gave me the foundation to understand that we pursue happiness only to find peace.

Caesar said, "I came, I saw, I conquered!"—the path of a great warrior.

That is *not,* however, peaceful and satisfying in and of itself.

Victor Hugo refined the statement by saying, "I came, I saw, *I lived,"* which differentiates his experience, just as a gourmand is different from a gourmet. The former can eat himself or herself to death; the latter eats to satisfaction.

While I have had pain, setbacks, and huge human losses with long-term repercussions, I certainly have *lived.*

We are all the result of our cumulative experience on the planet. It is all part of being alive.

Mine is a story of both love and despair. However, instead of declaring an angry defeat with "I've had enough," I choose to feel that enough experience will allow me to be peaceful.

May you all live the life I have had so far! *A rainbow* of glorious colors—fading colors, ups and downs—and may you "survive" and live life to the fullest…and travel the road to triumph.

**Christmas 1994 with our dogs,
T-Cell and Silly, at Chenoncette.**

T-Cell and Silly, at Chenoncette.

BIBLIOGRAPHY

Cose, Ellis, et.al., "AIDS at 25." *Newsweek* (May 15, 2006), Special Report Issue

Plant, B. Andrew, "Anthony Azizi Delivers His International Policy on AIDS." *A&U Magazine* (March 2006)

Grmek, Mirko D. *History of AIDS: Emergence and Origin of a Modern Pandemic.* Princeton, NJ: Princeton University Press, 1988.

Rofes, Eric. *Dry Bones Breathe: Gay Men Creating Post AIDS Identities*
and Cultures. New York: The Hawthorn Press, Inc., 1998.

Shilts, Randy. *And the Band Played On: Politics, People, and the AIDS Epidemic.* New York: St. Martin's Press.